AUNTIE'S CHARLIE

CHARLES CHILTON

AUNTIE'S CHARLIE

AN AUTOBIOGRAPHY

fantom
publishing

First published in 2011 by Fantom Films
fantomfilms.co.uk

A catalogue record for this book is available from the British Library.

Hardback Edition ISBN: 978-1-906263-72-0
Paperback Edition ISBN: 978-1-906263-76-8

Typeset by Phil Reynolds Media Services, Leamington Spa
Printed by MPG Biddles Limited, King's Lynn

Photographs appear on plates between pages 134 and 135.

CONTENTS

ACKNOWLEDGEMENTS

This book is principally the story of my life at the BBC. My first acknowledgement, therefore, must be to the Corporation for taking me on the staff at the age of fifteen. As well as enabling me to enter the world of radio, the BBC also acted as my university and introduced me to the world of music. I am eternally grateful to the Corporation and to the many writers, producers and musicians who helped me in those early days.

More recently, I have to thank Loulou Brown for exceptional help and encouragement, and for her painstaking editing of the work. I also have to thank Bradley Brown for his help in choosing and scanning the photographs to be included in the book. *Auntie's Charlie* would never have been published without the Browns' encouragement and enthusiasm.

FOREWORD

This is a book I've been looking forward to for years. Its subject is a unique man, the only truly multi-talented man I know: Charles Chilton. Forgive me if I call him 'Charlie' now and again; that's how I know him best.

His radio output is amazing. I know of no one who's been a specialist in so many different subjects. He has produced and written programmes about jazz, folk music, music hall, American history (particularly the Wild West – remember *Riders of the Range*?), London, the First World War and the mould-breaking *Journey into Space*. He also wrote for the very best children's comic, *Eagle*; and, with Joan Littlewood, put together the classic stage musical *Oh What a Lovely War*.

But radio was his great love. He was part of the golden period of radio, the days when a programme-making committee consisted of just the producer. Then there were no decisions by faceless panels of whoever – it was just the boss. The producer was the person who usually came up with the idea and saw the project through from conception to realisation.

How lucky the BBC was that a fifteen-year-old job-seeker stopped to look at Broadcasting House. He started as a messenger and, on his retirement forty-six years later, was described by the *Sunday Telegraph* as 'the one genius the BBC ever had on its staff'.

Yes, the Corporation was lucky to have him, and I was also lucky when he asked me to be part of a series he'd written and was going to produce for Radio 4: *Roy Hudd's Vintage Music Hall*. It was right up my street. I'd learned lots of the old songs from my Gran, but it was Charles who opened up the whole of that very special world for me. He introduced me to so many long-forgotten gems; but even more fascinating were his explanations, on and off the air, of how the songs so perfectly reflected the times, troubles and tragedies of the years when they were first sung. He was quite brilliant at bringing erudite research to colourful, entertaining life.

Each programme in the series was a recreation of an evening in a historic music hall and he insisted no expense be spared in presenting the songs in their very best light. He had the BBC Concert Orchestra playing the best arrangements, the best solo singers and a superb choir. I was allowed to sing the easiest songs and act as chairman. He himself, like all good directors, was a frustrated performer. The choir, the soloists and the orchestra played the rowdy music hall audience and Charles was in the middle of them, leading the chaos. His improvised heckles, shouts of encouragement and howls of dismay were all perfectly in character – and funny. On one occasion, because the song meant so much to him, Charlie himself sang and talked the song 'Oh What a Lovely War'. It made the hairs on the back of my neck stand up. His *was* the voice of a First World War soldier.

I had the great joy of being cajoled, bossed about and, best of all, being inspired by him. Sure, he was a hard taskmaster. He worked hard on the material and knew, unlike so many that followed him, exactly what he wanted – and insisted he got it. Years before, he'd produced some episodes of *The Goon*

Show. I'd have loved to have been a fly on the wall if Charlie and Spike had had a disagreement. They *both* knew exactly what they wanted. That's why the pair of them were the best.

So much of my knowledge of music hall, its stars, its songs and the stories behind them, I learned at Charlie's knee – or some other low joint! (He was the first person I ever heard use that line!) His stories of the great days of radio were, and are, priceless, and I bet they're all in *Auntie's Charlie*. I've been looking forward to reading them for years, and now I'm going to.

Let's turn the page and enter the world of a truly one-off, talented and down-to-earth (whisper it) genius.

Roy Hudd
July 2011

CHAPTER ONE
EARLY DAYS

My earliest memory is of a lion. It was crouching on a low cliff and was about to spring onto a man who stood below staring up at the animal. He wore nothing but a leopard's skin that wrapped round his loins and over his shoulder, a waist belt and an empty knife scabbard – empty because the man held the knife in his right hand. Tarzan stood firm, ready to receive the lion's attack. The lion leaped out and down towards the almost defenceless figure. Then the picture went dark and in its place appeared the legend, 'To be continued at this cinema all next week'.

What I had recalled was the final scene of an episode of a weekly cinema serial featuring *Tarzan of the Apes*. The man's professional name was Elmo, billed as 'Elmo the Mighty, King of the Jungle'. He was an American professional strong man turned film star. In 1921 Elmo the Mighty was playing every week at my local cinema, the Euston.

Some of my earliest memories are of the Euston, because in the early 1920s, when I was aged three or four, that's where my mother worked. She was a war widow, having married my father in October 1916. Very soon after the wedding he returned to the Western Front and was killed not far from Arras in the first hour of the German advance that began on 21 March.

I was born in June 1917, so we never set eyes on each other.

Back in England, my mother, barely eighteen years old, found herself a war widow with a nine-month-old baby to bring up. Local people were very sympathetic and did what they could to help her. Sometime in 1916, while still a civilian, my father had helped decorate the Euston cinema, and the proprietor offered my mother a job as a ticket sales woman cum chocolate seller in the programme intervals. There was, however, a problem about this employment: me. Where would I go while she was working? I could be farmed out to my grandmother Chilton, my father's mother, but not all the time. She was also a widow and had four children (two boys and two girls) to bring up. She did this by doing a great deal of charring and taking in washing, mainly at the Theatre Royal, Haymarket.

When my mother went to the Euston cinema to work, if she could, she would dump me at my grandmother's house. But if my grandmother was working at the Theatre Royal, my mother had no choice but to take me with her to the cinema. The tickets she sold were heavy metal ones, about two inches square that were issued by turning a handle on the ticket machine. Having issued the tickets, she would then leave the box office by way of a long, red curtain into the auditorium in time to vet the clients and take back the tickets she had just issued. She then fed the tickets back into the machine. Issuing metal tickets also automatically counted the number of people who paid for admission and the amount of money taken.

When my mother took me to work with her, I was strapped with a shawl I had been wrapped in as a baby into one of the more expensive seats at the back of the house, quite near the door that led into the back of the pay box. My mother constantly appeared and disappeared, to collect the tickets she had just sold and also to keep an eye on me in my expensive seat, where I was apparently fascinated by the flickering images on the silver – more probably plain whitewash – screen.

Quite suddenly, all contact with the Euston cinema ceased. My mother no longer worked there because she'd decided to re-marry a man who had been a front-line soldier like my father. His name was Bert Banbury.

At this time our home was a single front room in a Bloomsbury Georgian house. It had originally been built for middle-class occupants but had deteriorated into common, almost slum accommodation for working people, since the building of the great railway termini along the Euston Road.

The street we lived in, which still exists, was called Sandwich Street, and we lived at number 35. Our little parlour in Bloomsbury was on ground level, and everyone who lived in the house had to pass our door. My mother could tell by the tread of anyone leaving the house who the person was, and she would say, for instance, as footsteps echoed in the passage, 'That's Mr Woodford, going for his beer'.

Our room had one large window, which my mother cleaned and hung with spotless white lace curtains. On one side of the room was a black kitchen grate with a coal fire and oven on which she cooked the meals, and which kept us warm in winter. On top of the grate there were three iron plate circles. When you wanted to cook something in a saucepan, you would remove one of the iron plates and heat the saucepan in the hole. In summer, because there was no fire, all food was cooked on a single gas ring. (Some families cooked on fire ovens all the year round, so that during the summer they would have been very overheated.) Coal for the fire was kept in a box under the bed, which served as a coal scuttle, and the fireplace was surrounded by a wire fireguard to keep me away. A large, brass-knobbed double bed stood opposite the fireplace. Next to the farthest wall from the window were a chest-of-drawers and a washstand, and a little bed for me that was folded up during the day or which served as a chair for visitors. A small kitchen table was pushed up between the bed and the fireplace, and this is where we had our meals, with my mother and stepfather sitting sideways to the fire and me sitting on the bed facing it. There were two cupboards, one on either side of the fireplace. Here was where the food was kept:

bread, margarine, sugar, and tins of very sweet and very sticky condensed milk. Printed in large letters on the side of the tin was the warning, 'Unfit For Babies'. This was ignored.

My mother worked hard to keep her tiny home clean – at least I think she did. I was too young to be really aware of cleanliness, but I do remember her forever cleaning windows, scrubbing the floor, blackleading the grate, or whitening the doorstep.

Artificial light was created by gas. There was a gas bracket on each side of the fireplace that was lit with a match and which popped when the gas ignited. Light came from a heated gas mantle, made from a delicate cloth that glowed brightly when heated and fell to pieces at the slightest touch. Between them, the two gas brackets produced a greenish light that brilliantly illuminated the whole room – at least they would have done had we had them both on at the same time, which we hardly ever did. To save money we burned only one light, and that was often turned down to half its full strength.

In the evenings my mother would put me to bed at about 7pm, and then she and her husband would sit in front of the fire and talk, or play cards. On some occasions, however, they would give me a pencil and paper, tell me to be a good boy and go out, leaving me alone and rather frightened. I can still remember those evenings. Sometimes I would write letters to my Auntie Queenie, my mother's younger sister, in 'real writing'. This consisted of a scrawl and scribble that I couldn't read myself – which proved it was 'real writing' because I couldn't read that either. When I'd written my letter, I posted it; that is, I put it under the pillow and banged on the wall. Then I became Auntie Queenie and took the letter out and read it. Then I wrote an answer to myself. After a little while I usually fell asleep, but not always. Sometimes the fire roared or the gaslight went out for want of a penny. I would become frightened and scream until somebody else in the house came to comfort me. Whoever it was would say it was a shame to leave me alone like that, and would open the fire to stop it roaring or put a penny in the gas meter. At other times I would dress myself and try to go out, but I could never open the street door. I would then get frightened and howl in the dark passageway until one of the other tenants would discover me standing crying by the door, with only one shoe on and my shirt hanging out of my trousers.

Early in the morning my mother would pull me out of bed, wash and dress me, and send me out to buy bread and milk. Then we would have breakfast that consisted of bread, margarine and tea.

My mother sent me to school as soon as she could, to get me out of the house while she did her housework. I first went to school the day I was three years old. My school was almost opposite our house, and I would head off after breakfast, come home for 'dinner' (lunch), and then go back to school again, usually an hour too early. I used to sit on the doorstep until the school bell rang, watching the horses parked in the kerb and daring myself to go up to them to touch their heads.

Horses and carts often parked in our street, because it was so near the mainline railway stations in Euston Road and their goods yards. On Saturdays in particular a great number were parked because it was pay day, and there was a pub at each end of our street where the carmen who drove the horses and carts would drink away a substantial part of their wages. They wouldn't go home until the pubs closed at 3pm.

Where the horses had been standing would be new piles of horse dung littering the road. Local residents would soon emerge from the nearby houses with buckets and shovels to scope up the precious droppings and take them home to their back yards to lay on the carefully cultivated vegetable plots as manure. Our back yard was no exception; it had been dug up by my uncle who grew a number of vegetables and flowers, mostly rhubarb and hollyhocks.

We followed a way of life familiar enough to most cockney working families. We went to the cinema – I was not always left alone at home – but by the time I was six years old I went by myself. The cinema became part of my life. It seemed as natural to go to the cinema as to go to bed. By this time I loved Charlie Chaplin; all the children in my district did. We liked him so much that we included his name in one of our chants that we sang when our ball fell into the areas that lined the street that became our playground:

One two three O'Leary
My ball's down the airy
Don't forget to give it to Mary
And not to Charlie Chaplin

I loved that little man! I loved his walk, his funny hat and his stick. And how lucky it was that he should live so near me. I saw him at least twice a week and followed him around from pub to pub, where he performed outside the entrances to the main public bars. Besides his moustache, hat, stick and big boots, he carried a pole with a large spring at one end and an old army tin helmet on the other. Fastened down the side of the pole were tins, bells and other gadgets. Charlie would bounce this pogo stick up and down on the pavement outside the pub doors and hit the bells and other gadgets with his stick, singing the latest popular songs in time to the racket he made. When he'd finished his performance, he'd collect money from the drinkers inside and then go to another pub where I would follow him. My faith in the cinema shadows being real, live human beings was so great that it was some time before I could be persuaded that he was not really the Charlie Chaplin I saw on the screen.

Sometimes we went to the music hall in Camden Town. This was an occasion. We always took sweets and oranges with us, which we ate as we sat in the gallery and watched the show. The music hall people were very clever. There was a man who only had to kick his heels back when he was dancing before something went *chirrup* or *tonk tonk* or *boomph*. I nearly ricked my neck at home trying to reproduce these noises, and my mother would anxiously tell me not to fidget. I never told her what I was trying to do.

My stepfather worked in a piano and gramophone shop in Euston Road. Although we had no bath, we did have a gramophone. This new musical toy was to be found in nearly every working-class home. It was usually the only means of musical entertainment for a mainly musically illiterate people, and was to maintain its popularity until supplanted by the radio towards the end of the 1920s. My stepfather brought home many gramophone records, mainly consisting of popular songs of the day. My earliest musical recollection is of a song called 'Hullo Old What's-A-Name', sung by a tinny-sounding voice coming from a daffodil-shaped horn on the top of a chest-of-drawers.

My mother was always cheerful and was forever singing. She sang with the gramophone and I would sing with her, which made her laugh. She'd pick me up and say, 'When you grow up you'll be a singer and earn a lot of money for your mummy'.

As well as the pop songs of the day, we also had a number of classical records. They had a strange effect on me. Whenever they were played, I used to stalk stealthily round the room – under the table, over the bed – much to the distress of my mother and annoyance of my stepfather. What I was really doing was re-enacting films I had seen at the Euston cinema.

In those days films were silent, and a pianist, if not a small orchestra, accompanied every performance. Tragedy on screen was heightened by tragic music from the pit, while comic scenes were enhanced by comic music. Music and film, I thought, were part and parcel of the same thing, so that when I heard melodramatic music being played at home on the gramophone it would remind me of films I had seen at the cinema.

At that time the gramophone and the music hall were not my only contact with music. Two sons were born to my mother and stepfather. Each time a new half-brother was due to arrive I was sent off to stay with my mother's aunt in Sutton in Surrey, then a rural district within easy reach of London. My great aunt's husband, whose name was Larkin, was my favourite uncle. He was Irish and apparently the brother of a famous Irish revolutionary. One of his daughters had married a Salvationist. On Sunday mornings I would be taken along to the Salvation Army's open-air corner meetings, after which, with the band leading and me carrying a flag or banner with other young Salvationists, we would march to the Sutton Citadel for the morning service. My stays in Sutton were short but very sweet. My Irish uncle's market garden was a green paradise to me. It was very small as market gardens go, but my great uncle scraped an income from the sale of fruit, vegetables and flowers to local shops and householders, which, added to his army pension, just about gave him enough to live on.

In Sandwich Street on Friday nights we always had a big supper of fish and chips, which I greatly looked forward to. We would go to one of the fish shops in Camden Town, or would stay at home if it was raining and gather round the fire to play the gramophone. I would try to teach my baby brothers to talk or draw funny men on a sheet of paper.

One rainy Friday night in January 1924, we were spending an evening at home. I was learning something I'd been asked to learn by my school; my stepfather sat at the table reading his *Evening Star*; and my mother was washing her hair. My stepfather didn't say a great deal; the only time he spoke was when my mother made a splash, which annoyed him. When she had finished washing her hair, my mother sat down with her feet on the floor near where I sat. She wore high-heeled shoes with straps across the insteps. I tried to undo them.

'Don't undo Mummy's shoes, there's a good boy,' she said, not even looking down at me. But I took no notice.

'Leave yer mother's shoes alone when she tells yer,' said my stepfather so quickly and so sternly that I took my hand off the strap as though it were hot.

I sat sulking silently. Except for the noise of the burning coal and my mother rubbing her hair there was silence in the little parlour.

Quite suddenly my stepfather said, 'How about the supper, gel?'

My mother stopped rubbing her hair and said, 'Oh dear, why didn't you tell me before I started to wash my hair? I can't go out now. I'll catch me death o' cold.'

My stepfather couldn't go for it either: he had his boots off. Then an idea struck him.

'Couldn't he go?' he said, looking at me.

'Yes, I'll go,' I said eagerly, and with the help of the fireguard I pulled myself on to my feet.

'How can he go out this time of night?' said my mother.

'It's only round the corner,' said her husband, thinking of the fish shop.

'Yes, I know where Levy's is,' I said, glad of his support. 'I can go there, easy.'

I had lately been allowed to go out on outings. Not for ordinary errands such as getting bread in the morning, but for really important ones such as taking the rent round to the collector's office in Cartwright Gardens on the other side of the block. The day I'd done this, however, the rent was never paid. My mother gave me the money wrapped in an envelope and with the rent book in one hand and the envelope in the other I set off. But as soon as I got out of the house I tore open the envelope and threw it away. I wanted to be grown up and carry the money in my hand. I stopped to look at the horses on the way. I also looked at the shops. Then, as I neared my destination, I saw something absolutely wonderful that held me spellbound. There, standing in the kerb, was a large steam engine.

Trains had always fascinated me and here was an engine, a large red and green engine with a fire and a tall chimney. I couldn't leave it. *Soon*, I thought, *it'll move*. I couldn't let it move away and not see it go, so I sat down on the nearest doorstep to wait for the great moment. And there my mother found me when, growing anxious, she came out to look for me. The rent money was clasped naked in my hand, with the rent book lying on the pavement.

Perhaps it was the memory of this aborted errand that now caused my mother to doubt whether I could be trusted to buy the supper. But I pleaded with her and my stepfather said it would be all right, so she gave in to the pressure. She dressed me in my warmest clothes and made me wear a hat. Then, giving me a two-shilling piece and a slip of paper to give to the shopkeeper, she took me to the street door and opened it.

'Be as quick as you can and don't go anywhere except the fish shop.'

It had now stopped raining but the pavements glistened under the light of the street lamps, and the lights of the public house on the corner shone brightly. Besides the note and the money I carried a string bag in which to put what I'd bought.

I soon reached the fish shop, which was rather crowded but warm and steamy inside. I pushed my way to the counter, which was much taller than me, and called out in a loud voice:

'Fish and chips please, with two shillings and change out.'

Nobody took any notice, so I called out the same thing again and kept calling it out until the monotony of my sing-song voice claimed the server's attention and I was served.

My order was wrapped in a large sheet of newspaper and handed over the counter with my change. I put the warm parcel under my arm, pushed my way through the mass of legs, and stepped out into the damp night. Once outside I remembered the string bag, so I unrolled it and tried to put my warm parcel in it. I found that rather difficult because one hand was full of change. Eventually, however, I manoeuvred the bag and the parcel into a position where I thought I could drop it in and let the parcel go. Unfortunately I still held one corner of the wrapping in my hand so the bundle unrolled, sending the fish and chips loose into the bottom of the carrier.

This surprised, but did not alarm, me, as I merely put the paper on top of the pile and made for home.

I tried to carry the bag the way I had seen my mother carry it, by the handle, but in doing this the bottom of the bag flopped along the pavement so that our supper was dragged home through the wet evening loose in the bottom of a string bag.

When I got home my mother was pleased with me because I had been so quick. But she wasn't so pleased when she took the bag from me and found the fish and chips loose in the bottom of it, all muddy from having been dragged along the ground.

'There! I knew I shouldn't have sent him,' she said. 'We can't eat that. Look at it!' We looked. The fish and chips were covered with potato dust from the bottom of the bag; some were muddy.

'They'll be all right,' said my stepfather cheerfully. 'We can soon clean them up.' And he set to work scraping the dust off. 'The fish is quite clean inside; we can take off the dirty batter.'

My mother brightened up a little and left him to do the scraping while she made some tea and cut the bread. Instead of fish covered with golden brown batter we ate naked white pieces. In the meantime the chips had got cold and had to be warmed up in the oven before we ate them.

Not long after supper my mother said, 'Let's go to bed,' and I was undressed as far as my shirt that served as a nightgown. The little folding bed was retrieved from under the table and my elder stepbrother and I tucked into it. Just before I fell asleep I heard my stepfather tell my mother not to bother about washing up as it was getting late and might as well be left until the morning. My mother agreed.

During the night I was woken by the gas being lit and the sound of my mother vomiting into the slop bucket. She looked very pale and struggled hard against every heave of her stomach; clearly she was in a lot of pain. My stepfather stood over her anxiously and kept asking her how she was. She said that she would be all right in a minute, and sure enough she seemed to be better. My stepfather put out the light, told me to lie down and go to sleep, and got back into bed.

Shortly afterwards, however, he was up lighting the gas again and my mother was once more leaning over the side of the bed. This time her retching was worse and, in place of semi-digested fish, streaks of blood appeared. My stepfather put on his trousers and heated the kettle for a cup of tea. As morning approached my mother got steadily worse. She vomited blood. It ran out of her mouth, down the side of her face and stained her nightdress. As she lay back spasms of pain gripped her, distorting her face and making her pull up her knees and cry out. As I watched her I became frightened and began to cry.

As soon as it was light, my stepfather made me dress myself and go across to my grandmother who lived almost opposite us to tell her that my mother was ill and ask her to come over. I was to stay at my grandmother's house. I dressed myself quickly and went. The last glimpse I had of my mother was of her lying back on her pillow, with her hair and shoulders stained red by her own blood, a channel of which ran down the side of her mouth and wet the pillows and the sheets.

My grandmother went over to be with my mother while my stepfather took his two children to his mother who lived a few streets away. When he returned, my grandmother said he must send for a doctor. I had been forbidden to go home; watching from the window I saw my stepfather come out of our house and I ran outside to meet him.

'Can I come home?' I asked him.

'Not yet, son, Mummy isn't very well.'

That night I slept at my grandmother's house, but next day I decided to go home and crossed the street to where I lived. I found the street door open when I got there and walked straight in. I turned the handle of our front parlour door and pushed, but it was locked. That was indeed a surprise. I called out to my mother to let me in, but the only sounds in answer to my cries were the echoes of the passage. I ceased calling and looked through the keyhole. The room was deserted. My bed was still as I'd left it. The plates we had used for supper were still on the table.

Suddenly I felt frightened and afraid. I began to cry and beat on the door and cried out for my mother. The noise brought everyone in the house into the passage. Mrs Mahoney was there first because she lived in the next room.

'Now, now,' she said, 'what's all this noise?' She said this not angrily but kindly and gently. 'You mustn't go on like that; you'll have a policeman after you.' Then she took me by the hand and led me across to my grandmother.

Why should our room be empty? Where had my mother gone? Nobody seemed to want to talk to me about my mother. I was told to be quiet when I asked questions, or was given answers I knew to be false. When I was told she would be home soon and she didn't come, I stopped asking questions and simply waited.

Early in the evening my stepfather and uncle came home. 'How is she?' asked my grandmother. My stepfather said nothing, but buried his face in his hands.

I now know that my mother bled to death from a damaged stomach, which had been ripped open by her retching. I sometimes shudder when I see myself dragging a string bag along a wet street, thinking how grown up I was. My mother had allowed me to go out into the darkness to buy the fish and I remember how she tipped the stuff out on to the table, declaring it was not fit to eat. Then I try to comfort myself with the thought that it could not possibly be the fish that had made her retch and that it was not bad.

My mother was twenty-six years old when she died. I have never been able to find out what she died of. As a boy I asked my grandmother and uncle about this, but they looked embarrassed and hastily changed the subject. The official explanation was that she died of the virulent Asian flu that had swept through the country after the war. But in later life I often wondered whether she had died following an illegal abortion, not being able to bear the thought of having yet another child in that tiny room.

My mother was buried in Finchley cemetery in a public grave. She had a horse-drawn funeral. I remember the funeral well because on that day I saw the person to whom I used to write letters when I was lonely. Auntie Queenie, my mother's sister, then only aged eighteen, was there. She would always take me out when she came to see us and would let me wear her watch and her Girl Guide's hat. She would know about funerals. When I saw her I ran to her and laughed and hugged her. I asked her why there was going to be a funeral, and what we were going to do when it happened, and why had everybody, even my grandmother, met at my other grandmother's house (my stepfather's mother). I thought a funeral must be something like Christmas, because all sorts of relations had gathered together and all were dressed in their best clothes. Auntie Queenie sat on the stairs and I sat on her knee. Every now and then she would tell me to be quiet and 'Hush like a good boy'. I did and spoke to her only in whispers.

Very soon the coffin that contained my mother's body was carried out of a small parlour on the shoulders of the undertakers. Then my stepfather began to call out names as he was standing at the door. As we were called, my Uncle George, my Auntie Queenie, two other people whom I cannot remember and myself, stepped out into the street to a waiting horse-drawn carriage. I was surprised to see quite a crowd of people outside lining the pavements and crowding round the doorstep.

We climbed into the carriage and I sat on my aunt's knee in one of the corners. All the way to the cemetery and all the way back I clutched a teddy-bear-size rag doll in the shape of an Egyptian mummy. (This was the time when toymakers were cashing in on the story of Tutankhamun's tomb that had been discovered in Egypt in 1922.)

Quite soon we moved off. We left the street where my step-grandmother lived and turned into Judd Street and finally into our own street.

'Are we going to church now?' I asked my aunt. I was quite interested in all that was going on.

'Yes dear,' she said, 'but you mustn't ask too many questions. You must wait until we come back and then I'll tell you all about it.' She was embarrassed and didn't want to talk because all the people with us were weeping. I looked out of the window and counted the number of carriages there were in our procession. There were four more besides ours, but the one in front of us was different. It carried the coffin.

We soon reached St Pancras Church. Inside we sang a hymn and the burial service was read. The coffin rested on two trestles before the altar and the priest came right up to it when he talked. Then he gave a short sermon. I cannot remember what he said, but I do remember his voice echoing from the high walls. The church was cold and the congregation of mourners was exceedingly small. I didn't like it at all. It was so different to how it was on New Year's Eve when my mother had taken me there. Then we had sat up in the gallery because the church was full to capacity and was warm; everybody seemed different, nobody was crying as they were now and the priest's voice did not echo so eerily. I hung on to my aunt's hand and decided I didn't like funerals.

Very soon the coffin was carried out and we once more took up our positions in the coaches and began the long ride to Finchley. All the men we passed who wore hats took them off or raised them, and policemen saluted while women stood and watched.

We arrived at the cemetery after what seemed to me to be a very long ride and rode through the big iron gates that were opened for us. In the public graves section we stood round a very deep, narrow hole and the coffin was first rested on the edge and then slowly lowered into it. The weeping was now loud; few people bothered to cry softly any more. The priest read from a book and threw a handful of earth into the grave that clattered onto the coffin below. It seemed a very deep hole and indeed it was so, because my mother's body was the first to be buried in this grave. Before it was finally filled in, another fifteen coffins had been placed on top of her.

Seeing all that I saw did not frighten or bore me. I was interested in what was going on, and although I suspected that perhaps my mother was in the box now covered with flowers I couldn't bring myself to believe it. Why would anyone want to shut her up in a box and treat her like this? I looked up from the grave to the hundreds of gravestones round about us, all glistening in the weak January sunshine. I'd never seen so many white stones together before. They fascinated me. I began to ask my aunt, whose hand I was still holding, about them, but she checked me before I could get half the question out.

'Hush while the priest is talking.'

I hushed.

We returned home in the fast fading light with the horses trotting all the way. Their harnesses rattled and the straps clapped against the shafts. Everybody seemed a bit better now. Nobody was crying any more, but nobody talked either. When we arrived back at my step-grandmother's house, a few children had gathered to watch us alight.

We had a big tea in my step-grandmother's very large kitchen. There were lots of familiar faces. All my stepfather's brothers and sisters were there, whom I knew as my aunts and uncles; my aunt and uncle from Sutton; and one or two of my father's relations.

I sat next to Auntie Queenie, happy to feel that at last there was something nice about funerals. Here was a large tea with winkles, watercress, bread, jam, cake, shrimps, sandwiches and lots of other good things. It was just like Christmas. But after tea I was rather disappointed because everybody went home.

My aunt and uncle from the country asked me if I'd like to live with them. Remembering how much I'd enjoyed being with them I said that I would, very much. They said they'd see what they could do. But little did I know that there had been a battle over who was going to be my guardian. My grandmother claimed me because she said I was her son's boy. My stepfather claimed me because he said he had been good enough to look after me while his wife was alive and he could see no reason why he shouldn't go on doing so now that she was dead. My aunt and uncle from the country declared that they alone could really afford to take on an extra mouth to feed, which was true.

Eventually, however, it was arranged that I should live with my grandmother, my father's mother. My stepfather left the tiny little parlour that had been our home and went back to live with his mother. He took his children with him. I merely crossed the road to live with my grandmother at number 9 Sandwich Street.

I was six years old.

CHAPTER TWO
ANCESTORS

My grandmother Annie Elizabeth Chilton's maiden name was Kirkham. She was born in Worksop, Nottingham, in 1872, but her father and grandfather were both Londoners. Her grandfather, Joseph Kirkham, worked as a turnkey in the Westminster House of Correction. Granny used to tell me stories of how, if his children misbehaved, he would lock them up in a cell. Her father, Frederick John Kirkham, was born in Westminster in 1850. In 1869 he married Ann Elizabeth Plumpton at St Martin-in-the-Fields. Soon after he must have moved to Worksop. Granny told me that he worked there in a mine and twice had to be dug out of a mine disaster. He therefore decided to move back to London. In the 1881 census he is described as 'head painter' and living at 8 Grafton Street.

Later, the family's painting and decorating business, F. J. Kirkham and Son, was established at 28 Sandwich Street, with a builder's yard in nearby Hastings Street. It was here that many of the men in my family learnt their trade.

Granny's husband, Charles Chilton, had moved from Lambeth where his parents and his brother lived to make his home with his wife Annie in north London. One reason for this was that both his wife and mother worked at the King's Cross Laundry. They were married in 1890, settled in St Pancras and lived in a tenement house. The house he chose was in Harrison Street just off Gray's Inn Road. He earned his living in various ways, as a window cleaner, a builder and decorator and – what he considered his true trade – as a stagehand at the Haymarket Theatre. He would work for no other theatre, so when the Haymarket was dark he took to window cleaning or house painting. Granny was very tiny and when I knew her she had no teeth. She had been given false teeth but never wore them, although she managed to eat almost everything – except nuts.

Early in the twentieth century the Chiltons moved to 9 Sandwich Street. They rented four rooms, two on the ground level and two in the basement. My grandmother bore thirteen children, seven of whom died in infancy. Those who survived were Rose, Charles (my father), James, Annie, Lilian and Arthur (always known as Pat).

My grandmother used to tell me a lot about my father. He was clearly very headstrong. At school it seems he was very clever. At the age of eleven at elementary church school he was getting top marks in all his exams. He decided there was nothing more to be learned, so he didn't go to school. Instead he roamed the streets where he earned money, and in hot weather swam in the Regent's Canal.

My grandmother knew nothing of this. So far as she knew he left the house for school every day at the usual time. She thought he got there all right, which would have been very easy as he lived right next door to it. But living next door to a school is no reason for attending it, as I discovered myself some twenty years later. It all depends on which way you turn when you leave the house.

The first my grandmother heard of my father's truancy was when the school board authorities summoned her for keeping her eldest son away from his education. She was then in danger of losing her eldest son altogether, because the penalty usually paid for truancy was a few years in a reform school.

My grandmother was at her wits' end and appealed to my father's schoolmaster, Mr Whetham, for help. He gave it by appearing at the trial and speaking up for her son. He presented my father's school records to the court and asked them how they could possibly expect a young lad who had reached the top class at the age of eleven and had won top place in examinations not to be a little bored and restless. The boy was young, headstrong and impetuous, but if he as a teacher were allowed to take full responsibility for the child, he would see to it that he attended school regularly. The court granted him that responsibility.

The first thing Mr Whetham did when he got my father back to school was to cane him. This he did very thoroughly and with great deliberation. Then he set him to work helping to train the backward boys.

Out of school, from the time he was twelve or so until he left school and went to work aged fourteen, my father spent his time parading the streets, being noisy and having narrow escapes with the law. He hated policemen and lots of his time was spent in fixing booby traps for them, knocking off their helmets and tripping them up. On one occasion he hid himself above the lamp of a streetlight where he couldn't be seen and threw horse dung at a policeman below. In our neighbourhood hatred of policemen was fairly universal. His younger brother James felt the same way about them. He made a friend in the army whom he used to see a lot after the First World War, but subsequently that friend became a policeman and from then on James was no longer his friend.

When he was not up to his pranks, my father earned himself a penny or two. In Cromer Street Mr Ponser owned a barber's shop. Jack, as the barber was known, was very popular with many of the working men in the district. On Sunday mornings his shop would be crowded out with men who wanted a shave and a gossip while their wives cooked the Sunday meal. Jack had so many customers that he found he couldn't cope with them all. Help came from the Chilton brothers, Charles and James, who spent their Sunday mornings lathering faces for Jack to shave. For their trouble they received 2/6d each – a princely sum. But my father said, 'For every half a crown he gives us, he makes ten. He'll have a bigger dinner than us, Mum. He'll have a bigger dinner than any of those men he shaves and they have supplied him with it.' Whether Jack did have a bigger dinner I can't say, but I do know that later he was able to send his son to London University where he took a medical degree.

My father must have thought this lathering business was a bit boring, because one day he and his younger brother decided not to go. Jack came running round to where they lived in a panic as his customers were filling the shop and he couldn't get rid of them fast enough. Charles and James heard him arrive and crawled under the table in the hope that they would not be seen. But they were found. Under threats of a beating from their father they went back to lathering faces, their half-crowns split between themselves and their mother.

My grandfather was a very stern man. He often got drunk, and when he did so he beat my grandmother. To be beaten by one's husband was not uncommon in those days and my grandmother usually took her beatings silently without complaint. On one or two occasions, however, she rebelled and threw things at him. I don't think my grandfather was a good husband. Not only did he drink too much; he also had a fiery temper.

He defied convention and etiquette, and during an age when all men would give up their seats to women, he refused. He sat firmly on his seat in the tube and refused to budge until the train reached Russell Square, no matter who was standing – unless it were a woman of his own class. To the flower sellers of Piccadilly he would offer up his seat with great courtesy but for all he cared a woman in evening dress could stand for the whole of her journey.

One 'gentleman', as anybody who wore a top hat was called, asked him to stand up and let a lady sit down.

'Sir,' replied my grandfather, 'you've been to the theatre to be entertained. During all that time you and your lady have been sitting down, but I've been standing and working behind the scenes to entertain you. So now it's my turn to sit down, and I'm sticking here until I get to Russell Square.'

Which he did. Five minutes walk from Russell Square and he was home.

At one time my great grandmother, Lydia, who lived at Lambeth got herself a job as an ironer at the King's Cross laundry and came to the north side of the river to live with her son and daughter-in-law. She saw how her son carried on and was shocked. The first time she saw her son beat my grandmother she beat her son hard across the head with a 'copper stick' (a large wooden pole used in the laundry). That dealt with him for a while and he went out to drink a lot more. The two women stayed home and quietened the children. They had gained a victory.

'The trouble with you me gel,' my great grandmother said to my grandmother, 'is that you let him have his own way. You want to let him have some back some time, just as I did his father. They don't get their own way with me.'

My grandmother replied, just as she always did: 'Anything for peace and quiet.' But inside she felt that perhaps resistance would stave off a few blows.

My grandfather returned later that evening after the theatre had closed and sat down to his late meal. He complained about the food.

'Don't you like it?' asked my grandmother.

'No I don't. It's bloody cold.'

'Then take that then,' and without more ado my grandmother picked up the plate of food and broke it over his head. He was so surprised he didn't know what to do.

'You cow,' he said rising up from his seat.

My grandmother and great grandmother grabbed a broomstick and a copper stick, respectively. He stopped in mid-air and surveyed them. Then he went out and didn't come home for a week.

When he came back he told his mother to get out of his house. He said she was a bad influence on his wife and children. She went back to Lambeth and never came to Sandwich Street again. In later life I used to visit her in Lambeth and asked why she never came to see us. She said she could never find a bus to take her there. I discovered she was looking for a horse bus! She never recognised the motorised vehicles as buses and refused to travel on them.

As he grew older, the streak of delinquency in my father's behaviour disappeared. In 1913 when he was barely fourteen, he left school and went to work for his living. His first employers were a wholesaler's in Berners Street, off Oxford Street. There he became a messenger, errand boy and carman's help, all in one. He delivered goods on a tricycle. He carried goods by hand and rode on the tailboard of a horse-drawn delivery cart. His official title in this capacity was 'Van Boy'.

Except that he could read and write, his education, what there was of it, was of little use to him in this job. He didn't learn a great deal from it, either. True he learned his way around London, but he could have done that anyway – a London child who was at all adventurous knew all the main roads within three or four miles of his or her home long before leaving school.

No matter how ambitious he was, my father could see little prospect before him other than riding at the front end of his van as the driver instead of at the back end as the van boy. After a year he tried for something else. There were jobs inside the firm that appealed, so eventually, after much asking and being refused, he became a counter assistant. This meant he stood behind one of the wholesale counters packing up parcels and serving representatives of various London shops who bought their goods wholesale from his employers.

Being a counter-hand soon bored him. He asked for a different job, 'one with more future in it', but the firm couldn't give him such a job, so he left, determined to learn a trade or die. He had everything worked out. He would learn a trade and when he had learned enough to earn his living at it, he would save his money and start up as a master of his own.

But the First World War shattered any hopes he ever had. By the time he had decided to learn a trade he was sixteen, and the war had been carrying on for a year. The trade he chose was that of builder and decorator. My father was taken into Kirkham's as a paid apprentice and learnt enough to begin to decorate his own home. He redecorated all the rooms and papered and painted them in bright colours. Everybody agreed that he'd made a good job of it – except his father who, because he often did a little decorating when there was no work at the theatre, went round finding fault.

My father applied the knowledge of his trade to buildings in the district: people's houses, tenement rooms and public places. He was among the first men to redecorate the Euston cinema. There he was threatened with the sack because he spent so much time playing the piano instead of getting on with his work.

He and my grandfather erected a decorative ceiling in a public house, the Norfolk Arms, on the corner of Leigh Street and Sandwich Street, that's still extant today. It's a ceiling typical of its place and period: cupids' heads entwined with flowers and fruit gaze down at the customers at the bar. The pub has changed hands many times, and many alterations have been made to the basic construction, but the ceiling, the pride of the saloon bar, remains and, except for fresh coats of paint, it has never been touched.

My father would spend his evenings at the music hall or at the cinema. He took his mother, brothers and sisters with him. He read a lot of books when he could get hold of them and followed the war closely. One Saturday he came home from work in bright spirits. He washed himself, changed his clothes, greased his hair and brushed it flat on his head with a parting down the centre. He wore a stiff collar, put on his morning suit of striped trousers and single-breasted coat, and went out and had his photograph taken. The photo he had taken in his bowler hat was for a very special occasion, as my grandmother soon found out. He came back from the photographer late in the afternoon, just when my grandmother was about to go to Somers Town market to do her weekend shopping. He often went with her on these occasions, but today he was more than keen. He supplemented the produce my grandmother had bought with lots of extra things: winkles, shrimps, watercress (pronounced 'watercrease'), celery, cake and various other things that taste so good to cockneys at Sunday teatime. Thus laden they returned home.

'My gawd, son, why did you buy so much? We'll never eat it.'

'It's all right, Ma – it's for tomorrow.'

'But that'll last us till next Sunday!'

'No it won't. I'm bringing somebody home tomorrow to help us eat it.'

'Oh, are yer? I thought there must be something up. Who is it?'

'Me girl.'

'Who?'

'Me girl.'

'Well, gawd 'elp us, Maurice.'

Quite what that means I don't know, because my father's name was Charles, but my grandmother used that saying for all great occasions and this was certainly a great occasion.

She said she just 'sat there, flabbergasted'. Here was her son, barely seventeen, bringing home a girl to tea: courting.

'Well it's no use me sitting here doing nothing, is it?' said my grandmother suddenly. 'We've got to get the place looking nice for her.'

And this they proceeded to do immediately, Charles helping and being just as enthusiastic about it as his mother. While they tidied, swept and dusted they talked.

My father had met this girl about four weeks previously at the Euston cinema. He had bought a bar of chocolate from her two or three times and had chatted with her. Sometimes after the show finished he took her home. He saw her on her night off and took her to the music hall in Camden Town. By now he was walking out with her regularly, and he wanted her to meet his family, which was why he was bringing her home to tea on Sunday.

My grandfather took the news with a deal of indifference, but agreed to be present at teatime to meet the girl.

Sunday came. Everybody got up a little earlier than usual so that by four o'clock when the visitor was due to arrive, everything was ready for her, the table covered with a clean cloth and the meal all laid out ready to be eaten.

She was very punctual. She was introduced and everybody liked her. My grandmother took a special liking to her because she brought her sweets. Thus did my father bring home his future wife.

Her name was Gladys Lee, and she came from a gypsy family who lived in Ashford in Kent. Her grandfather, George Lee, was a horse dealer. He bought and sold horses of all kinds, travelling to the big fairs all over the country. He could neither read nor write. A dumpy figure who always wore a top hat and was known as Jockey Lee or Gentleman Jockey (he particularly liked the latter name), George made money from his horse-dealing, so much so that Victoria Park in Ashford once belonged to him. His son, William Lee, Gladys's father, was born in a caravan. Father and son never got on and eventually George turned William out of the house. So when he died George left all his money to the other side of the family and my mother never got a penny.

Gladys's mother died of cancer in July 1914. After her death, Gladys, who was then fifteen, was supposed to look after the younger children, but she preferred going out with the Canadian soldiers billeted in Ashford prior to being shipped to France. The children were neglected and not kept clean and at one point the cruelty inspector came round. After this the family broke up and an aunt of Gladys took her to London, to Argyll Street, King's Cross, where she met my father. They courted for a year and sometime during September 1916 must have discovered that Gladys was pregnant. On 2 October 1916 they were married. This was quite usual among the young folk in my area.

'I hear Sally's getting married,' says one girl to another.

''Oh really? I didn't know she was pregnant.'

My parents rented the room directly opposite the school that my father had attended, and almost opposite his mother's house. Here they lived with no more than a bed, a table and two chairs, and the bare necessities of life in the shape of food. 1917 was a very bad year because it was when rationing was first introduced as a result of the large numbers of ships that had been sunk by the Germans at sea.

It was a bad military year, too. My father had long toyed with the idea of joining the army because he hadn't wanted to be thought of as a coward. Very soon after he was married he enlisted in the Sherwood Foresters, an infantry regiment. He was posted to Grantham in Lincolnshire. I haven't been able to find a date for when he joined up, but once he'd finished his preliminary training, instead of going to France like the other trainees, he was left behind to be an instructor in arms and promoted to lance-corporal. He rather liked this work and filled a number of exercise books with neatly written notes and diagrams from which he lectured and trained his men. I have one of these notebooks which has the inscription 'Gunnery Course – Began Jan. 16th 1917 – Expired Feb. 2nd 1917.'

In the spring of 1917 he applied for drafting to the front line. He loathed having to tell people that he was stationed at home as an instructor and had seen no active foreign service. Finally, after a number of applications, he was allowed to go to the Front. Before he went he was given ten days' leave. He spent his leave taking his wife, who was now quite near her time, parents and young brothers and sisters to the cinema and music hall, buying them expensive presents and, as far as possible, enjoying himself.

He spent what should have been his last night at home at his mother's house, but when the day for him to return to his regiment arrived, he decided to wait another day. When he eventually reported back he was court martialled and punished with the loss of his rank.

On their way to France his company passed through London. Here the men were allowed a few hours to themselves before catching the train at Waterloo. My father, living only a few minutes from King's Cross station where they were dismissed, of course went home, together with ten or more of his comrades. He took them to his mother's house. She fed them as well as she could – there wasn't a great deal to be had – but it seems they were all grateful for what they received and affectionately called her 'Ma' and kissed her good-humouredly when they left. Once my father saw them settled in, he went across the road to his wife.

What happened in their little room I cannot say. They may have quarrelled or perhaps my mother was too conscious of her swelling figure to want to show herself to her young husband's comrades. In any case, when my father emerged from his home, he came out alone.

When he formed up with his men in a street off King's Cross station to begin the march to Waterloo his mother and father were there to wave him off. His father, though by this time quite ill, marched along the pavement at his side. He saw him onto the train and shook his hand goodbye. Then he walked back to Sandwich Street where he found his wife in tears and in need of consolation. Neither of them knew it but it was the last they'd see of their favourite son. And neither of them thought to visit his young wife sitting in her little room on her own, not twenty yards away.

At first my father rather enjoyed the fighting and felt that at last he was 'doing his bit'. Once he was gassed and spent time in hospital, but he didn't tell anyone about this in his letters. He wrote to his old schoolmaster and told him how things were going and how he was still in the trenches 'showing the Hun who was who'. When he came out of hospital he told his folks where he'd been, but by the time they'd received his letter he was back in the trenches again.

In his letters there were now suggestions of his wanting to come home and see everybody again, to take them to the cinema or music hall, and to eat winkles in the firelit parlour on a Sunday afternoon. He knew that he now had a son whom he very much wanted to see. His child had been christened after him, and he was proud to be a father and made no attempt to hide his feeling in his letters home. He was due for leave before long.

Christmas 1917 came without his having any leave. He was promised some early in the year but this was cancelled. Then he was told he would have some in the spring of 1918, but again this was cancelled.

In April he fought in a fierce battle near Arras. During the battle there were many bayonet charges and much hand-to-hand fighting. One night, in spite of a heavy artillery barrage put up by the enemy, my father's section was ordered 'over the top'. They went. Few of them came back. No trace of my father was ever found, not even an identity disc to prove he was dead. For many months he was reported as missing, until finally he was presumed killed.

After the war was over, an officer of the Sherwood Foresters visited my grandmother. He told her how her son had once saved his life by crawling out to a shell hole where he lay wounded and bringing him back safely to the line where he was able to receive medical treatment. He had never been able to thank him for this because when he came out of hospital the battle of Arras had been fought and my father killed.

This was something my father had never written about. He wrote jokingly of the coarse food and biscuits; of the jokes and tricks of his comrades; of his long-awaited leave; but never of this courageous rescue.

CHAPTER THREE
LIVING AT NO. 9

Number 9 Sandwich Street, the tenement house where my grandmother lived, had four floors and a basement. Each floor, including the basement, comprised two rooms let out to various families. The Chiltons rented the two rooms on the ground floor (the front and back parlours) and thought themselves lucky to have an additional back kitchen room in the basement, but this had been condemned by the sanitary inspectors and locked up as unfit for human habitation. Another family, the Bryants, occupied the front basement room.

When I moved in after my mother died in 1924, the two rooms rented by the Chiltons housed my Granny, my Uncle Jim, my Aunts Lil and Annie, and my Uncle Arthur (known as Pat). Granny, Annie, Lil, Pat (who, although my uncle, was only four years older than me) and I slept five in a bed in the back parlour. The women slept with their heads at the normal end, while Pat and I slept at the foot of the bed. So many legs and feet made it most uncomfortable, and the bedclothes, such as they were, were constantly ending up on the floor.

Meanwhile, my Uncle Jim had married his girlfriend, Aggie, because there was a baby on the way. In 1925 he brought his wife, Aggie, and baby to live with us. The baby, 'Young' Charlie, was born in 1924. (I was thenceforth known as 'Old' Charlie.) He was hit by a taxi in Judd Street about a year before he died aged ten in 1934. My mother's brother, George, who had come up to London from Ashford to work at

Kirkham's, also moved in, and paid rent to Uncle Jim. Things became uncomfortably overcrowded so Uncle Jim broke open the door to the condemned back kitchen, repainted it, and installed a large double bed so that we could live there illegally.

Our sleeping arrangements then were Granny, Lil and Annie, ground floor back parlour; Jim and Aggie, front parlour; and Uncle George, Pat and I in the back kitchen. The back kitchen became the room we used most. It had a cooking range that used coal, a gas cooker and a cold water tap above a yellowish sink. Every so often when the health inspectors came round the room would be re-condemned and a new padlock fixed on the door. When they had gone we would break the padlock and move back in.

After Lil and Annie got married in the mid 1920s and set up their own homes, Jim and Aggie slept in the front parlour with 'Young' Charlie. Pat and I slept in the back parlour and Gran slept in the front kitchen in the basement, which also served as the living room as the Bryants had moved out.

Money was always short. Uncle Jim worked as painter and decorator for Kirkham's. He paid the rent, and gave my grandmother eighteen shillings a week for all expenses. Up to the time of her death my mother had received a war widow and orphan's pension. When Gran looked after me she received a very small war orphan's pension of about 12/6d a week. She supplemented her income by washing and ironing for local people.

As I grew older I used to collect and deliver the washing and help turn the big wheel of the old-fashioned wooden mangle in the wash house. In the winter or in wet weather the newly washed clothes were hung to dry from lines in the steamy kitchen. Water dripped on us as we ate our dinner or lay in bed. We shivered from the lack of bed covers.

The pawnbroker played an important part in the lives of my Granny and later my Aunt Aggie, as it did in the lives of most families in our area. So did the tallymen who came round to the houses offering goods for sale very cheaply, but who charged a high interest that had to be paid later. Thus my Granny might buy some article of clothing for a few shillings, but the interest to be paid was twice as much. When the tallyman came to collect it, she wouldn't open the door.

'Tell him I'm out', she'd say to me.

Eventually, when she could put him off no longer, she'd pawn the article and with the money she received pay off at least some of her debt. She tried to hide all this from my Uncle Jim, but on one occasion he found out and discovered that she owed £30. He was furious and accused her of being a bad housekeeper, never bothering to think that perhaps the eighteen shillings a week he paid her to keep us all in food, gas, and coal was not nearly enough.

In the passageway that led from the foot of the kitchen stairs into the area (what we kids called 'the airy') hung a row of old coats, two or three hung on one hook and with six or more hooks in a row. In the semi-darkness they looked like a row of pot-bellied spooks. They were terrifying. I hated to walk past them. I was scared that if I went too close they would reach out, grab and suffocate me. In cold weather these old coats were raided and put on beds in place of the blankets we needed but didn't have, but they were poor substitutes. They were neither wide nor long enough to make efficient covers. We laid them overlapping one beside the other – sideways and lengthways – but with three restless people (Pat, Uncle George and me) sleeping, or trying to sleep, they soon became misplaced and slipped to the floor.

Hardly anyone ever wore any of these coats. They probably dated from the 1890s (when Granny and Grandfather were married) to just after the First World War, and had been hoarded ever since. I remember just one or two occasions when they were worn. That was in freezing weather when, having served as blankets at night, Pat and I each put on a coat to protect us against the cold.

They were far too big for us and we had to roll the sleeves halfway up our arms in order to have our hands free. We could do nothing to disguise their overlength, and went to school looking like a couple of Artful Dodgers.

In the winter we couldn't sleep for the cold, while in summer we were kept awake by bed bugs. The latter were wonderfully adept at hiding away in the smallest crack or crevice during the day, or while the gas was burning, and then advancing on us in hungry hordes as soon as it was dark – and crawling into bed with us to have a good, hearty meal. On hot summer nights entire families would sit out on their doorsteps rather than face the bed bugs.

When the house was built (around 1812) there were no lavatories, either indoors or out. Chamber pots were the common utensils for personal relief. They were kept in a small closet and emptied into a larger container kept in the back yard. This container was carried from the yard through the house to the area and up the tradesmen's steps to the street. The contents were then tipped into a horse-drawn cart that usually came along at night, in charge of the 'night men'. The cartload of effluent was taken to a laystall (a heap of dust and human effluent) near the great dust heap, a huge rubbish dump, at Battle Bridge (later renamed King's Cross) from where it was taken to nearby fields and spread on crops as manure.

Human sewage had to be carted away from houses because there were no sewers. Sewers only came to Sandwich Street (as they did to most parts of London) in the 1840s and 1850s. Once the sewers were in place, water-closets could be installed. They were built outside, at the back. There were two closets per house, one above the other. This, however, was hardly enough, for by 1850 all the houses in Sandwich Street had become overcrowded tenements, one family to a floor on average, sometimes one family to a room. There was one water-closet on the ground floor and another at basement level. As the Chiltons occupied the basement, we considered the lower lavatory to be ours. The rest of the tenement used the upper lavatory.

Our lavatory, which we called khazi, or shit house, was a horror. It was embedded in a mound of tightly packed earth. The door was flimsy and the space so cramped that when you sat on the seat and closed the door your knees were pressed right up against it. In one corner was a small shelf, on which you placed a candle if it was dark. After some years of living at number 9, I used to take a candle to the loo in the evenings, which I used as a quiet place for reading. You got used to the smell.

There was a rude verse that we used to recite:

There is a certain puff of wind
Which rises near the heart
And when it reaches the lower bowel
Is commonly called a fart
Now a fart is a very useful thing
It gives the body ease
It warms the bed on a winter's night
And chloroforms the fleas

Bathing was a big problem. A large tin bath hung on the wall by the back kitchen window. It could only be used if most of the family were out. The big problem was heating sufficient water to fill the bath. Pails of water were heated on the kitchen range, but these hardly half-filled the tin bath.

As far as Pat and I were concerned, having a bath on a washing day solved the problem. Gran did the washing in the wash house that was in the backyard. All the houses in our street had wash houses. They looked like small bungalows with at least two windows, but their main feature was the 'copper'. This was a brick-built contraption with its own fire, a copper cauldron and a tall chimney. It generated a lot of heat and enabled the washing to be boiled, which was not only a great step towards cleaning but also a means of sterilisation and de-infestation. In order to help the cleaning process, lumps of Sunlight soap were added to the water, along with large helpings of soda. This mixture bubbled away all day, while heaps of soiled clothing and other washing were plunged into it. After an hour or so, the washing was removed on to a large circular wooden board with the aid of a 'copper' stick (actually a long wooden pole). The boiled clothes were then plunged into a large wooden tub full of cold water to soak. After being passed through the mangle, the washing was hung on a clothes line to dry. Small items were washed in a tub of hot, soapy water and were laid on a corrugated washboard, soaped and scrubbed with a hard bristle brush. At the end of the day, with the copper fire still burning, the water, which had been bubbling away all day with its various changes of dirty clothes, was still hot. On bath nights this water was transferred into buckets, using a tin bowl with a wooden handle, and carried into the kitchen to fill the tin bath. And that was what we had our bath in. It was dark grey, rather thick like a thin blancmange, and smelt strongly of dirty washing.

The daily routine at Sandwich Street didn't vary much. Every weekday morning the men in the house had a cup of tea and then went off to work. I went to school. My grandmother did her washing or went to Somers Town to do her shopping. She preferred to go to the market because it was cheaper than the nearby shops. Lil and Annie also went out to work.

There was no breakfast except on Sundays. After I had washed and dressed in my short trousers, jersey, long socks and boots, I would go to school, which was literally next door. Of course, living so close to the school, I was late, almost every day.

My 'lunch' would consist of bread and margarine wrapped in newspaper. The bread would be from the bottom of the bread bin, old and stale. This would give Granny the chance to use it up with no comeback from me, because once I'd got to school, I couldn't complain. This 'lunch' was what we would now call elevenses. We ate it during the first playtime break (about 10.30). Some kids had lovely lunches such as Bovril sandwiches. One boy whose parents had a restaurant in

Woburn Walk had cakes or scones, things we never saw in our house except at Christmas.

Everyone came home for dinner at midday, which was cooked by my grandmother. Usually we had a joint of meat on Sundays – the cheapest she could find; breast of lamb I remember being a favourite with boiled potatoes and greens. On Monday we had cold meat off the joint. Sometimes we had stew, which I hated. It seemed to consist mainly of bones and water. Occasionally there would be a treat and she made a 'baby's head', that is, a steak and kidney pudding with suet crust cooked in a pudding basin.

The only time we had a sweet was on Sundays. Under the table in the kitchen where we ate there was a huge bread bin with a wooden cover. Any bread that had gone too hard to eat was thrown into this bin and made into bread pudding, my favourite. The stale bread was soaked in water, mixed with raisins and sugar, and cooked in the oven. I always looked forward to it.

When the men came back from work at 5pm we had 'tea'. There would perhaps be a kipper or bloater, or maybe bacon and eggs, always with lots of bread and margarine.

Granny had one luxury that she would never give up. She always treated herself to two ounces of butter each week and would never eat margarine. When asked why, she would say it was because she had had butter in hospital when she had pleurisy, and she liked it so much she was determined to have it at home.

Christmas was special, but we never had a turkey, and sometimes not even a chicken if funds were low. Once we had a duck that Uncle George had won in a raffle. I used to hang up a pillowcase in hope on Christmas Eve, but there was never much in it in the morning. One year my grandmother bought me a 6d box of tin soldiers, and on another occasion Pat filled the pillowcase with coal. Another time I remember Granny, Uncle Jim and Aunt Aggie went to relations in Lambeth for Christmas dinner. Pat, Lil, Annie and I were left at home. We sat down for dinner and found slips of paper at our places on which Pat had written 'Roast turkey and stuffing', 'Christmas pudding', 'Mince pies', etc.

I don't suppose I shall ever again come so close to poverty as I did in those days, or enjoy the things that poverty, or near poverty, made scarce, such as Saturday night supper. Sunday morning breakfast, for instance, was special simply because there *was* a breakfast – it didn't exist on the other six days of the week – and it was always a cooked breakfast. Saturday was pay-day, and Saturday and Sunday were the two days in the week we could afford to be lavish with food. I shall never forget the wonderful taste of hot beef dripping toast, bread pudding, pease pudding, faggots, black pudding, stewed or jellied eels and fish and chips – all luxuries that we looked forward to at the weekend.

Occasionally we went to the music hall on a Saturday night and had supper afterwards at one of the local restaurants. Tables were marble-topped and supported by cast-iron filigree legs with chairs to match. Cutlery had a rusty appearance. Huge cans of salt and a large bottle of vinegar stood on every table. The walls were usually wet and running with condensation. Yellow gaslight flickered, hissed and popped. You bought your plate of food, probably faggots and pease pudding, at a large counter and took it to a table.

Sweet Saturday night! The elders drank in the pubs until closing time – Granny would drink black beer, unless someone offered to buy her a port and lemon, her favourite – so we never got our luxury suppers until after 11pm. When the pubs turned out – usually my family went to the Norfolk Arms at the top of our road – everybody stood around talking in groups. Likely as not they would start singing and dancing in the street, 'having a knees up' they called it, especially if there was a barrel organ handy. Mind you, they might well be abusing each other and fighting before the night was over and then supper really would be delayed; we'd probably be lucky to get any at all.

Until I was aged eight or nine, books didn't play a part in my life. My main reading matter was comics such as the *Wizard*, the *Rover*, the *Adventure* or bundles of American comics that could be bought at Somers Town market. These were strip cartoons, such as 'Amazing Stories' taken from the Sunday editions of various US papers and sold for a few pence. 'Funny Wonder' was a British strip that featured Charlie Chaplin as the main figure on the cover.

It was Auntie Queenie who bought me my first real book: a sixpenny edition of *Robinson Crusoe*. As I got older, I discovered that left-wing papers such as the *Daily Herald*, in their efforts to expand their readership, ran a system whereby you could obtain free copies of classical books (that were out of copyright). This you did by collecting small squares with printed numbers on them that appeared every day at the back of the paper. You had to be sure to collect the numbers consecutively – if you missed one you didn't get the books. In this way I collected and read the works of Charles Dickens and of my great hero, H. G. Wells.

The attitude of my family towards books was unfavourable. Granny thought reading was bad for your eyesight. My Uncle Jim and other grown-ups thought it put ideas into your head, or was a waste of time when you could be doing something useful. I had difficulty in finding somewhere to keep the books I bought. Eventually I found a very old table in the back kitchen where I slept that had a shelf underneath it and I kept them there. They were difficult to get at, but at least it was a place I could call my own.

Music was something the family did indulge in, however. Most families at that time had a piano, and my Uncle Jim was no exception. He bought one from Woodhouse's in Oxford Street near the British Museum. Once a week Aunt Aggie, Granny or Lil had to walk there with the weekly payment. Uncle Jim never went himself. That piano was the joy of his life. It was kept in the front room against the folding doors. It was the only piece of furniture that was ever polished. But the only person I ever heard get a decent tune out of it was the piano tuner. When everybody was out in the evenings and I was alone in our part of the house, I used to sneak into the front room and 'play' the piano. All I could play was 'The Vamp'. I would try to play other pop songs but seldom managed even the single notes of the tune.

Uncle Jim also had a gramophone of which he was very proud. It had no horn. The sound came from an opening under the turntable that was closed off by two doors when not in use. Playing records was probably my favourite pastime. Once I earned a little money I spent a lot of it on records – cheap ones from Woolworth's, six-inch ones with white labels. I played lots of Sophie Tucker, Layton and Johnson, and selections from *Rose Marie*, *The Student Prince* and *The Desert Song*. I remember a comic song called 'Down at Our Hotel', one line of which went: 'He'd fallen through the mattress and they found him in the spring'.

Aunt Aggie was our pianist. Her right hand played the melody with about eighty per cent of the right notes. Her left hand wandered where it would, regardless of key or harmony. The nearest I ever got to playing an instrument was when I learned the fife in the Boys' Brigade. After I'd learned to play the fife, I could play duets with Aunt Aggie. We tried many pop songs together, but with lots of wrong notes from me and seldom the right chords from the pianist, the result was not very harmonious. But when we got together for a Sunday evening singsong, nobody seemed to mind. They all sang their heads off. Slow, sentimental tunes were their favourites: 'Old-Fashioned Lady', 'While London Sleeps', 'A Bird in a Gilded Cage'. I remember Uncle Jim's favourite, which was 'A Group of Young Soldiers':

> A group of young soldiers
> Sat round a camp fire
> All talking of sweethearts they had
> They all looked so happy
> Except for one lad

And he was downhearted and sad
Come join in our chorus
Said one fellow-lad
For surely there's someone loves you
But the boy shook his head
And sadly he said
Boys I'm in love with two
One has the hair of silvery grey
The other's hair is gold
One is gay and beautiful
The other's bent and old
Dearer to me my life would be
If either of them should depart
For one is my mother –
God bless her, I love her
The other is my sweetheart

My interest in music and gramophone records was to have a great influence on my future life.

CHAPTER FOUR
LIFE AT SCHOOL

I went to the St Pancras Church of England Elementary School in Thanet Street, North Bloomsbury, which also had an entrance in Sandwich Street. It was built as a direct result of the Education Act of 1870, and my grandmother was one of its first pupils. All her children attended the school, and also her children's children, which included me. As it was a church school we received a lot of religious instruction, though I can't say we received a good education.

In Sandwich Street St Pancras Church had a mission hall, above which was a chapel and below it a boys' club room. A playground connected the two buildings, the mission hall and school, so that one could walk from Sandwich Street through the Mission, over the playground into the school and thence out into Thanet Street.

The mission hall and chapel were there for the use of the school, as required. The hall was used every day by the school as an assembly hall. The chapel above it was used every Tuesday when the pupils (not the infants) had to take part in the children's Eucharist (sung version). A priest came over from St Pancras Church to supervise the service. We all assembled in the chapel and when the service was about to begin the organ played and the servers' procession emerged from the vestry. The service was led by a surplice-clad boy carrying a crucifix on top of a long pole, followed by the priest carrying the chalice. Two serving boys, also clad in white surplices, followed him. While the young congregation sang the hymn 'Father Look on us Thy Children', the procession slowly moved up the aisle. When it reached the altar steps the cross-bearer would turn towards his specially reserved seat and clamp the cross to one of its arms into a slot specially made for the purpose. The priest would proceed up the altar steps and stand the chalice on the altar. Then the two altar boys would spread out, one right and one left, and kneel at the altar steps.

When, as sometimes happened, the priest was unable to attend on a Tuesday, the headmaster, who was a very religious man and delighted in the pomp and ceremony of the church, was very happy to fill his role himself. If any boy made a noise or misbehaved in some way during the service he would receive the thrashing of his life from the headmaster, who during ordinary school lessons was really quite lenient with his punishments.

We boys preferred to be cross-bearers rather than altar boys. It felt quite important carrying the heavy cross and leading the procession up the aisle to the altar. Once there, we could sit down for the rest of the service. Altar boys, on the other hand, were kept busy passing the bread and wine from place to place and generally helping in the intricacies of the service.

By the time I was twelve my friends and I could sing the Eucharist by heart – and at the same time read a comic concealed in the prayer book.

On Sundays there was Sunday school. Classes were held in the lower rooms of our day school. Texts, such as 'God is Love' and 'Suffer the little children to come unto me', were given out at the end of each lesson for us to take home; they were on pretty cards with angels or flowers printed on them, with the text printed over the picture.

Special teas were given out at Christmas in the basement of the mission building, where there were three or four full-sized billiard tables at which the children sat and where they consumed their tea and lemon curd sandwiches. They each received a Christmas cracker and an orange to take home before leaving.

Our school was always trying to impose the public school sporting spirit onto us boys. The school song was 'Play Up, Play Up and Play the Game', which had been specially written for the school sometime during the 1920s. A picture of St Pancras guarding St Pancras Church, encircled by the legend 'Play the Game', headed our annual school reports.

> In exam time, if you get hard nuts to crack,
> Play the game
> What you've learned in term time, try to give it back,
> Play the game
> Keep the flag of truth unfurled;
> Show its colours to the world...

The song was based on the poem 'Vitae Lampada' by Henry Newbolt, which begins: 'There's a breathless hush in the close tonight...'

In fact there was no room for sports at our school. We had a small playground, but it was not big enough to allow us to play cricket or football, so once a week we went to Parliament Hill Fields or Regent's Park. Both these open spaces had playing fields for school use. Because Parliament Hill Fields could be reached by tram, and because, like the school, trams were under the umbrella of the London County Council, we were allowed to travel free on them. So it was there that we mostly went, especially during the football season.

There were no trams to Regent's Park, only buses. Buses were not controlled by the LCC but by a private bus company, the London General Omnibus Company (LGOC), so there were no free rides there. We had to walk there and back – often with two of us sharing the weight of a heavy cricket bag.

Most games against other schools were played in the evening. On one occasion our school played another school at Regent's Park. The game began at 4pm and was still going on at 5.30. At that time I had a paper round due to start at 6pm. It took almost half an hour to walk back from the park to home, so I asked the teacher, Mr Atkinson, if I could leave the game early to go on my paper round. But instead of letting me go he gave me a severe lecture on the duty to one's side and playing the game and all that, and told me that if I left the game to deliver papers I would be severely punished. So I had to stay to the end. I got to the paper shop nearly an hour late. The proprietor then gave me another lecture – on my duty to my commitment as a paperboy.

In line with public school tradition, our headmaster expected us to wear white flannels for cricket matches. An arrangement was made with Charles Baker and Son, clothing and sportswear outfitters, situated on the corner of Euston Road and Tottenham Court Road, that if eleven boys visited the shop together they would be supplied with the clothing cheaply. The school would pay them and the parents would repay the school at a rate of 6d a week. We were fitted out on a Friday. On Sunday I was made to wear the outfit as a Sunday suit. On Monday my grandmother took it to the pawnbrokers. On Wednesday there was a cricket fixture. I was the only one to turn up in ordinary clothes.

Clothes were taken out of pawn on Saturday (payday) so I was able to wear them on Sunday. On Monday they were taken back to pawn, but refused as being too soiled and worn. After that I wore the cricket clothes every day until they wore out. I don't think Granny ever paid her 6d per week. In August the cricket enterprise was forgotten as the football season took over, and there was no uniformed cricket team the following year (1929–30).

I liked two things at school, music and writing – what is now known as composition: 'How I spent my holidays', 'My cat', 'The adventures of a penny' and so on.

In 1929, when I was about twelve years old, I delighted the school staff and myself by winning first prize in an all-London Elementary schools' essay competition. The vicar was also delighted. The subject of the essay was 'Cleanliness and hygiene in the home'!

Music took place twice a week – singing in an afternoon and violin lessons at Monday lunchtime. I was all for the violin. A three-quarter size one could be had for 6d a week, with lessons for 4d. Only 10d to become a prodigy like that kid Menuhin that the hoardings said was astounding everybody at the Albert and Queen's Halls. But alas it was not to be. I had a violin for precisely three weeks. Then it was taken away as my grandmother had not kept up with the weekly payments.

Once a week we found our own way to other schools that boasted woodwork or metalworking teaching facilities. The metalwork school was in Stukeley Street, off Drury Lane. In those days there were two ways of getting to Drury Lane from King's Cross, either by bus from outside St Pancras Church, or by walking. We introduced a third way. I say 'we', because I was a member of a gang.

Our gang called each other by our nicknames: Baily, Evvy, Higgy, Marty, Alby, Pongo, and Chilly (me).

The gang was led by Baily who was the oldest of us and our ringleader. He was short, with dirty cheeks and ragged trousers. He wore no socks but covered his feet with a worn-out pair of plimsolls through which, in one of them, his big toe protruded. He wore an open-necked, grey shirt that had once belonged to his father and an old jacket on which he had a number of badges and brooches fastened at the lapels. He was the ringleader because he was the best fighter. He was small but fearless, his courage always showing during a fight with other boys or with schoolteachers, to whom he proved to be a big problem. His mother had thirteen other children to clothe and feed besides him. He wore his hair short, very short, indeed, in an 'all off' hair cut. Not one of the hairs on his head was more than half an inch long except in the front where a little of it, a very little, was allowed to form a fringe.

Baily came from the poorest part of the slum dwellings in Somers Town. The rest of the gang's circumstances were a little bit better and we dressed in similar fashion. Unlike Baily we wore socks – socks that should have reached almost to our knees but which actually hung loosely around our ankles – and boots. True, the boots were rather worn and, in my case, had holes in the soles; but at least they didn't look as bad as Baily's plimsolls with his big toe sticking out. Our hair, although it was often cut as short as Baily's, was allowed to grow to a reasonable length as winter approached. Those who looked after us thought hair could serve as a hat. We too wore ragged trousers, shirts (somewhat cleaner than Baily's) and jackets and ties.

Our way of getting to the metalwork class was both exciting and dangerous. On Tuesday afternoons, four of us would sit on the kerb of the corner formed by the junction of Southampton Row and Tavistock Place.

At the crossroads where Tavistock Place, Tavistock Square and Southampton Row meet, a policeman would direct and control the traffic because at that time there were no traffic lights. We would sit with our knees tucked well under our chins to keep our feet away from the threatening wheels of the traffic. We were very interested in the policeman. When he held up the traffic in the main road and had his back to us, we would glance at each other and grin, holding up our thumbs at each other and looking hard at the long line of traffic that had stopped. Occasionally one of us would shout, 'There's one!' and we'd all jump up and run down the pavement until we reached what we'd seen – a motor lorry. We would stand on the pavement and examine the rear of the vehicle.

'No good,' we'd say, and we'd go back to our original places on the kerb.

The policeman would lower his hand, the traffic would move on and we would look disappointed. But it wasn't long before another motor lorry would be held up that was exactly to our liking.

'This'll do,' we said, and we waited together in a group on the pavement by the lorry's side, just as though we were waiting for a bus. The lorry that would do would be a large Morris Commercial, with a cloth-covered carrier and a small tailboard. The tailboard, of course, was chained up, but the top of it was not out of our reach. Underneath the carrier was a spare tyre, held parallel with the ground by a specially designed rack.

The policeman would lower his hand.

'There they go,' one boy would say and, as the gears were slipped home, we would all step into the road. As the lorry moved off we would run to the rear and board it. Two of us would make a leap for the tailboard, which we would grasp and pull ourselves up until we lay across its edges on our stomachs. The other two would grasp the top of the tailboard and place their feet on the spare tyre; then, hanging by our arms and resting on our stomachs, the four of us would be whisked passed the policeman and up Southampton Row towards Kingsway. The policeman would see us but could do nothing. He couldn't stop the lorry – had he shouted, his voice would never have been heard above the noise.

Getting off a lorry was a very uncomfortable business. If we were to be in time for school it was imperative that we got off at Holborn. Once, when we reached the crossroads where Holborn crosses Kingsway, the policeman controlling the traffic was allowing our lorry to pass.

'The bloody fool's not gonna stop!' said Evvy who was on the offside and could see. 'We'll have to shout.'

And shout we did. As soon as we were level with Holborn underground station we shrieked and yelled making our presence known to the driver who, hearing us, hurriedly stopped to deal with us. This, however, was just what we wanted. As soon as the lorry had braked to a reasonably slow speed we jumped down from our places and ran for all we were worth across the road, dodging traffic, which gave rise to much squealing of brakes and curses from drivers. We were over the road before the lorry driver had time to leave his seat, so he moved off. We kept running and reached the school just in time for our metalwork class. At 4.30pm, when school was over, we would make our way back to await a suitable vehicle to escort us home.

Every Tuesday it was always the same, wet or fine, summer or winter, until riding on lorries got into our blood and we hardly moved from one place to another without riding on one. In the summer evenings we went for long rides up Hampstead Road to Highgate and beyond. We went to Hampstead and Parliament Hill Fields in the same way. We called this form of fun 'lorry jumping'.

One day we boarded a lorry carrying bottles of mineral water. Baily took a bottle, opened it, and tipped it up, trying not to pour too much of it down his neck which was not easy as the water was bumping about a lot.

'Want some?' he said, offering the bottle to Pongo.

'Yes, I'll have some,' he replied.

Baily took another bottle from out of a case, opened it and began to drink again. This was too much for the rest of us. It wasn't long before each of us had a bottle and was drinking away steadily.

The lust for stealing rides on lorries grew, and so did the lust for stealing. Not only mineral water, but also small goods such as tins of biscuits, fruit or anything that could be carried in our pockets became our targets.

It was in this way that our gang satisfied our lust for adventure. Unlike boys who live in the country we didn't climb trees or ride horses or poach, but did things that served just as well. For a month or two, stealing both goods and rides was our sole occupation out of school. None of our schoolteachers or parents knew anything about this, but such things are always found out in some way, and found out they were.

One of the regular habits of the gang was going to the cinema on Friday nights. This we did immediately school was over when we ran hard down to the picture house, both from excitement and because if we got there before 4.30 we could get in at half price. Most of us could afford to go to the pictures (the entrance fee was 3d) as we had a newspaper round, delivering newspapers in the early morning. Baily and Evvy, however, were too lazy to do anything like that.

One Friday, Baily and Evvy told us about some lorries that were chock full of goods, which, they said, were so easy to lift that the stuff almost fell into your hand. So vividly did they describe the fun that could be had that all of us in the gang decided not to go to the cinema that evening but to go lorry jumping instead.

In the afternoon of that day, however, Higgy, always a thoughtful boy, decided that he wanted to go to the pictures after all, and during the history lesson told me so. I then decided to go to the pictures too. I scribbled this information on a scrap of paper and handed it back, under the desk, to Alby who sat behind me. He in turn handed the note to Pongo who passed it on until all the gang knew of my and Higgy's intentions. Very soon another scrap of paper was handed about written by Pongo. This said, 'I am to', Pongo not being a very good scholar. A similar note came from Alby. But no note came from Evvy or Baily. Instead they made grimaces at their friends which plainly said, 'Don't go to the pictures, come with us.'

When school was over and we went to the cinema, Baily and Evvy went down to King's Cross Station without us.

On Monday morning when the school reassembled, neither Evvy nor Baily was there. We boys didn't take much notice of this as members of the gang were often late; it was the most effective way to miss prayers, which were always boring. The best thing to do was to wait in the lavatory until prayers in the hall were over and join the other boys when your class marched past the lavatory on its way to the classrooms. You slipped into line and adopted an 'have been to prayers' attitude. No one noticed you hadn't attended prayers, because the roll was not called until after the classes had settled in their various classrooms. On this day, however, although Higgy and

I appeared from the lavatory and slipped into line, there was no sign of either Baily or Evvy.

When we reached our classroom the register was called. Mr Atkinson, a stern man and well up to the tricks of his pupils, called the register slowly. When he came to Baily's name he called it twice and then looked up.

'Where's Baily?' he asked nobody in particular but addressing himself to the whole room. Nobody replied. 'Higgins, do you know where Baily is?'

'No, sir,' said Higgins standing up and being very polite, fearful that the master might know he hadn't been at prayers. 'I haven't seen him since Friday, sir.'

'Right, sit down,' said the master. 'Does anybody know where he is?' Nobody did. So, rubbing his chin thoughtfully he went on calling out names.

After the roll had been called we were told to get out our Bibles so that the Scripture lesson could begin. I was sharing the same desk as Higgins. We bent down to get our books from the shelf underneath our desks and stayed down a little longer than was necessary.

'Have you seen 'em?' I asked, surveying the upside-down features of my friend.

'No, have you?' answered Higgy. 'P'raps they've run away from 'ome to join the Navy. They always said they would.'

'They wouldn't 'ave done that without tellin' us, would they? We were all gonna run away together.'

A sharp word from Mr Atkinson brought us sitting bolt upright in a flash with our Bibles lying before us.

'The class will not wait for you,' he said sternly. 'Higgins, stand up and recite the 23rd Psalm.'

Higgins stood up and did his best, but he was never much good at reciting, and having been picked out to recite unexpectedly early on a Monday morning when things much more important to him were foremost in his mind made matters a lot worse.

He stood out in the gangway between the desks and began.

'The Lord is my Shepherd. I shall not want.' And there he stuck. With the room so quiet and the master watching us so attentively, it was impossible for me to prompt him as I might have done. So Higgins stood mute. Then, as though to pull himself together, he shrugged his shoulders and began again.

'The Lord is my Shepherd. I shall not want.' And once more he stuck. This time I made an attempt to help him.

'He shall,' I whispered, hoping that two words were enough.

'He shall,' said Higgins with great confidence and then stopped again. 'He shall; He shall,' he said, his voice fading away. 'I can't remember any more, sir.'

'Can't remember any more?' said the master angrily. 'You haven't said anything yet. What did the headmaster say at prayers this morning?' Now Higgins was stumped completely. He hadn't been at prayers.

'I forget, sir,' he said falteringly.

'You forget!' roared the teacher. 'No wonder you can't remember a psalm; you can't even remember what was said to you less than half an hour ago. You'll learn the 23rd Psalm before you leave here today and tonight, instead of gallivanting around the streets, you'll write out a hundred times, "I must know the 23rd Psalm".'

I grinned. 'And the same applies to you,' said the master, glaring at me.

The grin instantly left my face.

Mr Atkinson told us to open our Bibles and get down to learning the psalm. The rest of the class had to do likewise. Comparative quiet reigned over the class and the teacher busied himself with odd things in his register. Then quite suddenly the door opened and in walked two policemen, a man in a large overcoat and bowler hat, and the headmaster.

The effect on the class was electric. Every boy sat bolt upright as though a pin had been stuck in him. Every boy forgot what he was supposed to be doing and stared hard at the policemen, fearing that it was because of him that they had come. Every boy thought of the many bad things he had done: of the windows he had broken; of the money he had stolen at home; of the times he had played truant; of the football he had played in the street; and of the time a policeman had tried to catch him for doing so. Thirty young boys instantly repented of all the things they had done wrong and swore to themselves that they would never do anything wrong again so long as they lived – not even swim in the Regent's Canal – so long as they were let off this time.

Mr Atkinson stood up when they entered and moved towards them. The headmaster came forward, introduced the man in the bowler hat (who made no attempt to take it off) and talked in low tones. The policemen talked in low tones too, so low that in spite of the breathless silence of the class, we could not hear what was being said, except for a few words such as 'King's Cross Station' and 'Friday night about eight o'clock'.

When at last they had finished they turned towards the class and the policemen and the man in the bowler hat looked at us carefully.

'Can you recognise any of the boys amongst this lot?' said the headmaster to the man in the bowler hat. The only reply the man in the bowler hat made was to suck his moustache – he had a thick black one – and look thoughtfully round the room. He did this until his eyes rested on the area where our gang sat.

Fixing his eyes on Pongo he said, 'What's your name?'

'Pond, sir.'

'And where were you on Friday night?'

'I went to the pictures.'

'Oh you did, did you? And what did you see?'

'*Don Q*'

'*Don Q*, eh? And who's in that?

'Douglas Fairbanks.'

It was obvious that Pongo had in fact been to the pictures.

'Humph,' said the man. 'Do you know Evans and Baily?'

'Yes sir,' said Pongo, thinking it would be wise to be honest right now.

'Do you ever play with them?'

'Sometimes, sir.'

'Not very often, eh?'

'No sir, not very often.'

Now this was a downright lie. The remainder of the gang knew this, and so did our teacher, Mr Atkinson. He'd often had complaints about the gang.

'Why don't you play with them very often?'

'I don't like them, sir.'

Mr Atkinson winced, but the headmaster, not being as intimate with the gang, noticed nothing and the policemen stood still like dummies, expressionless.

'Who do you play with?'

'Chilly, Higgy and Alby,' said Pongo, boldly speaking the truth.

When the names had been translated and the owners of them pointed out to him, the man in the bowler told Pongo to sit down and asked the remaining three to stand up. He questioned each of us in turn. Alby said that his mother forbade him to play with Baily and that his only regular friends were the other three. Higgy and I followed his example. Higgy said he wouldn't play with Baily as he didn't like him, and I stretched the point a bit more and said that Baily and I always fought whenever we met. The bowler-hatted man eyed me suspiciously when I said that, but I met his gaze with a saint-like respect.

'Were you ever near King's Cross goods station, young feller?' asked the man with a bowler.

'Where's that?' I asked innocently. 'Is it near the main station?'

Again the man looked at me hard, and in turn was met with a steady gaze until, withdrawing his stare, he told me to sit down, which I did with no outward signs of disturbance but with my heart beating wildly and my knees weak.

Bowler Hat then turned to the headmaster and said, 'No, I don't think so. I thought maybe Pond, but I must have been mistaken.'

With that, and a parting gesture for Mr Atkinson telling him he was sorry for the trouble he'd caused, he and his little party left. The relief of the class could be felt.

'All right – the show is over. Back to your work,' said Mr Atkinson, and from then on the class assumed the atmosphere of a normal working day. The lessons changed and the time dragged on until, at long last, midday came and with it the break for dinner.

When the bell rang for work to cease the master said, 'Put your books away, stand in the gangway, and be prepared to march out quietly.'

When all was ready he gave the command to move but said that the gang, or rather what remained of it, had to remain behind. When the rest of the class had gone, the four of us were lined up before the teacher's table. We stood there looking rather sorry for ourselves and extremely contrite. He looked at us hard and then slowly pulled open the bottom drawer of his desk and took out a stout cane.

'I expect you know why I held you back,' he said. 'I'm going to punish you, punish you like I hope you've never been punished before. You're lucky to be treated in this way. I wish Evans and Baily were here to share your good luck, but unfortunately, or perhaps fortunately, we shall never see them in this class again. This morning, each of you stood up and told lies. You denied being friends of boys with whom you have associated ever since I've been a teacher at this school – in fact you expressed a definite dislike for them. For that I cannot blame you. You realise, I suppose, that on Friday night Evans and Baily were caught stealing from a wagon outside King's Cross Station by the detective you saw this morning? But I'm sure they were not the only offenders. They often had four companions with them. The detective had seen all six of them hanging around. He thought he recognised you, Pond, as one of them.'

Pongo shifted uncomfortably. 'But you denied associating with Baily or Evans, which made him change his mind. Whether he was right or wrong in his supposition I cannot say, but I'm telling you now that if I ever hear of any of you four hanging about King's Cross Station or' – and this he said slowly so that he should not be misunderstood – 'stealing rides on motor wagons, I'll take the hide off you. Now, Pond, bend over.'

Pongo bent over and received ten of the best that made him jump and, at one point, utter one of his biblical quotations, which was all he knew of the Bible – for which he received another shaker. Higgy, Alby and I in turn received our share, knowing better than to shout in case the wrong word came out.

Pongo was so concerned about his punishment that he didn't go home to dinner. Instead he walked very rapidly round and round the block. The rest of us went home but stood up to eat our dinners, telling our parents that we'd been sitting down all morning and thought we'd like to stand up for a change. During the afternoon at school we moved about and tried various sitting positions, first on one side and then on the other; then forward on the seat and then as far back as we could go until, finding no relief that way, we started all over again. Only one sat still: Higgy. He'd brought a cushion with him.

We never saw Baily and Evans again, but we heard a lot about them. They were sent to a reform school, and from there Evans joined the Army and Baily the Navy. I reckon the only thing that saved the rest of the gang from going the same way as them was Higgy's passionate admiration for Douglas Fairbanks and his decision to go to the pictures rather than go lorry jumping.

CHAPTER FIVE
UP THE PICTURES

Moving pictures were an important part of life in my environment. Most people that I knew went to the pictures at least once a week. The cinema was greatly preferred to the theatre, and attendance at cinemas was much greater than at church.

The cinema had such fascination for us boys that occasionally some of us skipped school to attend it. Once we were caught coming out of the pictures when we should have been at church for an All Saint's Day service, another ritual insisted upon by our headmaster. When asked why he had not been to the service, my mate Baily said he didn't really see there was much harm in what we had done. There wasn't all that much difference between the church and cinema. When asked to explain he said, 'Well, in church they say "Stand up for Jesus" and up the pictures they say "Sit down, for Christ's sake!"'

When the Stoll theatre in Kingsway went over to showing films, it put on a much talked-of epic called *Wings* (1927). Baily and I longed to see this film, but had no money. That, however, didn't deter us. We arrived at the Stoll and found the gallery queue, which was quite long. A fire-eater was entertaining the waiting crowd. As soon as he'd finished, my mate and I started our act. While Baily stood on his head and waved his legs about, I walked round and round him with bent knees, crouching shoulders and hands behind my back in imitation of the then popular cartoon character Felix the Cat.

While I walked and Baily waggled I sang the Felix song, 'Felix Keeps on Walking, Keeps on Walking Still'. Then I stood on my head and he sang. Afterwards we went down the queue and collected money from the waiting crowd. Some laughed and gave us pennies 'for our cheek'. Others swore at us – one clipped us round the ears – but in the end we gained 1/6d, more than enough for the entrance fee and a fish-and-chip supper afterwards.

The cinema we went to most often during my childhood was the Euston in Euston Road where my mother had worked. It was not a 'picture palace'; it was hardly more than a large hall with a sloping floor and a large, white screen. There were no curtains to hide it or to reveal when the show began. The sloping floor was very steep. Clients sitting in the cheaper seats down in the front had to crane their necks when looking upwards to see the screen.

We kids mostly went to the Saturday matinees. These began about 2pm and the admission price was the same for all: 3d. Before the advent of talkies, metal tickets like the ones my mother had sold were still the means of entry. Sometimes older boys managed to hold on to their metal tickets instead of giving them up to the ticket collector. They were slipped into their pockets and taken home, as they were considered to be of great value among the boys in my area, who rated each metal ticket worth ten 'glarnies' – highly prized glass marbles.

The programmes were not modified to accommodate children's tastes. What you got on Saturday afternoon was exactly what adults saw during the rest of the week. The only modification made to the Saturday matinees was to the orchestra. This usually comprised two violins, one of whom was the leader, a cello, bass, maybe a trumpet and clarinet-doubling flute, a pianist and percussion. The percussionist was also the effects man. He supplied the sound for special scenes and incidents such as gun shots, the clink of rapiers during sword fights, horses' hooves, motor horns, bells, high winds (a wind machine) in storm scenes, etc. But on Saturday matinees the orchestra was reduced to piano and percussion.

The shutters went up half an hour before the programme began. At least an hour before they did so, a queue would begin to form, its ever lengthening tail-end stretching westwards along the Euston Road alongside the newly built Euston Market.

At the sight and sound of the shutters being rolled up, there would be a great surge of young people towards the box office, just inside the cinema entrance. Two attendants would hold the crowd back with cries of 'Have your money ready' and 'Don't push'. Bigger boys and girls who had arrived late and had gone to the back of the queue would now rush to the front of the line, or as near to it as they could get, hoping to push in out of turn. In the shove and jostle in front of the box office, many of the younger cinema fans had their entrance money knocked out of their hands by these older children.

Once I went up the Camden Hippodrome, another of our favourite cinemas. My mate Evvy and I went to an early evening performance rather than a Saturday matinee. It was midwinter and already dark. Although we arrived at the Hippodrome a good hour before the programme began, there was already a long queue outside the gallery. We weren't too far from the paybox, which was just inside the door at the foot of the long flight of stairs that led up to the gallery (the gods). But the queue continued lengthening, and by the time the pay-box was due to open it had stretched all the way down to Bayham Street.

Evvy said: ''Ere, I'll hold the money, gimme yours.'

'What for?'

'Soon as the doors open, I'll push to the ticket box and get the tickets. You rush upstairs and try to get two good seats at the front in the middle.'

I gave him my three hot pennies. He placed them in the palm of his hand and wrapped his fingers round them. Not easy to do. The old-time penny was the largest coin then in circulation, and for a ten- or eleven-year-old boy to hold six of them in one hand wasn't easy.

The pass over of the pennies had hardly been made when we heard the bar of the gallery door being released and the two halves swung open revealing a commissionaire sent to control the queue, who called out, 'Get your tickets please'. There was a great surge of humanity pushing and shoving from impatient people queuing at the back of the line. It was like a wave from the tail to the head, with the front queuers being pushed towards the newly opened door, almost knocking some people off their feet, and knocking Evvy completely off his. As he fell, he put out his hands to break his fall, thus releasing the six pennies which hit the pavement and went rolling in all directions, most of them down the sloping pavement across the kerb and into the gutter. I broke ranks and went after them. As soon as Evvy could get to his feet he did the same.

We searched diligently, heads down and hearts full of desperation, lest the queue should have disappeared into the cinema and all seats sold before we found our entrance money. I found one penny, then another, but all my searching produced no more. The queue was getting shorter and time was running out.

Suddenly Evvy gave a shout: 'I've found my three; see you inside.' He disappeared into the queue to regain his lost place at the head of it. That was the last I saw of him. An hour's further searching did not produce the vital lost penny. Eventually, well aware that the show had long been under way and that even if I got in I would have missed the best part of it, I did my best to hold back the tears and headed for home.

At the Saturday matinee shows there was a long wait, about half an hour, between getting in and the show actually starting. The cinema felt naked or dead. The only lighting came from somewhat dim suspended lights hanging down from the high ceiling. There was, however, one huge, bright spot: the screen at the far end of the hall, suspended high in the wall. While waiting for the show to begin, boys and girls would run up and down the sloping aisles between the rows of seats, looking for and greeting their friends in high-pitched voices, shouting to be heard above the constant din.

Rising above all this racket was the loudest voice of all: that of the chief commissionaire trying, somewhat hopelessly, to bring this young over-excited crowd to order and to silence.

'Keep your seats. The show will not start until you are all sitting down. Anyone not sitting down in two minutes will be thrown out.'

What he said, however, made little or no difference. The noise would go on as before, with children running up and down the aisles. Some would munch peanuts bought from pedlars who had targeted the queue outside. Some would suck sickly coloured lozenges that were sold in tight little packets called 'Val' lozenges.

Suddenly the lights would go down, the piano would strike up and the huge screen would be bathed in brilliant light, displaying a certificate of approval for the film that was to follow. In large, brilliant white letters on a deep, grey-black background it would announce the title of the first item on the programme. A great cheer would go up. Individuals still adrift from their seats would go running back to them, crashing into other lost souls as they did so, for the sudden plunge into darkness made it difficult to see one's way. The cheers would die away and everybody would look hopefully and expectantly at the screen. Now the only sound would be the piano and the drums.

The first item was always the newsreel – Pathé Gazette: interesting for adults but boring for children. It showed the main political and social events, usually of the previous week. Ship launches, football, cricket and other sporting events. The Boat Race and the Derby were popular, but photographs of politicians and suchlike held no interest for the kids. Picture records of record-breaking motorists (Donald Campbell) and long-distance flyers (Amy Johnson) were, however, always popular. The song 'Amy, Wonderful Amy' was always played when she appeared on the screen. It was immediately taken up by the children, who would sing it loudly and enthusiastically, not so much because they admired Amy, but because they knew the song and providing a vocal accompaniment to the cinema pianist was a kind of knee-jerk reaction.

Amy seldom appeared for more than a minute or two, whereas the song would last much longer. By the time Amy had disappeared from view to make way for another item, the song would be only halfway through and the pianist would be playing another theme to fit the following news event. The audience, however, would ignore this and would continue to sing 'Amy' lustily to its end.

> Amy, wonderful Amy
> How can you blame me for loving you?
> Since you've won the praise of every nation
> You have filled my heart with admiration
> Amy, wonderful Amy
> I'm proud of the way you flew
> Believe me Amy
> You cannot blame me Amy
> For falling in love with you

The newsreel always ended with a special feature, which the boys all looked forward to: 'Fashions of the Fair Sex', in colour. It was really a bit of publicity for the fashion designers and fashion houses, which they probably paid Pathé Gazette for. It showed models wearing the latest fashions: cloche hats, low-waisted dresses, short skirts, bobbed hair, Eton crops and other fashions of the day.

The 'colour' was probably intended to show the fashions at their best, which black and white images could not do, but it wasn't really up to the job. It was rather pale and washed-out, and seemed to consist mainly of reds and blues. In those days there was no Technicolor.

The films we saw in the late 1920s were, of course, silent and mainly American. It was at that time that the first film 'stars' were born. Many of the personalities of American film actors and actresses became even more important than the films they appeared in. Mary Pickford, Gloria Swanson, Pearl White, Greta Garbo, Harold Lloyd, Lillian Gish, Douglas Fairbanks and Charlie Chaplin were some of our favourites.

One of the greatest film successes immediately after the First World War was an anti-war film called *The Four Horsemen of the Apocalypse* (1921). It starred an actor who had been a dancer, one who had specialised in the newest dance craze which he had helped to popularise: the tango. In fact it was because a tango dancer was needed that he was chosen to play in the film. This man was an Italian, a USA immigrant whose name was Rodolfo Alfonzo Raffaello Pierre Filibert Guglielmi di Valentina d'Antonguolla. The movie moguls who employed him thought his name was too long to fit into the screen credits so they shortened it to Rudolph Valentino. The film was a tremendous hit and made him world famous.

In his next film (*The Sheik*, 1921) he played the part of an Arab and a sheik. Valentino's eastern style of lovemaking revolutionised the entire technique of courtship among young film fans. His good looks, grace, virility and charm made him the idol of countless women, including my Aunt Lil who was besotted by him. Many music hall performers sang a song based on the film entitled 'The Sheik of Araby'.

> I'm the Sheik of Araby
> Your love belongs to me
> At night when you're asleep
> Into your tent I'll creep
> The stars that shine above
> Will light our way to love
> You'll rule this land with me
> I'm the Sheik of Araby

We boys had our own rude version of this song. We added the words 'with no pants on' after each appropriate line!

In 1925 Valentino visited England to attend the premiere of one of his films, *The Eagle*. The crowds who gathered to see him gave him a hysterical ovation. He died in 1926, aged 31. Thousands of people attended his funeral – women wept at his graveside.

The female equivalent of the Sheik was the vamp, short for vampire or *femme fatale*. She, too, originated from the Middle East, from Egypt, and held the same power over male members of the cinema audience as Valentino held over the female. The lady fated to portray the vamp on the screen was Theda Bara, which is an anagram – very nearly a palindrome – of 'Arab death'. Her publicity said she was half-Egyptian and half-French, but actually she came from Ohio. Her real name was Theodosia Burr Goodman. The film director Frank E. Powell, who discovered her and put her in her first film *A Fool There Was* (1915), trained her in the arts of feminine seduction.

A popular song called 'The Vamp' became a great hit in the variety theatres.

Vamp and swing along (keep a' doin' it)
Vamp and sing a song (don't you ruin it)
Do a nifty step
With lots of pep
And watch your rep-
-utation
Do a bumble bee (buzz around a bit)
Shake a wicked knee (he will fall for it)
Vamp all night and day
Keep vamping till you vamp your cares away

Then there was the 'It' girl, Clara Bow. She was a direct descendant of the vamp. She was given the name of the 'It' girl by the popular romantic novelist Elinor Glyn, 'It' being Glyn's term for sex appeal.

In 1926 Warner Brothers produced a film called *Don Juan*. It was advertised as a 'synchronised' film. I didn't know what this meant when I went to see it, but I soon learnt. It had sound. Not the sound of actors talking, but the sounds of rapiers clashing in sword fights and carriage wheels turning: that is, sound effects. These were embedded in the film. At first people were happy just to hear the 'noises'. But they soon wanted to see and hear what their favourite players made of the new medium. Would Chaplin talk? What did Greta Garbo sound like?

One day in 1929, I was surprised when a girl at my school called Florence Richardson asked me to go to the pictures with her.

'I haven't any money,' I said.

'Don't worry, I'll pay.'

Flo was always rather a naughty girl and never had any money, but the lure of going to the pictures was great so I agreed.

'What's on?'

'Oh there's nothing good on locally, only silent pictures. I want to go to that cinema in Tottenham Court Road where they do talkies.'

So we went. The cinema advertised its programmes as 'All Talking, All Dancing, All Singing', for by this time Warner Brothers had produced *The Jazz Singer* (1927) starring Al Jolson, a musical in which Jolson sang his famous song 'Mammy'. Cinemas all over England were becoming wired up for sound and the end of the silent film was approaching.

But the film we saw in Tottenham Court Road was not a musical. It was in fact a rather dull detective story starring an actor called Jack Holt. The sound effects we heard were mostly of the villain's wooden leg when pursued by policemen! Afterwards we went back to Flo's house. Her mother was there.

'Where the hell have you been?'

'To the pictures.'

'Oh yes, and where did you get the money?'

Flo looked embarrassed.

'I'll tell you where you got it; out of the tin on the mantelpiece, you little thief!'

And with that her mother gave Flo the belting of her life. I hastened back home.

Some silent film stars resisted the 'talkies'. Greta Garbo appeared in a new silent film, *The Divine Woman* (1928). Lillian Gish appeared in the silent film *The Wind* also in 1928. Chaplin was also still making successful silent films in the same year. 'Stage is stage,' he would say, 'and cinema is cinema. My forte is mime, not talking.' But soon even our local cinemas, which were some of the last in London to be wired up for sound, were advertising 'talking' pictures.

The coming of the talkies brought with it American wisecrack, the sharp retort, and the extraordinary new language that now invaded homes by way of the cinema. Phrases such as 'You're telling me'; 'I'll be seeing you' (changed by some of us when Mussolini invaded Ethiopia to 'A-bi-syn-ia'); 'I guess'; 'That's okay by me' – usually delivered with a nasal voice – became part of British life. Our accents and vocabulary at home, school or in the street were related to the latest film seen and heard at the local cinema. It was the bane of parents and teachers who hated the idea of children growing up as copies of celluloid Yankees. By mid 1929 when sound films had spread across Britain, there was hardly a town or village in the country without some child saying 'okay', when previously he or she would have said 'yes'.

Musicals were the most popular talking films. I remember one made in England named *Elstree Calling* (1930), imitating an American musical. It featured the enormous xylophone and vibraphone player Teddy Brown who would finish his solos by getting up and staring straight at his cinema audience and shouting 'Sing', which they all did. He had been a successful musical hall performer and had lived in one of the flats where I used to deliver newspapers, but I never saw him there although many of my friends swore they had.

But it was American films that we preferred. They were exciting, loud, and full of adventures. The Tarzan films, starring Johnny Weissmuller as Tarzan, were the best. Who knew? If you learnt to swim like Tarzan, maybe you would become a film star too.

CHAPTER SIX
ON THE STREETS

The streets in those days were much friendlier places than they are today. The traffic was mainly horse-drawn; there were very few cars. But there was plenty of noise. Vendors would cry their wares – lavender, fish, primroses, vegetables, fruit, toffee apples, 'hokey pokey' (the cockney expression for ice cream, which was probably a corruption of the Italian words *O che poco*, meaning 'Oh what a little'). Every vendor had his or her own individual cry. There were all sorts of street musicians, from single, unaccompanied voices to troupes of performers complete with drums and barrel organs, who would provide a whole show lasting fifteen minutes or longer.

Dozens of kids would sit on the kerb at one side of the road, while the entertainment took place on the pavement the other side. Childish voices would join in the singing while adult heads gazed from the windows and pennies rained from the skies. Statue dancers, bell ringers, piano players, tap dancers, Egyptian dancers, banjo players, trumpeters, one-man bands – they were never-ending and always welcome.

Most street entertainers were forced to work the poorer districts and beg from their own kind, because there were never street entertainers in the grander squares. Large notices attached to the railings would frighten them away. 'No hawkers, no vendors, no street musicians.'

The streets were our playground. We spent our time exploring the streets and squares around us, and got to know every nook and cranny. At one time our gang headquarters was in the cellar of a large house that had once stood where St Pancras Town Hall is now. After the house had been demolished, the land where it had been remained vacant for a long time. Like all big houses in the area, it had a large basement or cellar. We discovered a way of getting into this: via the manhole through which coal used to be delivered to the household. We would prize open the lid of the manhole and drop into the cellar below. The large room made an excellent headquarters for our gang's activities.

But sometimes we had a problem. Baily, our gang's leader, had a small, three-year-old sister. His mother insisted that Baily should look after her and take her with him wherever he went. So when it came to going down into the cellar the manhole cover would be opened and some of us would jump down. Baily, at the top, would then drop his sister into our waiting arms. But getting her up again was much more difficult. First, we would have to make a mound of the quantities of rubbish lying around in the cellar, which one of us would climb on top of to climb out. Then one by one we would grab hold of the opening and ease ourselves out into the pavement above. One of us in the cellar would have to hold up Baily's sister to another boy waiting to grab her from above. It entailed much pushing and shoving and the need to get her and ourselves out quickly before a policeman spotted us. We played games, re-enacted films and quite often lit a fire, but if we did this, likely as not the coppers would be on to us in no time.

For us boys living in London, this period was a time of great exploration and discovery of parks, museums (especially the British Museum), squares, gardens and other treasures left to us by the Regency builders of more than a hundred years before. We went to anywhere that let us in free. I suppose I was about twelve before I began to notice architecture. Then suddenly I realised that the Victoria and Albert and Natural History museums had the appearance and atmosphere of ancient cathedrals, as did the Presbyterian gothic-style church in Regent Square where I went for Boys' Brigade functions. The South Kensington Museums were popular because they had many hands-on exhibitions that excited our imaginations. And I particularly liked the London Museum, which at that time was housed in St James's Palace.

We didn't visit the British Museum in order to enhance our appreciation of architecture. Rather, we went because we wanted to see the Egyptian mummified bodies that had been discovered in the desert. They fascinated us. I remember taking my Auntie Queenie, who used to come up from Sutton to visit me from time to time, to the British Museum. As we walked past the great rows of classical statues she would say, 'Oh aren't they rude!' I suppose that's why we liked them.

In 1931 radio was just reaching its first peak of popularity. The number of licences taken out exceeded five million, and the number of listeners was at least four times that figure. There was no audience research in those days, so the number of listeners to any one programme had to be guessed at. But the drop in cinema audiences on Saturday nights when Ambrose and his orchestra took the air already indicated the powerful draw of radio.

I, along with millions of others, became an ardent radio fan, thanks in my case to a school friend of mine, Ronald Reed, who had won a scholarship aged about twelve to the polytechnic in Regent Street and was studying radio engineering. He was not one of the gang because his mother was rather protective of him and wouldn't let him roam about like I did. Nevertheless, she was fond of me, perhaps because like her son I had lost my father in the war. Ronald used to make radio receivers by the dozen even when a schoolboy – crystal sets in match-boxes, one-valved jobs with headphones and coils of wire that moved around when you turned knobs. He made me a set – a one-valve receiver with headphones that was battery-operated. He also made transmitters. He would get me to go to one end of the street with my receiver to receive what he transmitted from the other end.

'Hello Charlie, can you hear me?'

'Yes, hearing you loud and clear.'

We communicated with each other in this way with great enjoyment, but this suddenly came to an end. The trouble was that everyone in the district who had a radio could hear us too and their reception of the BBC was ruined, so we received many complaints and were lucky the police never found out about what we were doing because it was totally illegal.

Ronald Reed became a BBC engineer and during the war worked as a member of MI5. In 2008 I was surprised to be rung up by Donald Rumbelow, one of the guides for the original London Walks, asking whether I had seen the reference to myself in a recently published book by Ben Macintyre, *Agent Zigzag*, which tells the story of the double agent Eddie Chapman. I quote:

> The man dispatched to handle Zigzag was Captain Ronnie Reed. Reed's father, a waiter in the Trocadero restaurant, died in the Battle of the Somme in 1916 and his mother brought him up in a tenement in King's Cross. From the St Pancras Church of England School, he had won a scholarship to the Regent's Park polytechnic school, where he studied engineering and developed a passion for radio. He could build a wireless from scratch and with his school friend Charlie Chilton (who went on to become a celebrated radio presenter and producer) he would broadcast to the world from his bedroom with a home-made transmitter. Ronnie would sing a warbling rendition of Bing Crosby's 'Dancing in the Dark' while Charlie strummed the guitar. The outbreak of war found Reed working as a BBC radio engineer by day, [or] flying through the ether by night with the call-sign G2RX...

Although our street broadcasting came to an end, I had a great time at home with my radio. I would listen to it for hours, mostly in bed at night. My favourite programmes were pop songs – what the BBC called dance music. There were the

Savoy Orpheans, Ambrose and his orchestra, and Roy Fox and his orchestra. The latter was a great favourite because Nat Gonella was in his band. Nat was also a King's Cross boy.

One way of exploring the streets of Holborn and St Pancras was by bicycle. Cromer Street was famous for two things: a faggot-and-pease-pudding shop, and number 99 which was Reddington's Cycle Shop. Reddington's did not sell bicycles but hired them out, at a rate of 6d an hour or 3d for half an hour. There were two sizes of bicycle: adult and half size. The half-size bicycles were not fairy cycles but smaller editions of regular bicycles. This meant that children (mainly boys between ten and sixteen years old) could enjoy a cycle ride as well as adults.

Once, having hired the necessary bikes from Reddington's, a small group of us, instead of returning our bikes to the shop when the half-hour was up, decided to spend the day cycling to Southend-on-Sea to enjoy the air. The distance from London to Southend is about forty-five miles. We set off after breakfast and thought we would be at our destination by lunchtime. But by late afternoon, hungry and exhausted, we had only reached Dagenham, which is about halfway to Southend. It was already growing dark. We decided to turn back. We thought of Reddington's having to wait until we arrived back with the long overdue bikes. By the time the streetlights came on (about nine o'clock at that time of year) we were still toiling our way up Commercial Road towards central London.

There were no lights on the hired bicycles. A policeman stopped us and told us to light up or walk. We walked. We feared the law too much to risk riding without lights. Walking, however, meant we were not likely to reach home much before midnight. Meanwhile, back home our families were out looking for us. Reddington's, of course, had no idea where we were. The hours slipped by and Reddington's gave up waiting and shut up shop. By now we must have been in debt to the tune of twelve shillings or so – more money than any of us had even seen at any one time.

We turned the corner of Sandwich Street at about one o'clock in the morning. Our families were still up waiting for us, most of them sitting on the doorstep enjoying the summer night air. Instead of joy at the sight of our safe return we were greeted with clips round the ears and cries of 'Where the hell have you been?' 'Who's gonna pay for the price of those bikes – it'll cost a fortune!' Actually it cost nothing. After having been grumbled and raged at, and blamed for all the upset we had caused, we were told to take the bikes back to Reddington's, leave them outside the shop, then run back home before anybody spotted us and demanded payment. This we did, and it was not difficult to do because all the people who worked at Reddington's had long gone home to bed and the shop was tight shut. We left the bikes against the shop door and ran for home. For weeks I didn't dare go down Cromer Street for fear of being stopped for payment.

Another time, some of the gang (Evvy, Higgy, Baily, Marty and I) were playing cricket in Sandwich Street outside the rag shop when a bloke pulled up in a car right in front of where we had our wicket painted on the wall. Baily had just hit the ball down the airy of number 7 and was six and out. While he was handing the bat over to Higgy who was in next, I shinned over the railings and down the airy to get the ball. I had to be quick because Mrs Brown, who lived in the basement of number 7, said she was going to douse the next kid that climbed down her airy with a pail of water.

I'd hardly grabbed the ball and thrown it back up into the street when I heard her coming through the door that leads into the airy, yelling blue murder, calling me a cheeky little sod and telling me she'd give me a bleeding ball if she got hold of me. I was already climbing up the cellar door when she appeared. She didn't have a pail of water with her – I don't think the old cow could have lifted it – but she did have a broomstick which she aimed at my backside. I grabbed at the railings and heaved myself up, but I wasn't quick enough. She caught me a smack at the back of my left leg and called me all the names under the sun. Before she could get a second blow in, however, I had hauled myself up and over the railings and out of her reach.

I jumped down to the pavement, landed on my knees and took a chip out of the left one, so now it was hurting both back and front. Nevertheless I'd got the ball before she could pinch it so we could carry on with the game. But play had stopped. Baily, bat in hand, was tearing down the street, the rest of the team hard on his heels. And the cause of the flight was heading towards me. Still lying on the pavement licking a bleeding knee, I didn't have a chance to get away. He was on me, dragging me up on my feet almost before I knew what was happening.

I thought he must be a copper, or an inspector from the Ministry of Pensions who'd come to put me in a home because my boots had holes in the soles and let in water. If he was a copper he must have come about the button factory business. I had a pocket full of buttons – more than I'd got from the button factory that the gang had recently raided, in Harrison Street off Gray's Inn Road, because I'd won most of Evvy's lot as well previous night playing 'Banker' (a card game) outside the pub. I had at least two hundred buttons, and wouldn't give Evvy back more than 'six for dumps', which was why we had had a fight and why my coat had split at the seam and was showing its lining.

The safest thing to do when you're caught is to cry. Sometimes this makes the copper sorry for you and he lets you go. Or else he'll let go of you to fish for a handkerchief, which gives you a chance to get away. But this bloke either didn't have a handkerchief or he'd been caught that way before, because he didn't let go of my arm but asked me if I was hurt. Then he asked me if I'd like to earn myself a tanner (6d) – so I knew he couldn't be a copper or the pension bloke.

I wiped my eyes on my sleeve, told him yes, and asked him what I had to do. I thought he wanted me to keep an eye on his car, which was parked nearby. I'd be willing to do that – if he let me sit in it at the wheel. And I'd guarantee I'd keep Higgy and the rest of the boys off and stop them chalking rude words on the back.

But he didn't want me to look after his car; he wanted me to sing. I thought he must be crackers, but it seemed an easy way to earn a tanner. I treated him to a quick chorus of 'Yes! We Have No Bananas' and asked for the money.

He wasn't satisfied, however. He knew that one. And besides, he said, it wasn't the sort of song he was looking for. To me it seemed a good enough song for anybody's money, but in the hope of pleasing him and getting the tanner, I thought I'd give him something a bit stronger. I'd barely got into the rude version of 'Last Night on the Back Porch' (the one Evvy's old man sang outside the pub after time: 'But last night in her nightie, I loved her best of all') when he told me that that wasn't what he wanted either.

It looked like the tanner wasn't going to be easy to get hold of. I asked him what kind of songs he wanted. He said he wanted traditional songs, songs of the London streets, especially those sung by children. Did I know any songs that we sang while playing games, and, if I did, would I sing those and he'd sit on the doorstep and write them down in a book?

We moved down to number 3 and sat there on the doorstep. (There was still the risk of the pail of water if we sat on number 7's.) It turned out that when this song bloke had got out of his car, he'd made straight for Baily who, thinking as I did that it was a copper, made straight for the far end of the street with the rest of the boys after him. But when they saw this geezer helping me up off the pavement and realised they were in no immediate danger, they hung around a nearby lamp post to see what was going to happen to me. When nothing did, curiosity got the better of them and they came wandering back. Five minutes later we were all sitting on number 3's doorstep.

What this bloke was after were words and tunes of street games; but any fool knows that it's the little kids, and mostly the girls at that, who played that sort of game. At our age (then about twelve) we preferred Release and Tin-Can-Copper-Knob, which don't have many words to them – certainly not sung ones. But if this bloke was willing to pay a tanner each to us for singing him all the games we could remember and telling him how they were played, we didn't mind remembering them.

We started with the skipping games. All the girls and most of the young boys know the skipping games. First we gave him All-in-Together. That's where two take an end and everybody else jumps in the rope while it's turning, one at a time. When everybody's in you all start singing:

All in together
All kinds of weather
The rope must be empty
When I count twenty
One, two, three, four…

and so on. Anybody left in the rope by twenty takes an end. They take an end if they hit the rope on the way out, too. T'ain't easy to do, I can tell you.

Then there was Cold Meat and Mutton Pies. That's another one where everybody goes in the rope all at once, and you sing:

Cold meat and mutton pies
Tell me when your mother dies
I'll be there to bury her
Cold meat and mutton pies

Cold meat and mutton chops
Tell me when your mother drops
I'll be there to pick her up
Cold meat and mutton chops

You just go on turning and singing until someone stops the rope and then they have to take an end. Nobody likes to take an end – they'd rather skip.

Some skipping games are 'calling in' games, such as:

Somebody under the bed
Whoever can it be?
I feel so jolly lonely
I call my ...... in

Here the girl calls her sweetheart into the rope with her.

And now that ......'s in
...... won't go out
I'll call my ...... in
And he can push him out

And then another boy jumps in and pushes out the first one. The good thing about this game is that sometimes he pushes too hard and then there's a fight. Girls' skipping games are soft, and a lot of them are about courting and getting married:

Blackcurrant, redcurrant
Raspberry tart
Which day will you marry
Your sweetheart
Monday, Tuesday, Wednesday...

Whatever day the rope stops at – that is, when the rope gets tangled up with the feet – is the day to get married. If you stop on Friday you have to skip again, because Friday is an unlucky day. It's also unlucky to have a funeral on a Friday.

By now I reckoned this bloke should have coughed up his tanner but he didn't. He said that with five of us giving him 'material', as he called it, it was going to cost him half a smacker (2/6d), and that he expected a good deal more than eight measly skipping games before he started dishing out any lolly. So we thought up a lot more skipping games for him – quicker than he could write them down. He was a clever bloke and all. He wrote down the music as well as the words.

One we gave him was this:

Oliver Cromwell lost his shoe
At the battle of Waterloo
Left, right, left, right
Attention, halt, one, two

When we'd given him this song, the bloke stopped writing and asked whether we knew our history. I told him we did history at school but what had that got to do with anything?

'Well,' he said, 'then you must know that Oliver Cromwell could never have been at Waterloo.'

The thought had never occurred to me. I'd always sung the song that way and the kids that still played skipping games still sang it that way. It wasn't my fault if Oliver Cromwell wasn't at Waterloo – and I wasn't going to change the words of the song just because he couldn't get there. Then he asked us if we knew any more songs that had historical references as he found them most interesting. We couldn't think of any at first, but then Baily thought of the Skotchy-lander.

There was a Skotchy-lander
Who went to Waterloo
The wind blew up his petticoat
And showed his cock-a-doodle-do

While Baily sang the words, the rest of us made a noise like bagpipes, which you do by holding your nose with one hand and bashing your windpipe with the other while ah-ah-ing the tune with your throat. The song bloke wrote something down in his book about it, and then Mrs Bellini from number 3 told us to go and make a row on somebody else's doorstep as we were waking her baby up. So we moved over to an empty house in Thanet Street, where at that time we had our gang headquarters. We invited the song collector in but he said he'd rather stay out in the fresh air, thank you, so we sat on the empty house doorstep and tried to think up more songs.

By now he'd spent an hour with us, and I thought it was about time he coughed up that tanner. But getting any money out of this geezer was like trying to get shit from a wooden horse. He wanted still more songs for his money. Didn't matter what they were, he said.

We couldn't think of any more skipping games. Would he like some of the songs we sang on the corner at night? Yes, he said.

Evvy started us off with 'The King's Cross Boys'. It was a good choice because it hinted about the tanner that was due to us.

> We are the King's Cross boys
> We know our manners, we spend our tanners
> We are respected wherever we go
> As we're rolling down the Old Kent Road
> The doors and windows open wide
> I-tiddeley-I-ti, eat brown bread
> Ever seen a donkey fall down dead?
> We are the King's Cross boys

Then we did the second ending with the dancing bit in, and we all got up and showed him how to do it.

> This is the way we bang our feet
> Bang-diddi-bang-bang down the street
> We are the King's Cross boys

He thought that was a good one and wrote down the music and words, but didn't say anything about the tanners. So off we went again, feeding this bloke all the songs we could think of as fast as he could write them down. We sang him the Salvation Mission song:

> Will you come to the Mission
> Will you come, will you come
> Will you come to the Mission
> Will you come, will you come

Come to the Mission
And sit upon the floor
And we'll tell you Bible stories
Like you've never heard before

We started telling him some of the Bible stories. But after hearing the one about the clergyman who said, 'Let fire come down from heaven,' and the parrot up the steeple who said he couldn't send down any fire because the cat had pissed on the matches, he said it wasn't the sort of thing he was looking for and could we think of a few more songs.

Marty sang him 'The Soldier and the Sailor' and we all joined in the chorus:

A soldier and a sailor were walking one day
Said the soldier to the sailor, 'Oh come, let us pray'
'Oh what shall we pray for, what do we hold dear?'
Said the soldier to the sailor, 'Let us pray for some beer'

'If you send us a pint, Lord, then can't we have ten?'
'Let's have a bloody brewery!' Said the soldier: 'Amen'

We sang him more than one verse and chorus, including the one about praying for some girls, which made us all laugh but which seemed to shock the song collector.

We gave him a few more shocks before we were finished – especially with the one that starts, 'My wife's a cow – my wife's a cow-keeper's daughter.'

A country girl is pretty
You ought to see her dance
She'll cock her leg right over the fence
And show her dirty arse

Ask old Brown to tea
With all his family
If he don't come, we'll tickle his bum
With a lump of celery

AUNTIE'S CHARLIE

The song collector seemed shocked but what did he expect?
He'd asked us for the songs that we sang, so we'd sung them.
But we still didn't get our tanners, not until we'd been through
a couple of what he called school chants such as:

Pounds, shillings and pence
A lady fell over a fence
Cut her belly on a piece of jelly
Pounds shillings and pence

Then there was a song about a copper:

I went down the Lane
To buy a penny whistle
A copper came along
And pinched my penny whistle

I asked him for it back
He said he hadn't got it
You're a bloody liar
You've got it in your pocket

And the drunk's song:

I was drunk last night
And drunk the night before
I'm gonna get drunk tonight
If I don't get drunk any more
The more I drink
The better it is for me
'Cos I belong
To a boozer family

Glorious, victorious
One bottle of beer between the four of us
Thanks be to God there ain't no more of us
'Cos one of us could drink the bloody lot

By now it was beginning to get dark and the song bloke said he had to go. Had we got any more songs for him? We couldn't think of any more, we said – the quicker he went the sooner we'd get our tanners – but if he came round again tomorrow we'd think of some. He said that if we thought of any more after he'd gone, we ought to write them down so we wouldn't forget them, and that he couldn't come round again tomorrow because he was going over to Lambeth to see if he'd pick up some more songs from there. Then he got in his car and drove away.

But he did give us the tanners as promised, and we went down the Euston and spent them on threepenn'orth of pictures and a packet of Weights and a box of matches to smoke while we were in there. I hoped he'd come round again the following month.

CHAPTER SEVEN
IN THE COUNTRY

In my part of London I was fortunate to have many open spaces in which to play, such as Hampstead Heath, where teachers from my school took me every Tuesday morning, and Regent's Park.

There was one occasion, when I was aged about six, when some friends and I were told to go for a picnic in 'the park'. A little group of us set off up Euston Road. After we had walked what seemed a long way, we came to a lovely open space with pretty bushes and flowers. This had to be it. We sat down on the grass and ate our picnic. Only later did we realise we had camped in somebody's front garden. It must have been one of the original houses in Euston Road, built before the arrival of the railroads, when the rule was that each house had to have a thirteen-foot garden between it and the 'New Road' (now Euston Road).

There were many squares around which grand houses for rich Londoners had been built, with beautiful gardens to remind them of the country. During the summer, my school used to take the infant classes to Cartwright Gardens after lunch. Tables were taken from the school, turned over and hammocks tied to the four legs so that we could lie there and sleep or, as I remember doing, watch the clouds go by. It was part of the campaign to improve the health and lifestyle of young Londoners that was very much in vogue at the time.

Swimming was something else we all enjoyed. A school swimming day was on Tuesday mornings in the summer, at

Titchfield Street baths off Tottenham Court Road. We would walk there from Thanet Street in a crocodile, and file into the baths while the teacher negotiated the official (free) entrance at the ticket office. Every boy was half undressed by the time he reached the baths, because there was always great rivalry as to who would be the first in the water. Later, this no longer happened because all the boys had to have a foot inspection before plunging into the water. Boys with dirty feet (most of them) were made to wash them in the footbath behind the diving board. None of us had swimming trunks, but we were allowed to swim naked up to puberty.

Another swimming site was the Hampstead or Highgate ponds – an official bathing place with an extremely high diving board. Bathing in the ponds was free in those days. We also swam naked in the Regent's Canal, where we earned a few pence for demonstrating 'a long swim under water' for a penny or two. People on the bridge would throw pennies in the water for us to dive after and rescue. Once someone had thrown an old pram into the canal, and when an unfortunate boy dived in he landed on the pram and came out bleeding profusely from his wounds.

There was also the Foundling Hospital. In 1926 that great institution, founded by Captain Coram with the help of Hogarth and Handel, had moved its orphanage quarters out of London to Redhill; it later moved to Berkhamsted in 1935. What was left were the cloisters and the extensive grounds and gardens. There was much discussion as to what should happen to this space. Lord Rothermere, one of the Harmsworth family who owned the *Daily Mirror* and other publications, led a campaign for the Foundling area to be saved for the nation and raised some £475,000 to turn it into a playground for children. A swimming bath was built and schools were encouraged to take classes in the cloisters – part of the experiment of teaching children in the open air, which was fine in the summer but chilly in the winter months. We didn't appreciate the classes; all we wanted to do was to get out and play football or have a swim. When Queen Mary officially opened the swimming pool at the Foundling Hospital in 1929, thirty or more boys marked the opening by plunging into the water. They dived into the deep end and swam towards the shallow end where a British Movietone News camera filmed the boys. To be sure of seeing myself on the newsreel, I waited until everybody had dived in before following suit. The newsreel was shown at the King's Cross cinema. I went there when the programme began on Saturday morning and stayed until the place closed. I saw myself four or five times.

The area is still a playground for children today. On the entrance gate a notice reads: 'No adults admitted except in the company of a child.'

My first real introduction to the countryside was through the Country Holidays Fund. Various villages and families willing to take children were chosen by the organisers and, in 1927, Pat and I set off with two other children from our school for our first summer holiday. The London Poor Children's Holiday Fund had arranged this. Granny should have paid 6d a week to book up for a fortnight in the country, but whether or not she did so, I don't know.

We went to a village called Horsley, near Stroud in Gloucestershire. The woman (unfortunately I cannot remember her name) who took us into her home was a kind, motherly soul who, I think, was particularly nice to me because I was an orphan. She had a husband who was a professional gardener, but no children, so suddenly having four London boys in the house together all at once must have been quite a shock for her. There was a large orchard at the back of the house where we could pick and eat apples and a sloping field that led down to a river where I could see fish swimming and jumping. This fascinated me.

I remember with shame that we went with some village boys to look for some traps they had set for rabbits. One had been caught. A boy held it down on a stone and we all hit its head with sticks until it died. Although I had nightmares about what had happened, it didn't stop me eating the delicious stew our landlady made from the dead rabbit.

I enjoyed living in Horsley so much that I didn't want to go home. Neither did the kind lady who had looked after us want me to go. She wrote to my grandmother offering to adopt me. Granny, however, was furious because I was *her* property, and because if I were adopted she would lose the 12/6d she received from the government for my upkeep. So home I went. For a long time I kept dreaming of the country and the kind lady; so much so that one day I thought I saw her serving in one of the shops near our house. I stood outside the shop staring at the woman, until at last she got cross and sent me packing.

My next country holiday, also provided by the Country Holidays Fund, was in 1929 to Castle Acre in Norfolk. This time there were about fourteen of us. We met at King's Cross station, most of us carrying pillow cases filled with our belongings. (Not many of us could afford suitcases, and anyway pillowcases were much more practical as you could sling them over your back.)

At Castle Acre we stayed at two farms. The farms were owned by two related families and mainly seemed to consist of large carthorses that were moved from one farm to another. Sometimes we saw these beautiful great beasts arrive at our farm with several small children riding on their backs. Our main interest, however, was in the ruined castle. This had not yet been taken over by the National Trust and, together with the ruined monastery nearby, made a wonderful free playground. We climbed the castle walls and probably pretended to be Saxons and Normans who fought each other. Castle Acre was on the edge of the Fenlands, where there were deep creeks containing crystal-clear water in which we swam every day.

Once we went on a day's outing to Swaffam in a horse-drawn bus. When it was time to go back, however, I found that I hadn't enough money for the bus fare. The driver wouldn't allow me on the bus and no one would lend me the money. I saw the bus drive off and, all alone and tearful, started on the five-mile walk back to Castle Acre. Tired and rather frightened I trudged along, feeling very sorry for myself, when suddenly I noticed something on the ground in front of me. It was a shilling. Forgetting how tired I was, I bent to pick it up and found other coins scattered around it; it was a veritable gold mine! Eventually I collected about two shillings and ninepence. The way back suddenly seemed much shorter and I walked quickly and cheerfully. When I got back to Castle Acre I found I had missed tea, but that didn't matter to me: I was rich! The other boys were jealous and crowded round asking where I had found the money.

'On the road,' I told them.

'Some money dropped out of my pocket the other day,' said one boy. 'It must be mine.'

But however much they asked, I wouldn't part with a penny of my lucky find.

Back home I found a new interest that was once more to take me into the countryside. In 1928 I regularly attended the Presbyterian Church of Scotland in Regent Square. This was actually a miniature copy of York Minster and was very beautiful. Although very sadly a German bomb destroyed it in 1945, in the 1920s it was in good condition and ran a thriving company of the Boys' Brigade. This organisation had been founded by William Smith, a teacher in the North Woodside Mission Sunday School in Thurso, Scotland. It was where John Reith, of the BBC, worshipped. He would sometimes inspect us boys who would line up while he walked up and down the lines chatting to us.

Possibly the happiest time of my youth was spent between the ages of ten and eighteen, when I was a member of the 39th London Company of the Boys' Brigade, as were other members of my gang such as Higgy, Pongo, and Evvy. I joined because of the band. Once a month on Sunday mornings, members of the Boys' Brigade marched around our streets to the accompaniment of their band. It brought them many recruits, including me. Every year in September, when recruiting began, there were nearly two hundred boys wanting to join. By Easter, the number would have dropped somewhat, but those who stayed on became enthusiastic members of the organisation. I still remember the thrill of the marches we made.

There was something doing every night, which was just the stuff to keep young lads out of mischief. On Monday nights there were first-aid classes, and I eventually became an instructor in the technique. A doctor from Barts teaching hospital gave the classes. He taught as well as performed, but his teaching was perhaps a bit ambitious for us boys. Once he told a boy to go and find him a cat. The boy found one and brought it back to the classroom. The doctor chloroformed it, cut it open and cut out its heart to show us what a heart looked like and how and why it was such a vital organ of the body. Someone told our teacher, Mr Atkinson, about this, and he told the RSPCA. There were many protests from boys' families who thought it was really wicked to cut up a cat.

This same doctor took us to Barts hospital for anatomy lessons and practical experience in the dissecting room. We were shown the bodies of elderly men and women lying on tables covered with cloths, which he would whip off. Sometimes there would be only a head; at other times, partly dissected bodies. I think he hoped to inspire us to want to become doctors, although, of course, this was rather more than a little unrealistic. The idea appealed to me, however, and once I asked my granny to buy some sheep's hearts for dinner so that I could study them before they were eaten. The family thought I was mad.

On Tuesdays there was band practice in the basement. Here we practised the music to be played on the following Sunday march. The 39th London Company had a fife and bugle band. We were envious of other companies that had brass bands, and even more envious of the companies attached to some Scottish churches that had bagpipes. (Some boys from our area went to Finsbury to join a company there where the boys played bagpipes and wore kilts.) Our conductor, however, was an ex-army musician who didn't play any brass instruments. Nevertheless, ours was a good band, and we played at the Albert Hall when the Boys' Brigade celebrated its fiftieth anniversary in 1933. I learned to play both the bugle and the fife.

Wednesday was drill night. We learnt army drill and marched in fours. It was a replica of the army, without rifles, run by ex-Sergeant Major Clegg. Thursday was gymnastics. We practised in the Scottish church's hall, and had a horse we jumped over, did exercises to music on parallel bars, and on rings hanging from the hall roof. I was in the team that was to take part in the fiftieth anniversary display at the Albert Hall, but the night before the display I broke my arm while practising leaps over the horse and so could not take part. I was devastated.

Friday night was Club night, when we played billiards or board games, while at the weekend we played football or cricket. On the second Sunday in every month there was a Church parade and a long march after the service around beautiful Georgian streets and squares that echoed to the sound of our beating drums, blazing bugles and shrieking fifes, with barking dogs snapping at our heels.

In charge of our Company was Captain Cunningham (known as Cug), a kind and gentle man. He worked at the headquarters of the Blue Star Shipping Line, and when he first founded the 39th Company at the end of the nineteenth century he gave the boys a holiday on one of the company's ships. Later, the shipping line presented an old ship's lifeboat, called the Neptune, to the 39th Company. It was moored on the Thames at Strawberry Hill in Richmond. We used it for weekend trips up the river.

I remember travelling on this boat, which had been adapted for sailing, towards Oxford. When the wind was right we used the sail, a marvellous experience. Sometimes we rowed and sometimes we had to walk along the riverbank and tow. There were places along the bank where we used to camp at night. We would get out, tie the boat to the bank and put a tent over it and a tarpaulin so that we could sleep in it.

There were also annual two-week camping trips under canvas organised at Felixstowe and Clacton in Suffolk and at Seaford, Cuckmere Haven, in Sussex. They always took place during the last weekend in July and the first week in August so as to include the Bank Holiday, and thus enable boys already working to join in. Two weeks' camp with rail fare was 15/-. We paid 2d a week subscription to the band, and this paid for music lessons, but it was the church and its members that financed the camping projects. I remember singing the following song while on the march from the train station to a summer camp. The tune is a bugle call that the Boys' Brigade played.

Here comes the Boys' Brigade
All smothered in marmalade
A tuppenny ha'penny pillpot [pill box cap]
And half a yard of braid

The first camp I went to was at Felixstowe. There were sixty to seventy boys, five officers and two women. One woman was the cook and the other was available in case anyone became unwell. We had to erect the tents in a long line, military style. Because of the emphasis on straight military lines, one tent was erected on what seemed to be a ditch, which ran straight through the tent. One night there was a thunderstorm and the tent was flooded out. Luckily, it was not my tent. Everybody had to do one day's guard duty, to guard against anyone stealing items from the tents. There was one guard for every tent and one officer, a grown-up, in charge of all. Each guard had two hours on and four hours off. The guards marched up and down the field in true military style.

For breakfast we had hard-boiled eggs, bread and butter, and tea. I remember the eggs being put in a big cage that was dropped into a cauldron of boiling water and boiled for about five minutes. If we weren't on duty we could do what we liked during the day, except that there was always a bathing parade an hour before lunchtime, which we had to be back for. Once, for supper, we had fish cakes. A boy took a bite and said 'Pooh! They've gone bad!' No one would eat them after that. Cug was upset. He lectured us on the hardships endured by fishermen to get us this food.

Our company had a permanent camp at East Tilbury, where we went for weekends, leaving on Friday night and coming back on Sunday. The camp's ground was right on the East Tilbury marshes, near an ancient village where an Elizabethan fort called Cole House Fort once stood, and where Elizabeth I delivered her famous speech. We had two wooden huts with stoves so that we could go there in the winter. They were nice and warm, but when a lot of boys applied to come on the camp, army bell tents had to be erected and it was very cold sleeping in these. At night we would have a big campfire.

During the First World War the place had been used as an army base. Along the river's edge the gun emplacements were still there. They were a great place in which to play. We swam in the moat.

At summer weekends when we got up in the mornings we would go to the many creeks surrounding the camp and get a basin of water to wash in. It was salt water, which made it difficult to lather. Sometimes after heavy rain the creeks would fill with water and we could swim in them. Once I felt something on my hand – I pulled out an eel.

Camping at East Tilbury during the winter introduced me to a type of entertainment about which I was later to write a musical documentary programme for the BBC: the Black-Faced Minstrel Show. Captain Cunningham, now an old man, was enthusiastic about the minstrel shows, which had started in the USA and became popular in England for nearly fifty years during the late nineteenth and early twentieth century. In the winter months we formed a minstrel troupe, sang Stephen Foster songs such as 'Oh! Susanna' (1848), 'Camptown Races' (1850) and 'Old Folks at Home' (1851), blacked up and entertained the people of East Tilbury. Back in London we would give performances of the show in Presbyterian church halls.

I was still an active member of the Boys' Brigade two years after I had joined the BBC. The official leaving age was seventeen, but in my eagerness to join at the beginning I had lied about my age, saying I was eleven (the earliest starting age) when I was actually only aged ten. So in fact I was eighteen before I left the organisation. I shall always be grateful to the Boys' Brigade for the happiness and education it gave me.

CHAPTER EIGHT
WORK BOYS WORK

During my schooldays, the odd jobs I had were many and various. I tried my hand at paper rounds, milk rounds, laundry rounds, working in a greengrocer, in a fish shop and in a rag shop.

Paper rounds were not very popular. The morning rounds meant you had to get up very early and the evening rounds interfered with activities such as the Boys' Brigade. At one point I had some roller-skates, and at the weekend I used to deliver the papers skimming round the various houses and flats in the grander squares around the British Museum.

If you worked for the laundry, you had to supply your own wheeled cart, made from a box that had contained sugar – a 'sugar box' – and two pram wheels. Although I delivered and collected the laundry on my skates, it was nevertheless a dull job and I needed to be working in the evenings and on Saturday afternoons – bad times for a boy. In winter it interfered with activities with the Boys' Brigade, and in summer with school cricket.

There were a number of dairies in our area with Welsh names, for example, the Cambrian. There were two in Leigh Street and one in Sandwich Street, all three run by people who mostly spoke Welsh. Milk was kept in large, glazed earthenware pots on the counter and was sold by the pint, half-pint and quarter-pint.

Milk could be bought out of hours from a dispenser fixed to the dairy door. The supply was kept in a large urn behind the door and fed to a tap outside that operated once a penny was placed in the slot. A handle was pulled down and milk delivered into your own jug. Occasionally the 'old iron cows', as they were known, went wrong and delivered the milk whenever the handle was pulled down so that there was an almost never-ending supply of milk. The word would quickly get round and a queue of people with large jugs would lined up at the iron cow for their free supply of milk.

Milk that was delivered was measured out in tin or pewter pint or half-pint cans with wire handles and lids that clipped tightly shut. It was carried in a brass churn that was placed in a three-wheeled cart. The tap at the bottom of the churn protruded from the rear of the two-wheel end of the cart so that milk could be extracted. The milk cans hung round the cart edge by their handles.

Beneath this apparatus was a cupboard or large sliding door in which eggs and butter could be carried. Cans of milk were delivered (any time from 5am to 8am) to the doorsteps of houses or flats and the previous day's cans would be collected for washing to be used again. There were no bottles.

The milk cart was also trundled out during the late morning when many residents appeared with their own jugs or even their own milk cans to buy their milk directly from the milk tap (operated by the milkman) on hearing his yodelling call. Boys were employed to help the milkman on his rounds – to deliver the cans of milk to doorsteps in the streets and in the high blocks of flats. They washed up the empty cans from the day before and also helped to wash them when the delivery times had finished. The work started at 6am and was completed by 8.30, when it was time to get to school. For this work (including Sundays when many more cans were delivered) the pay was 1/6d to 2/- a week.

In the cold, snowy and freezing weather a milk round was a hell of a job. Hands and fingers froze (few boys had gloves) and chilblains would appear. At least half the boy force dropped away in winter, leaving the milkman to cope on his own or rely on the help of his wife.

Even the large brand dairies (for example, a large Express Dairy depot with carts and horses was housed in Tavistock Place with a dairy in Marchmont Street) employed boys for early morning deliveries.

An attempt was made to regulate this child labour and no boy less than twelve years old was officially supposed to be employed on a milk round. But for the most part the rules were ignored. I did my first milk round when I was ten. I gave up milk rounds during the first winter because I found that delivering newspapers was a much warmer occupation.

When I worked for a greengrocer this involved Saturdays only, but it was not good for sports or Saturday afternoon pictures. Sometimes it meant early morning visits to Covent Garden in a van to collect fruit and vegetables. I remember delivering potatoes with a basket on my head. I also remember washing the icy celery or doling out hot beetroot. I was never allowed to serve in the shop, the one thing I really wanted to do.

Levy's Fish Shop also employed boys. The work was mainly at night, cutting up the chips, or tearing up sheets of newspaper for customers to carry their purchases home (tuppence and a penn'orth). It was hard work, but the best paid work available.

Work in the rag shop was well paid, too, but rare. Old newspapers and rags (old clothes) were collected and weighed on a huge pair of scales that hung from the ceiling. The basement was chock full of rags that were sorted by rag pickers, and periodically collected by dealers in junk and re-pulping materials. Owners of the rag shop dealt with rubbish, but were the richest family in our street.

As I grew older my Uncle Jim, who worked like all the other males in our household for the family business of Kirkham's builders and decorators, used to get me to help him with various jobs around the house. Decorating, plumbing, woodwork, and even de-bugging the house became regular chores. Rather too much was expected of me because I was a member of the family.

I had one other job during the late 1920s and early 1930s, which was to help two elderly blind people who lived in Leigh Street. I had to lead them to the Nonconformist Whitfield Tabernacle in Tottenham Court Road, for which they gave me 2d. It was perhaps the most boring job I ever had as I had to sit through the service before leading them home again – only to discover that I was accused of taking money from blind people by other boys who didn't lead anyone.

When the time came for me to leave school in 1931, I was aged fourteen. I had no inkling of what I wanted to do or be. My school reports and leaving certificates were good, but certainly not brilliant. I had shown no particular aptitude for creative writing, although I suppose winning a prize for 'Cleanliness and Hygiene in the Home' must have demonstrated a certain imaginative streak in me considering our home conditions!

My fourteenth birthday was on 15 June 1931. I'd only ever been to one school. At the end of the summer term I set out to face the world with an elementary education, two prize books for winning the essay competition on hygiene, and a school report that stated that I had attended school regularly for eleven years, that I was useful, helpful and willing and that I had a clean record.

The day after school ended my grandmother took me straight down to the Labour Exchange to find a job.

In those days, parents wanted boys and girls to have good, 'steady' jobs. Few found them. Popular jobs were being a van boy, telegraph boy, hotel page ('buttons'), messenger boy (on a bike), delivery boy on a three-wheel box bike, butcher's, grocer's or greengrocer's boy, or labourers to builders and decorators.

During one of my last days at school the children in my year were asked what sort of job we would like to have. No one answered. We didn't know. Then one bright spark said 'electrical engineer'. After that we all said we wanted to be electrical engineers. At the Labour Exchange I was told there were no electrical engineering jobs for unqualified fourteen-year-old boys. Did I like metalwork? Yes. So I was offered a job as a sheet metalwork apprentice at the Alan Manufactory Company in Gray's Inn Road.

'Good,' said my grandmother, 'then he can get home to dinner.' She thought I had done very well for myself.

The company manufactured electric signs. My wages were 7/6d a week, with a 2/6d rise after three months. I thought the wages were very low.

Mr Alan, my new employer, said, 'You are learning a fine trade,' and my grandmother agreed. So I began what was the most miserable time of my life.

I remember how time dragged; the work was extremely dull. You got burns from sulphuric acid and one boy cut the tops of his fingers off under the sheet metal guillotine. Many of the younger men were crude in the extreme, and had a passion for plaguing the boys' lives with obscene jokes.

Work began at 8am and ended at 6pm; on Saturdays it ended at 1pm. All we got for an annual holiday was one week unpaid; most of the men couldn't afford to take this.

At first I went home for dinner; but, soon after I joined, the firm moved its premises to Faringdon Road which made it too far to walk home for dinner and back. I lived on tea and yellow-dyed margarine roll for lunch.

The 'apprentice' business was a con to get boys into the firm to work as cheap labour – at least that's what we boys thought. There were four of us. We were doing men's work. I was assigned to Joe Summers, a real sheet metal worker who, because of the depression, had descended from higher things to electrical sign making. He told me to get out.

'Find a real trade or you'll regret it,' he said. 'If you don't, you'll be a semi-skilled labourer all your life.'

What I did was easily mastered. Before I was fifteen I'd made a number of signs of my own. One of them was in the shape of a thistle, which glowed in the sun during the day and blinked on and off at night. It hung over the Thistle Restaurant in the Haymarket for years until it was finally destroyed by a bomb blast in the 1940s.

I hated working in the sign factory so much that, but for the delights of the Boys' Brigade in the evenings and at the weekend that calmed me down and raised my spirits, I think I would have run away rather than have endured it. The last straw came towards the end of 1932. By then I had obtained a bicycle on which I rode to and from work every day. But one evening the foreman of the sign factory, who was given to amorous adventures, borrowed it, knowing he was going to miss the last bus home. He promised to return the bicycle the next day but didn't. Neither did he return it the following day or the next. In fact a good few weeks went by and still there was no sign of it. And he got angry with me each time I asked him to return it. I'd had enough.

'Unless you return my bicycle,' I told him about two Saturdays before Christmas, 'I shall not be coming back here to work.' The following Monday I stayed home, and, oh, the pleasure! The next day one of the men called at home to say that the foreman had promised to bring the bicycle back by Saturday. But now I hadn't the slightest desire to return. I would not go back, even if the foreman got down on his knees and begged me to – even if the governor himself came and pleaded with me. I didn't go back, but no foreman came and fell on his knees and no governor came to plead. I never heard anything more about the bicycle.

My grandmother was horrified and in tears, but I was adamant.

'Don't worry,' I said. 'I'll get another job.'

I thought of all the jobs I'd done during my school days, and decided to have a go at one of them. I chose the Express Dairy because there you began at 6am and finished early. I got an application form, filled it in and sent it off. They told me they would contact me in a few days.

Meanwhile I went walking in the West End, where I knew there were a number of employment agencies that displayed vacancies in their shop windows. I suddenly found myself in Portland Place and there, looking like a great battleship, was the new BBC Broadcasting House. Eric Gill, the sculptor, was still carving his statue of Prospero and Ariel over the entrance.

That, I thought to myself, would be a fine place to work. They must need boys for some sort of work, surely? Plucking up courage I pushed through the heavy doors of the imposing entrance and went to the reception desk.

'Yes?' said the rather grand receptionist.

I asked if they had any jobs vacant for boys.

'Jobs?' he said, 'You can't just walk in and ask for a job; you have to go to the Labour Exchange.'

Crestfallen, I walked back towards the entrance. I was about to go out when someone tapped me on the shoulder. It was a tall, military-looking commissionaire. (All commissionaires employed by the BBC were ex-servicemen and many had been wounded during the First World War.)

'If I were you, son,' he said kindly, 'I would go home and write a letter.'

So that's what I did. I sat down and wrote to the BBC, asking for a place in the organisation. My letter is still on my file at the Corporation.

To my utter surprise, a few days later I received a letter offering me an interview. I went to see a Miss Freeman, who dealt with applications from clerical staff and boys. She asked me many questions about my life and family. I told her that my father had been killed in the war and that my grandmother had brought me up. I had on a new suit and shoes, which I'd bought but hadn't paid for. Miss Freeman didn't know that, but thought I must be a very thrifty boy to buy my own clothes out of the 5/- or so that I earned a week doing odd jobs.

I was delighted and amazed when Miss Freeman then said that the BBC would like to offer me a job that would be confirmed a few days later by letter. I would work as a messenger boy, at 15/- per week, plus 2/6 dress allowance.

As I turned to leave the office, one of my sock suspenders broke and tripped me up. I fell flat on my face on the floor. It didn't matter. I was over the moon: I had a job at the BBC.

When I got home there was a letter from the Express Dairy – they had turned me down.

CHAPTER NINE
FIRST YEARS AT THE BBC

In January 1933 I started work as a messenger boy, working in the Publications Department of the BBC. I have never quite understood how I got the job, but it was probably due to the fact that I was a war orphan. I had to wear a dark suit, stiff white collar, black tie and black shoes. We were allowed to wear grey flannel trousers on Saturdays only.

John Reith, the BBC's Director General, had been badly wounded in the war and was anxious to give employment to ex-soldiers, especially if they had been wounded or disabled in some way. Some of the extremely badly wounded ex-soldiers worked in the Publications Department. One of my first jobs as messenger boy was to deliver a new supply of envelopes to these men. I received a terrible shock when first I saw their terribly burned and disfigured faces: many of them lacked noses, ears, hair, even lips. They were so badly disfigured they stayed in their office, never going out for meals, even to the BBC canteen. I used to get their meals for them and got to know them quite well. They were very kind and friendly.

I was put to work in the publications store, at that time situated on the second floor immediately above the concert hall. My main tasks were to deliver advance and current copies of the *Radio Times*, the *Listener* and *World Radio* to various people, including the Director General, and to help dispatch these and other BBC publications to schools, clubs, listeners' circles and discussion groups. We also sent out descriptive pamphlets to accompany any series of talks that were being broadcast.

In those days there was considerable prestige to be had from working for the BBC. It was apt to surround you with an aura of self-importance.

'Do you really work for the BBC?' friends and relatives would ask. 'Have you actually been inside a studio? Do you know any of the announcers?'

In 1933, Broadcasting House was still not complete. Building work was going on and Eric Gill, obscured from public view by a large tarpaulin tent, was working on his controversial sculpture of Prospero and Ariel above the front entrance. When the group statue was unveiled it showed that Ariel was naked, obviously a boy – and sexually very well endowed. The *Daily Herald* said that, 'Maidens are said to blush and youths to pass disparaging remarks regarding the statues of Prospero and Ariel,' while G. G. Mitchelson, at that time the MP for St Pancras, claimed that the figures were 'objectionable to public morals and decency'.

The new, much publicised building attracted many visitors. People curious to see the 'home' of the famous would hang around the steps of All Souls Church opposite the entrance, hoping to catch a glimpse of their favourite radio artists passing in and out. Some came on the place by accident, were intrigued by its strange shape, and stood trying to figure out its purpose. Was it a museum, or a government office? Once a man, blood streaming down his face, rushed into the entrance hall and asked for the casualty department.

Groups of visitors traipsed round the building daily and, under the monotonous voice and watchful eye of the official guide, wondered at the Talks studios on the third floor with their false fireplaces and rows of dummy books, to make people giving the talks feel comfortable and 'at home'. Lord Reith insisted on 'talks' as he considered 'lectures' to be too heavy. They would also have seen the Control Room on the eighth floor, the Variety studio in the basement, the Dance

Band studio on the sixth and seventh floors and the chapel on the third floor; and, in addition, the silence rooms down in the basement where you could relax in silence (with wonderful paintings on the walls), the listening rooms, where you could hear the programmes being broadcast, and the echo rooms, with a loudspeaker and microphones installed to create the echoes. A strikingly pleasant feature of the BBC before the Second World War was the abundance of flowers in all parts of the building, especially arranged daily by one women employed to do just that and nothing else.

Until the outbreak of war, each studio was individually decorated and the characters of each, ranging from the Military Band to News and Religion studios were strictly maintained, reflecting the fact that when Broadcasting House was originally built, each studio was designed for specific purposes. Every morning the illuminated cross in the chapel (Studio 3E) would be switched on for the morning service and again at night for the Epilogue. Only religious programmes and serious talks about classical music (mostly given by Sir Walford Davies, under the title 'Music and the Ordinary Listener') were allowed to emanate from 3E.

I was present when the consecration of the Concert Hall took place in 1933, Lord Reith thinking that God might thereby look kindly on the BBC's music programmes. Very reasonably, the Bishop of London was asked if, at the same time, he would also consecrate the chapel. He agreed; but once in Studio 3E he asked what was underneath. On hearing that it was a men's lavatory he refused to perform the ceremony.

In 1937 I bought a clarinet in order to try to get on closer terms with all the music I was hearing. I sought permission to practise it in a studio unoccupied at lunchtime. I was allowed to use the chapel, but only if I practised 'serious' music and not jazz.

My first meeting with Reith was accidental. I was in a lift with another boy named Charlie Leegood. We were possibly on our way to deliver some pamphlets or copies of the *Radio*

Times, or maybe returning to the second floor where the publications store was based. We caught the lift on the lower ground floor or the basement. The lift stopped at ground floor level and a very tall, rather scruffy, somewhat terrifying looking man with a large scar near his left eye and a strong Scottish accent got in. In spite of our having told the lift attendant that we wanted the second floor, the lift went directly to the third floor. When the lift stopped I made a move to get out and walk down the main stairs one floor, but found I couldn't move because Charlie Leegood had grabbed my long brown storeman's coat (BBC issue) and was holding me back. The tall, scar-faced man strode out before everybody else, while the ex-army lift attendant held a salute until he disappeared behind the door leading to Room 32l, the Director General's office.

My second meeting with Reith was when I delivered an advance copy of the *Listener* into his in-tray. He was sitting working at his desk, on a dais, and took no notice of me whatsoever. I later learned that you never entered the Director General's office unless let in by his secretary. (She wasn't there when I arrived.)

Delivering BBC publications to so many offices meant that I got to know Broadcasting House like the back of my hand. Sometimes I would try to sneak a look in when I passed a studio to see what was going on.

There was a campaign to boost the sales of the *Radio Times* and its fellow publications. The idea came from someone high up in the Corporation and much of the practical work involved fell to me and the boys with whom I worked. For three days a week we sat at a table filling envelopes, addressed to every newsagent in the country, with posters advertising the three journals. 'High and Low Browse over the *Radio Times*', 'Plan your Listening in Advance'. I remember a series on religion, and the title of the pamphlet that accompanied it read, 'The Way to God – threepence'! Inserting a poster in an envelope was one of my major occupations during this period.

To this day I never see a *Radio Times* poster outside a newsagent's shop without recalling the rough texture of the posters and the smell of the printing ink.

Then came the day in 1934 that I had dreaded. I was just approaching the age of seventeen and the BBC had a policy of making boys leave at that age to make way for younger ones. Older messenger boys, even though they might be fast envelope fillers, were not required. The only hope of staying on was if a suitable job became vacant. I was summoned to an office and told to look for another job and I left feeling very depressed. I had known this day would come when I first joined the BBC; but when you're aged fifteen, seventeen seems a long way off, far too far away to worry about.

For the first time I realised that any fool could stuff envelopes with bits of paper. You didn't need an Oxford degree for that. Education – that was my trouble: I didn't have any. An elementary education at a Church of England school didn't count for much in the BBC.

There was a job going in Publications, but it went to Charlie Leegood. (He became a big noise in the Publications Department as Manager of Subscriptions, in charge of distributing all publications.)

At this time the BBC broadcast many programmes of music on gramophone records, arranged and presented by announcers such as Christopher Stone who, with his relaxed style, became a great favourite with listeners almost as soon as he started his record programme in 1927. But the BBC had no gramophone library of its own. It relied on records supplied by companies such as HMV and Decca. This led to some questionable practices. Christopher Stone would bring along records to the studio supplied by the record companies that he wanted to play in his programmes. They were quick to advertise the fact that the BBC were playing their records and would publish lists of records Stone would be playing in his forthcoming programme.

The BBC decided to stop this practice by forming its own Gramophone Library. This opened just as I was about to lose my job as messenger boy, and there was a job available as assistant librarian in the department. Needless to say I applied for it.

The head of the Gramophone Department, Bowker Andrews, whose brother Kenneth worked in Publications, interviewed me. Bowker Andrews turned me down because I gave the impression I was so happy in Publications where I worked that I wouldn't want to work anywhere else. So he crossed my name off the list and decided to give the job to someone else. I was told officially that as I had not been chosen for the library job I had better go down to the Labour Exchange in Great Marlborough Street and see what was on offer. But I felt so upset at having to leave the Corporation that I didn't go.

Luck was with me. After my interview with Bowker Andrews he told his brother what he had done, and Kenneth, who knew me quite well, told him it was the BBC I wanted, not just Publications. So I was interviewed again and got the job.

Before the permanent Gramophone Library was set up in 1932, there were some 4,000 records available to programme makers, stashed away in various places throughout Broadcasting House. Children's Hour kept its own small library, about 150 records, in its office. The 'permanent library' of about 1,600 discs was the responsibility of the House Superintendent, Mr Chilman, who looked after the commissionaires and the cleaning staff. He was the 'social amenities' man. Productions Department (mainly drama programmes) possessed a library of about 2,500 records, 1,700 of which were described as 'effects', by which they must have meant incidental music because there were few recorded effects – 'noises off' – available in those days.

Each department tried to store its records in some sort of order and make a catalogue. Some, like those in the Children's Hour and House Superintendent's offices, were catalogued by title only, while 'Drama productions' records were indexed by categories as well as titles. Whatever system was used, however, the identification of the content of all three libraries relied more on the memory of their users than on the catalogues.

In 1932, when the centralised Gramophone Library was set up, it was decided to create a comprehensive cataloguing system that had not hitherto existed. Each record was to be indexed under three separate categories: title, composer (if known) and artist or performer. Sound effects records were to be filed and indexed separately. A careful account was to be kept of how often each record was used and for what reason.

Basil Adams, the first librarian, originally joined the library as a 'card writer'. Initially, only very basic details were put on the cards. For example, the label of a record that read, 'Medley of Sea Shanties' would be listed under just that title, with no details as to what sea shanties had been recorded on the record. Minuets, rondos, arabesques, etc. were listed without any reference as to what symphony, suite, divertimento or other work they might be part of. If it wasn't on the label, it wasn't on the card.

It was soon realised, however, that if the catalogue were to be a valuable research tool for producers and other broadcasters it would have to carry much more information than that conveyed by commercial record labels. Symphonic works would have to be identified not only by title but also by subtitles, number (opus and sequence), key and movements. All medleys would have to be itemised. All minuets, waltzes, gavottes, gigues, marches, allemandes and other dance movements would have to be identified not only by composer but wherever possible by the main work for which they were originally written. Opera cards, displaying title, composer and artists would have to list the order of acts and the arias sung in them. There would have to be a title card for each aria that would also contain details of the opera whence it came. In other words, there would have to be a fully comprehensive, cross-referenced catalogue.

When I was working in the Gramophone Library, Miss Thorpe was in charge of the index with the two Miss Londons (sisters) as the main indexers. They had both previously worked for HMV on its record catalogue and so brought valuable experience to the job. Miss Margaret Dean-Smith was employed as an expert in folk song and folk music in general.

When I first started to work in the library, records were housed in shelves stretching from the floor to the ceiling. I did not do any indexing, although I soon became familiar with the system and was able to help programme compilers find the records they wanted. My main job was to find the records required, get them down from the shelves and into the appropriate programme boxes, deliver them to the programme compilers, and put them safely away on the shelves afterwards. I also had to send out records ordered by the various BBC regions that had no gramophone library of their own.

I found myself in a completely different world from anything I had known before: a world of every possible kind of music. I also got to know, and become friendly with, types of people I'd never come across before. Some had great artistic talent and some had university degrees. There were also the more familiar clerks, librarians and indexers.

Basil Adams was in charge when I first started work in the library, but he moved over to television and Raymond Angel became the librarian. The latter was a first-class musician and teacher, and it was from him that I began to acquire some knowledge of music.

There were a number of gramophone programme compilers. For instance, Maurice Brown, who specialised in chamber and orchestral music; Max Robertson, who specialised in opera; Anna Instone, orchestral music; Leslie Perowne, dance and light music; and Basil Lam, who was mainly concerned with modern music. These talented people not only compiled the programmes for announcers to put over, but also engaged famous conductors, bandleaders and music critics to present special programmes.

It fell to me to put on the records for these outsiders, and, in most cases, for the announcers. Thus I became personally involved with almost every type of gramophone programme put out during the years 1935–1939, including, of course, my own favourite, the late night programmes of dance music.

In those days records were fragile ten- or twelve-inch discs that rotated at 78 rpm. BBC studios had various numbers of turntables on which the records were played. In the small news studios that were used for straight record programmes there were only two, but in the larger studios, used for variety programmes and the like, there were banks of from six to eight turntables on which complicated routines could be worked out. Experienced announcers and presenters manipulated the turntables themselves, but newcomers preferred it if someone like me played the records for them. This meant setting up the records in the right order and lowering the needles onto the discs in the right place, the location of which had previously been marked on the record by means of a yellow chinagraph pencil. There also had to be seamless changes made from one record to the next without a gap in the music. This was necessary for long works such as symphonies or other musical pieces that were recorded on several records. Sometimes, too, a compiler would want to play only extracts from a variety of records and to have these extracts faded in and out at the appropriate moment. This was also my job. I became quite good at manipulating complicated programmes of this type and was consequently much in demand by the record programme presenters.

I remember one episode when Joseph Macleod, a poet who worked at the BBC, was a new announcer. We were in the studio with all the records nicely lined up and for a while all went well. Then Joseph announced: 'The title of my next record is "The Silver Swan".' I started the record, but out came something called 'The King's Hunt'.

'What'll I do?' Joseph asked anxiously.

'You must apologise for putting the wrong side on,' I said.

'But I didn't put the wrong side on, *you did.*'

'Yes, but they don't know that. They think you did.'

'Oh very well.'

'Ladies and gentlemen,' said Joseph, 'I am so very sorry for putting on the wrong record. But here now is "The Silver Swan".'

I turned it on, but to my great dismay out came yet another tune that was not what was wanted. Joseph apologised again, while I hastily looked at the next record on the turntable and saw that it was labelled 'The Silver Swan'.

'It's all right,' I said, 'I've found it!' I lowered the needle on to the next disc, but what came out was certainly not 'The Silver Swan'.

'I refuse to apologise again,' said Joseph. 'Let's move on.'

So we did. At the end of the programme Joseph mopped his brow and said, 'What a bloody stupid way to earn a living!'

Afterwards I discovered that the record company had wrongly labelled the record 'The Silver Swan'. This incident made me much more careful after that to check the order and the labelling of all the records.

In the 1930s the BBC was a much smaller organisation than it was later on. Most people knew each other, and the atmosphere was relaxed and friendly. Although I was aware of my lack of education, all the people I worked for treated me as an equal.

I learnt much about music from the programme compilers who contributed in various ways to my musical education. Anna Instone, for example, showed me that music was not just a jumble of notes put together haphazardly but an art form. At lunchtime in the library, Raymond Angel would go through the scores of various works with me. Maurice Brown introduced me to chamber music. The first piece that I ever sat right through and enjoyed was Mozart's Clarinet Quintet in A. He took me to the Proms to hear Brahms. It was good to get a free seat, have an hour's lesson on what was coming and to be told what to listen to for best enjoyment.

All the programme builders loved opera but none more than Max Robertson. He took me to the first opera I ever saw, *The Tales of Hoffman*. I was flabbergasted when I recognised some of the tunes.

There was another way in which I got to see opera. During the opera season at Covent Garden you could go there from 5am onwards and buy a stool with your name on it that entitled you to a ticket in the gallery. You had to pick up your stool an hour before the performance started but were assured of getting a seat. The programme compilers weren't so keen on the 5am bit, so they got me to go and buy a stool for them that they would pick up later. For doing this I was rewarded with a free seat at the opera that the programme compilers would pay for.

Basil Lam spent hours with me talking about Shakespeare and English literature as well as music. I attended his lectures on musical appreciation because I put on the records for him. I also put on the records for Francis Toye, an opera-crazy critic, who loved and was very knowledgeable about Rossini. Leslie Perowne, who was in charge of popular record programmes, helped my education by bringing me his old textbooks on English grammar that he had had at his public school, Haileybury.

'Have you read your *Alice*?' he would say.

'No,' I would reply. So he would buy me a copy.

I was still very conscious of my lack of education and asked Bowker Andrews what to do about this. He arranged for me to attend evening classes in the mid 1930s in English and French at the polytechnic in Regent Street, which the BBC paid for.

Thus, in so many ways, the BBC became my university.

CHAPTER TEN
ASSISTANT TO THE ASSISTANT

One celebrity for whom I put on records was Spike Hughes, British jazz musician, composer, radio critic and music journalist. He was also a lover of violin concertos, especially when played by his friend Joseph Szigeti; but it was his love of jazz that was to have the greatest influence on me. Spike had played jazz in New York with his own orchestra, and was passionate about the jazz that was flourishing in dance-halls, on disc and on the radio in the United States through the 1920s.

In Britain during the late 1920s and early 1930s all dance music in two or four time was popularly and mistakenly called jazz. But in fact jazz proper did not penetrate the British conscience until the late 1930s. This was because there was so little opportunity to hear it. The one organisation that might have introduced jazz to the masses was the BBC, but that august body thought true jazz was not fit material for British ears, so they banned it from the airways.

The Gramophone Library contained almost every record published in Britain since the advent of electrical recording (1928). All popular dance music and all jazz records, of both white and black players, were to be found on the shelves.

By the time I joined the Gramophone Library, books on jazz were beginning to be published, mainly in France. With Spike Hughes's help I read all the books I could find on the subject. Although the BBC banned the playing of jazz on the air it did in fact have some 'race' records, as they were then known, in the library. These were recorded in the USA and sold in England under the label 'Parlophone' (part of EMI). They featured black bands and artists and in the USA were mainly bought by black people.

In my enthusiasm for learning about jazz, I would arrive at work at 7.30am, together with the cleaners and commissionaires, in order to get acquainted with as much of the music as I could before the rest of the library staff arrived. I discovered the rare 'race' records and many other American jazz bands' discs, both black and white, that had become part of the American scene. I decided to become a jazz expert.

Sometimes when I was playing jazz records to myself in the library, boys of about my age would listen outside the door. They were jazz enthusiasts like myself, and together we decided to form our own jazz band. We called ourselves 'The Six Swingers', swing being the name often given to jazz at that time.

We were to have appeared in a BBC programme that was called *Amateur Hour*. This fell through, but eventually we were given a spot in *In Town Tonight*. The following is from the *Evening Standard*, 24 February 1937:

> Three months ago C. W. Chilton, while filing records in the gramophone library, had an idea. He plays the guitar. He decided to find out if there were any other members of the BBC staff who played instruments. The result was a group called 'The Six Swingers'. This band includes an electrician's assistant, an operator in the Effects Department and other members of the staff.

The *Melody Maker* had this to say on 13 March 1937:

> With the help of two outsiders these keen youths of Broadcasting House made up a satisfactory combination. Sid Rowe, a toolmaker, extracted some not unoriginal sounds from his fiddle; the receptionist boy who haunts the ground floor at Portland Place brought along his saxophone. In the rhythm section were Curly Russell, an electrician, on piano;

Chilton, the librarian, doubling guitar; Joss (an outsider) on bass and Mr. Flanagan on drums who, as you might expect, hails from the effects department of the BBC.

I won't say they sounded very different from any other amateur band but there was a refreshing enthusiasm about their performance of 'China Boy' on which they were faded in and 'Dinah' during which they were faded out almost before one had had the chance to hear them. Surely it would have been better to let them have at least one complete item instead of two scraps like that?

My interest in jazz was to have further repercussions. There was at that time a great deal of debate about the worth or otherwise of jazz in the music world. Maurice Brown, who was then a documentary gramophone programme producer and compiler, mounted a series in which people from all walks of life gave their ideas of what the value of jazz was. One presenter I remember was a student from Eton College. He ran a rhythm club and jazz society there, and arrived in a dinner jacket saying that he wasn't quite sure how to dress for broadcasting.

I was also invited to take part in this special series. I gave a talk entitled 'What is Swing Music?' illustrated with gramophone records, of course.

It was about this time that the Gramophone Department was 'dispersed' as they called it. Maurice Brown was sent to Features and Drama, Anna Instone to the Music Department and Leslie Perowne to the Variety Department. The Gramophone Library became part of Recorded Programmes.

Not long after that I ceased to be assistant librarian and became a gramophone programme builder and producer. My official title was 'Assistant to the Assistant, Gramophone and Variety Department'.

The assistant I was assisting was Leslie Arthur Perowne. He was the son of the then reigning Bishop of Worcester. Leslie was also fond of jazz. When talking about record programmes the press never failed to comment on the holy connection between the Bishop's son and jazz. Leslie had asked me to assist him because he had too many programmes to compile on his own. Together we were responsible for the compilation of some thirty or more gramophone programmes a week, to be presented by the duty announcers. Also we were expected to mount two or three feature programmes on special subjects such as music hall, ballads, instrumentalists, composers of pop music of the day and even a little jazz.

Every night of the week except Sunday we were responsible for programmes of recorded dance music. They were broadcast from 11.30pm to midnight, after the transmission of dance music from restaurants and hotels had finished. They filled up the time until the BBC closed down at midnight.

I made a speciality of Wednesday night. I turned it into a jazz fan's half-hour and called it 'Swingtime'. My signing off record at midnight was a piece by the New Orleans trumpeter Henry Allen. It was called 'Feeling Drowsy'.

Within a short time of this programme being launched I was receiving dozens of letters from appreciative jazz fans. I received some quite good press notices too. One critic said how refreshing it was to hear a 'shirt sleeve voice' coming over the BBC.

I was quite elated. Then one Thursday morning I was summoned to the office of the head of the Variety Department, Mr John Watt, who wanted to talk to me about 'Swingtime'. Apparently he hadn't noticed it until a couple of press notices prompted him to listen. I was expecting a rise in salary, or at least a bit of a promotion. Instead, almost before I could cover the distance from the door across the carpet to the desk, I received a fierce scowl and a loud roar:

'Chilton, you will never broadcast again!'

I was flabbergasted.

'Why not?' I asked.

'Why not? We can't have that cockney voice coming over the BBC, even for jazz.'

'But I don't have a cockney voice; I have a London voice.'

'Same thing.'

'It's the voice of the capital of the great British Empire,' I said.

'Look,' said Watt, 'this seems to be quite a popular programme, so you'll continue to compile it. But from now on your scripts must be read by a staff announcer.'

So, for the following three weeks, the BBC's golden-voiced chief announcer Stuart Hibberd read my scripts. He had a lovely accent, but it was not really suited to voicing such jazz titles as 'I'm Tired of Fattening Frogs for Rattlesnakes', 'He Might be Your Man but he Comes to See Me', or 'Gut Bucket Blues'! In fact Stuart Hibberd was very helpful and kind to me. He and Leslie Perowne and many others helped me to rub off the rough edges of my cockney accent and guided my pronunciation any time I asked. I had always been a good imitator and was sure I could get the accent right if I tried hard enough. Whenever I had the chance, I sat in the studio with the announcers listening carefully when they talked. As a result I was able to tone down my accent sufficiently for John Watt to reverse his decision.

The favourable reception of what little jazz we managed to get on the air on records led Perowne and I to be more ambitious. We compiled a series of programmes for mid afternoon listening called 'Kings of Jazz'. This was well received, not only by listeners but also by some of the heads of BBC programme departments. One of our contributors was Harman Grisewood, the BBC's Director of the Spoken Word, no less, who had a limited liking for jazz. Perowne and I took advantage of this, and pressed him to talk to, and persuade, the hierarchy to give us more and better time-slots for true jazz programmes. He said he would see what he could do. To our delight, Harman Grisewood discussed the subject of more jazz to be broadcast with the august Sir Walford Davis, Master of the King's Musick. The latter seemed quite amenable to the idea, but wanted to find out what kind of jazz we had in mind.

What we had in mind was to do a series about Louis Armstrong.

This was controversial. In the summer of 1932 there had been great excitement among jazz fans when the news broke that Louis Armstrong was to tour Britain. For the first time a genuine New Orleans black performer would be heard in the flesh. His initial appearance was to be at the London Palladium, and the BBC was to broadcast the event. There was a lot of publicity. Millions of people tuned in. When the time came, Louis Armstrong began his act by coming through the curtains and taking a bow.

There was loud applause from the packed house. He blew a few notes on his trumpet, the curtains opened, and then he cut loose.

The *Melody Maker* said that: 'Every number was received with tumult. The packed house absolutely rose to it.' It certainly did, but what the reporter failed to mention was that the audience rose in order to walk out. By the time the act finished the Palladium was half empty.

One critic wrote: 'That sweating, shuffling figure in the spotlight hitting endless high notes seemed to have little connection with the creator of the intensely moving music of "West End Blues" or "St James's Infirmary". After "Tiger Rag" he went running round the stage like a madman.'

Most critics were devastating: 'A disgusting and abortive exhibition likely to nauseate all decent men,' wrote one composer. The Armstrong broadcast from the London Palladium proved to be something of a problem for the BBC and turned the Corporation against black jazz, and this music was almost (but not quite) put on the banned list of items considered unsuitable for public consumption.

So when, some five years later, Perowne and I wanted to do a programme about Armstrong, Sir Walford remembered the great fuss there had been about the broadcast in 1932. He asked us whether we would want to present his music, and we said we would, and that we were planning a whole series about him. In that case, said Sir Walford, he would like to hear something of what we had in mind.

Armstrong was still too hard to take for some people, and I reckoned Sir Walford would be one of these. Then I had an idea. I suggested to Perowne that we play substitute Armstrong.

'What do you mean?'

'Somebody who plays quite like him but is not really him – you know, like Nat Gonella. He plays and sings lots of Armstrong's solos and we've got Gonella on record doing this, but he's not so raucous as Armstrong.'

'You want me to deceive Sir Walford?'

'No, no, it's not deception – well, not really. It's the same thing once removed, that's all – easier on the ear for the uninitiated.'

'There may be something in what you say.'

I thought I had won him over. I was not allowed to attend the final judgement, but when Perowne went up to face the great man, among the many records under his arm he carried two or three of Nat Gonella's. The answer wasn't long in coming; Perowne was all smiles.

'Well, what happened?'

'We've done it! The Master of the King's Musick sees no harm in the music of Louis Armstrong. In fact he thinks that some listeners might even enjoy it.'

So around 1937 the sound of genuine jazz began to be heard across British airways: live bands from the BBC's own studios and record recitals presented by jazz musicians. We even managed to transmit a live impromptu jam session direct from New York by star jazz players working there.

When I first joined the BBC, I was still living at number 9 Sandwich Street with my grandmother, aunt and uncle. But I longed to get away, particularly because if I left any clothes or belongings at the house Aunt Aggie would pawn them and I would never see them again. (By this time my grandmother was no longer in charge of the household; Uncle Jim had banned her from having anything more to do with it.)

Leslie Perowne came to my aid. He suggested I took a room at the local YMCA. I wasn't really eligible; but with the help of his father, the bishop, Leslie was able to arrange this and in 1937 I moved in. I shared a room with a young man called Jimmy Gatt who became a great friend. (He was mad keen on flying and joined the RAF at the beginning of the war as a pilot.) The YMCA suited me down to the ground. I had somewhere to keep my clothes and books; there was a canteen and a swimming pool; and a very friendly atmosphere. At weekends some of us would go hiking, staying at youth hostels all over Britain, or go on long bicycle rides into the country. Sometimes I would go to the BBC Club premises at Motsburgh Park, where I was persuaded to play rugby. I didn't much enjoy it but tried my best not to show it.

Nevertheless, in spite of enjoying myself and making friends with people at the YMCA, I longed for a home of my own. I had previously met a couple living in Sandwich Street who were very kind to me and had welcomed me into their home many times. I got to know their daughter Bess, and in 1938, aged twenty-one, I asked her to marry me. She accepted, and very soon afterwards we got married and set up home together in a rented flat in Alexandra Mansions in Judd Street.

I now wish we had never done this. It didn't work out. Bess never understood my compulsion to educate myself, to succeed in the completely new world of radio and music, and everything that kept me working for long hours and left her lonely at home. She never wanted to meet any of my BBC friends. 'They aren't like us,' she used to say.

CHAPTER ELEVEN
THE WAR YEARS

In 1938 the BBC began to gear up for the war that was to come a year later. In the Gramophone Department Leslie Perowne and I were told to compile a lot of record programmes to be kept in reserve for use when hostilities started. These were kept in large, black record cases and I had to take them to the BBC's premises at Wood Norton in Evesham for storage.

The programmes were selected by the programme builders and packed in boxes, together with lists of running order programme notes for the announcer. I had to sort the records out into the correct running order. They were very dull, heavy records, with not a single piece of light music, no pop songs, no variety, and not a laugh anywhere. All the records were taken to a wine cellar, where I found the empty shelves very useful for stacking the boxes of record programmes in order. In fact, during the uneasy year between the Munich Crisis of 1938 and declaration of war in September 1939, life at the BBC went on much as before.

In the summer of 1938 I was introduced to a tall, lanky young man who wanted help with some record programmes. I couldn't place his accent; and then learnt that he had come to England from America for six months while awaiting confirmation of American citizenship. His name was Alistair Cooke.

He was born in Salford, Lancashire in 1908 and christened Albert. His father was a metalworker and a Methodist lay preacher. Alistair aspired to greater things. He changed his name from Albert to Alistair; gained a scholarship to Cambridge; and in 1932 won a Harkness fellowship to Harvard. He became a successful transatlantic journalist, moving between London and America in search of work. In 1934 he became the film critic for the BBC. Back in America he became acquainted with John Lomax, honorary consultant in American folk song and Curator of the Folk Song archives of the Library of Congress. Alistair persuaded Lomax to lend him a bagful of folk music recordings with which he was to present a record series called *I Hear America Singing* for the BBC.

That's where I came in. I was assigned to assist him in the series and to help him choose records (many from the BBC Gramophone Library as well as those that he had brought with him) and play them on the turntables.

Alistair's attitude towards me was rather condescending. Besides helping him with *I Hear America Singing*, I also helped him with various other projects that were outside the BBC when he gave lectures to various organisations illustrated by gramophone records. Alistair depended on me to find him songs about the American West that he didn't know. The producer Maurice Brown, the chief producer of gramophone record programmes, once asked him whether he had taken me out to dinner to thank me for all the work I was doing for him. Alistair then took me to a rather grand restaurant in Regent Street where he ordered fish and chips for me, no doubt thinking that that would suit a low-down cockney lad.

Nevertheless, I think Alistair appreciated what I did for him. Before he left to return to America he presented me with a copy of John and Alan Lomax's book *American Ballads and Folk Songs*. In it Alistair wrote:

To Charles Chilton who turned the tables on me
with more patience and skill than anybody will do again.
July 5th – September 20th 1938
    With my best wishes, Alistair Cooke

Before he left to go back to the USA at the end of 1938, Alistair asked me if I had ever thought of emigrating. I replied that I hadn't.

'Perhaps you should.'

'Why?'

'There's going to be a big war.'

I told him I had no wish to emigrate.

Alistair duly returned to the States. Later there was a certain amount of criticism levelled at him by the British press, who accused him of deserting his native country in time of war.

Alistair opened my eyes and ears to the social and historical importance of popular song. Used in the right way, songs can often say much more than plain words, and be a hundred times more evocative. I did little more than play Alistair's records for him, but watching him work gave me a new insight into radio presentation and use of material. I've based all my own work on his ever since. Turning the tables for Alistair Cooke was one of the milestones in my radio career.

I also followed in Alistair's footsteps in another way. He was always late with his script. He was often still writing it when we should have been rehearsing, and once we made it only by the skin of our teeth; the red light was flashing before we sat down, and we hadn't rehearsed anything.

After he had gone back to the USA, I'd made up my mind to specialise not only in jazz but also in American music as a whole. I turned my attention to documentaries on American themes – railroads, gold rushes, pioneers, negroes and cowboys – that provided me with raw material for a new kind of gramophone show, one that had actors taking part as though they were in a play, but with all the music and songs supplied by the turntable. Jazz was not forgotten in my new enthusiasm.

During the first months of 1939 I was compiling thirty-seven programmes a week from fifteen to sixty minutes in length. Some of these were merely straight announcements of record titles. Others contained detailed 'notes' for announcers, that is, information about the music and its performers on the records selected.

As well as compiling daily record programmes for announcers to present, under titles such as *Reveille* and *Morning Star*, Leslie Perowne and I were also presenting full-blooded productions with actors and narrators such as the weekly series entitled *Kings of Jazz*. These illustrated the life and work of famous jazz personalities, including Louis Armstrong, Fats Waller and Bix Beiderbecke.

With the declaration of war in September 1939, however, everything changed. Everybody at the BBC, except for the most skeletal of staff, was sent home. This was because it was expected that London would be subjected to intense and concentrated air raids. In fact, however, for about six months after war had been declared there was a non-active period known as the Phoney War when nothing much happened within the UK. The government and the BBC, however, behaved as though all the expected moves of the enemy had taken or were taking place. Theatres, cinemas, football grounds, public museums – all places where large crowds could gather – were closed. The BBC was reduced to one service – the National Service – and all creative programmes ground to a halt.

There were endless official announcements about gas masks, food rationing, call-up notices, tips for defence against bomb blast, and how to keep your air-raid shelter dry. In between the announcements came long periods of heavy, serious music played on gramophone records from Evesham, although nobody ever said that was where they came from, interspersed with long sessions – up to twelve hours a day – of Sandy Macpherson at the theatre organ. Staff at the BBC had to attend lectures on first aid, gas attacks, fire drill, gas-mask practice and Broadcasting House defence policy.

First aid was easy for me, as at the time I was a member of the St John Ambulance Brigade and I already knew what to do. We had lectures and practised on the lower ground floor of Broadcasting House near the band room of the Concert Hall. Gas lectures were held in a former drawing room of one of the grand houses in Portland Place. We learned about the types of gases that might be dropped on large inhabited areas and were introduced to the government civilian gas mask soon to be issued to every person in the British Isles. We had to test them. We were shut in an airtight room and told to put on the masks. The room was then filled with tear gas. On the count of three, we took the masks off, the room doors opened and we all rushed out coughing and with eyes streaming into the unpolluted air again. The gas masks were certainly proof against tear gas. So if that was all Hitler was going to use against us, we were safe.

In Incendiary Drill we learned how to deal with fire bombs by throwing a couple of spades of earth on them, or dousing them with a jet of water ejected by a stirrup pump. This was one part of defence drill that proved to be very useful during the Blitz in 1940. We were also formed into defence patrols of two or three people whose task it was to patrol every floor of Broadcasting House to make sure nobody was trying to sabotage the dynamos in the basement or in any other way trying to ruin British broadcasting. We had no arms for this duty – only a sawn-off broomstick some two feet in length.

As the weeks passed and the war appeared to be at a standstill, the country became fed up with the dreary programmes. Thousands of letters arrived at the BBC requesting at least some light entertainment on the national network. The government relented. The BBC began to soften and sweeten its grim output with all kinds of radio entertainment and plenty of variety shows whose artists took pot shots at the enemy in their own inimitable style.

The Home Service was set up, with programming reminiscent of pre-war broadcasting. The news was read on the Home Service at 9 o'clock every evening. It commanded more listeners than any other programme, because in wartime everybody thirsts for news. For security reasons, henceforward all newsreaders had to announce their names; and the likes of Stuart Hibberd (the BBC's Chief Announcer), Frank Phillips and Joseph Macleod became household personalities.

In January 1940, however, listeners were surprised to hear a brand-new newsreader on the Home Service wavelength. A German propaganda station in Hamburg was interrupting the BBC News. The newspapers and satirists quickly turned the German announcer, who was actually a British citizen called William Joyce, into a figure of fun. Because of his assured, somewhat overdone, upper-class accent, Joyce was nicknamed Lord Haw Haw.

Reith had left the BBC in 1938, and the new Director General was F. W. Ogilvie. Reith didn't think that the BBC should pander to public taste, rather that it should broadcast what it (for 'it' read Reith) thought was good for its listeners. But Ogilvie set up a listener research department. From this source he learned that the favourite radio item with the British Expeditionary Force, at that time inactive in the Phoney War, was Lord Haw Haw. Troops listened to him direct from Hamburg from where a stream of propaganda was directed towards them.

In order to counteract the German propaganda, it was decided that a special programme for the Forces should be created and beamed from England to France. Before the programme and its wavelength were set up, however, Ogilvie did what Reith would never have done. He went out to France to consult with the troops to find out exactly the sort of programmes they wanted. What he found they wanted was a purely light entertainment channel, including jazz and popular music, which is what they got, even on Sundays. Reith's policy of playing only religious or 'serious' music between church services or 'uplifting' talks on Sunday was abandoned.

The Forces Programme began broadcasting in January 1940, twelve hours a day from 11am to 11pm. The programme was also broadcast in Britain, where it became more popular than the Home Service.

Thus at the beginning of 1940 the Gramophone Department was almost back to normal. I, however, was twenty-three years old and in line for call-up. Measures were already being taken to recruit new staff in place of those who would have to join the forces. I was determined to make the most of the time I had left.

Jazz was what the troops wanted, so jazz I would give them. I had the idea of forming the BBC's own Rhythm Club. I put up the idea for the programme and it was accepted. In May 1940 the *Melody Maker* reported:

> The present BBC weekly series *Kings of Jazz* which terminates this Sunday (June 2) is to be followed straight away with an entirely new series to be entitled *The BBC Radio Rhythm Club.* Charles Chilton who has been responsible throughout for the *Kings of Jazz* broadcasts is to inaugurate the Club on June 8 in the Forces Programme at 10.20pm. He tells the *Melody Maker* that this new series is to include not only swing records but several other features that promise to make these programmes of especial interest to all jazz fans.
>
> Its primary intent is to explain jazz and to this end it will comprise rhythm of all kinds, contrasting styles and combinations, white and coloured jazz etc. and will by no means confine itself to the work of one artist only as hitherto.
>
> In addition to records, for instance, the BBC's own direct recordings of broadcasts by the leading American swing bands will be extensively featured.
>
> The Club also hopes to welcome from time to time notable personalities in the jazz world who will be put through their paces by Charles Chilton. On June 8 Roy Rich, himself a keen jazz fan and already well known to listeners for his dance record presentations, will be in the studio with Chilton representing the listening enthusiast. Membership of the club

> will be extended to all who listen and letters and requests from
> listeners will be eagerly welcomed.

By the middle of 1940 the Radio Rhythm Club had firmly established itself. The Club's public was large and enthusiastic, consisting not only of hardened swing enthusiasts and experts but also of people who, until the formation of the Club, had hated any form of swing music.

Many of the letters from listeners contained ideas for programme features, and quite often made a suggestion that I had long been nursing myself, namely programmes of British swing music. Such programmes presented a difficult problem because there were few really good British swing records – certainly not enough to provide material for a number of programmes. The only solution was to form a British swing 'combination' group for the Radio Rhythm Club, one that played swing and nothing else, and one that existed purely for swing lovers – and yet at the same time appealed to the general public. Such a combination would be very difficult to find, but in August 1940 I met the man who made my dream possible.

I went to hear a little band of swing musicians who played at the St Regis Hotel, London in Cork Street. I at once knew this band was almost exactly what I was looking for. Its music was fresh and the players were keen and of an exceptionally high standard. Most of their enthusiasm came as a result of the leadership of a smiling Welsh clarinet player whose arrangements, especially regarding the handling of riffs (musical phrases that are constantly repeated), gave me great pleasure. The clarinet player was Harry Parry.

Broadcasts of the St Regis Quintet followed soon afterwards. The reaction of the listening public was just what I hoped for. So I approached Harry about forming a Radio Rhythm Club Sextet. He was more than keen. He modified the St Regis Quintet, replaced the trumpet with a vibraphone, and sat up many late nights making arrangements for the new band.

The first performance of the Radio Rhythm Club Sextet was on 28 September 1940. Its members consisted of Harry Parry, clarinet; Joe Deniz, guitar; Tom Bromley, bass; Ben Edwards, drums; Roy Marsh, vibraphone; and, on piano, a young, blind musician, destined for a great career in the music scene: George Shearing.

The success of the Radio Rhythm Club, which was to last for about five years, marked a milestone in my career; and its inauguration was to coincide with something that brought an even greater change to my life. I fell in love.

In September 1940 Pen Colbeck, a young girl fresh from secretarial college, came to work as a shorthand typist in the Gramophone Department. She was from a very different background to me. Her father was a colonel in the British Army. She was put to work all alone in a little office in Duchess Street, where she had to type out lists of the records and notes to be included in the many standby programmes we were compiling for use in emergencies. One morning I entered her office and found her rather lonely and dispirited. I took her to have a coffee and to meet the rest of the department. She knew nothing of jazz or pop music, but was as eager to learn as I was ready to teach her. We worked together on the Radio Rhythm Club and other programmes I was producing, and she soon learned how to cope with all the many functions of the department.

Meanwhile, the Phoney War had long since finished. France had surrendered, Hitler was on our doorstep and bombs were dropping over London. During the raids, especially in October 1940, it was obvious that Broadcasting House was a prime target. Dozens of firebombs were dropped around it. Then, when the buildings of the surrounding streets were well alight, fixing and illuminating the exact position of the building, the bombs began to fall. They all missed, except one that struck the Langham Hotel, not twenty yards away. The whole north-eastern corner of the hotel collapsed, taking all the bedrooms and their occupants with it.

One night I was on firewatch duty with Fred, a painter in the building's maintenance department. We had to report all sighted fires or bombings to the Control Room on the lower basement floor. The BBC man in charge of the Control telephone was called Mr Topping. When all the fires were blazing at their fiercest and bombs were dropping uncomfortably close, Fred decided to report the position. He moved the handle of the phone and a rather grand voice at the other end said: 'It's Topping down here.'

To which Fred replied, 'It's bloody horrible up here!'

Broadcasting House received its first direct hit on the night of 15 October 1940. I was on the roof, on firewatch duty, with the director of BBC defence, an ex-admiral. Gunfire was heavy, and he was just enjoying telling me how everything reminded him of the Battle of Jutland when we heard a sound like an approaching express train. There was a thump and a slight vibration of the building.

'We've been hit!' said the admiral.

'But it didn't go off,' I said. 'It must be a time bomb; let's go and find it.'

We found it in the Music Library on the fifth floor, almost five feet long with crumpled tail fins.

'We must drag it to the end of the building, so that when it does go off it'll do the least damage. Go up to the fire station and get a rope,' said the admiral.

The fire station was on the seventh floor, two floors above. There I contacted the chief fireman and told him what had happened, asking him for a rope.

When I explained what the rope was for, he said, 'I'll take this to the admiral. You go round every floor and tell anybody who's working here to get down to the basement – and quick.'

At the end of fifteen minutes or so I had cleared five floors and had reached my own department, the Gramophone Library. As I pushed open the door, the bomb went off. Bruce Belfrage, down in the basement, was reading the news. The sound of the bomb, which must have been heard over most of the world via the Overseas Service, made Belfrage hesitate. As the roof didn't cave in he continued after a pause of only a second or two.

The bomb had exploded while the fireman was dragging it along the corridor. The admiral had gone for extra help. Part of the western side of Broadcasting House was blown out. The Tower, the internal soundproof part of the building, collapsed as far down as the fourth floor. Seven people died, including the fireman.

The next morning, tired and weary, I was having breakfast in the canteen when Pen arrived. She was distressed to hear what had happened and at my exhausted appearance. She put her arms around me to comfort me. The next day I asked her to have lunch with me at a restaurant called the Shanghai. She had never eaten Chinese food and enjoyed trying to eat with chopsticks. We laughed a lot and talked a lot, and I fell more in love than ever, although I don't think Pen was aware of it at this stage.

Soon afterwards, there was much talk of evacuation. It was decided that the Gramophone Library and half the Gramophone Department should be evacuated to Wood Norton at Evesham. Other departments such as Variety and Drama went to Bangor and Bristol. Charles Maxwell, a compiler (another recent addition to the Gramophone Department), I and Pen (as secretary) were to go to Evesham together with the Gramophone Library staff and Recorded Programmes.

Wood Norton was a large country house that had already been converted into offices and studios. Our office was in one of the wooden huts built in the estate with Recorded Programmes staff in the hut next door. Studios were in the main house. The Gramophone Library was in a larger hut near where our office was. The lodge of the former estate housed three announcers, like us evacuated from London: Frank Phillips, Raymond Raikes and Norman Wooland.

We were lodged with families in the town and the BBC ran a service of buses from the station to Wood Norton. At another house in the town was the BBC Club headquarters with a canteen and bar where we could congregate in the evenings. In our little wooden hut, cosily heated by a central wood-burning stove, each morning we were greeted by the strains of 'The Teddy Bears' Picnic', played over the intercom to make sure everything was working in case of an emergency. Here Charles Maxwell and I compiled our daily record programmes; but to produce and present the Radio Rhythm Club Sextet I had to go to London. George Shearing, however, and his wife Trixie would sometimes come to Evesham when I wanted to record him, and we grew to be great friends.

But my time at Evesham was to be short-lived. On 11 November 1940 we started work at Wood Norton; on 20 November I received my call-up papers. Earlier in the year I had said I would like to join the RAF. Now I had to go to a recruiting station in Hertfordshire to determine what sort of work I should do.

'What do you do in civvy life?' I was asked.

'I am a producer at the BBC.'

'Right; wireless operator and air gunner.'

The date on which I had to report was 12 February 1941.

Pen and I would often walk back to the town after work instead of taking the bus. On one of our long walks, which meant we went by way of the riverbank instead of through the town, I told her that I loved her. She said that she loved me too, but that she was anxious and aware of the problems we would have to face. That was the beginning of a long, six-year love affair.

I knew I could never go back to Bess. Bess had said she would never divorce me. Pen's parents were devastated when they knew about us. In those days a quick divorce could be had only by proving that the guilty party had committed adultery – that is, by being discovered together in a hotel room by a witness such as a chambermaid. Otherwise one had to wait

TOP LEFT Charles and his mother
TOP RIGHT Charles' mother and father
BOTTOM LEFT Charles' father
BOTTOM RIGHT Charles' granny

TOP Charles and friends at Castle Acre, 1929
BOTTOM The Boys' Brigade

TOP Charles with David Jacobs in their office at Radio Seac, Ceylon, 1945
BOTTOM MC Roy Plomley (far left), Charles and performers in *Accordion Club*, 1947

Riders of the Range: cast members including Rustler the dog

TOP Charles being sworn in as Honorary Deputy Marshal of Tombstone, Arizona, 1950
BOTTOM Charles with American folk singer Josh White

TOP LEFT Charles and Penny in Indian costume
TOP RIGHT Charles with David and Mary playing the guitar
BOTTOM The cast of *Journey Into Space*

THEATRE ROYAL

Angel Lane, Stratford, E.15. Maryland 5973/4
House and Box Office Manager : Alexander Gray
Prices Stalls 15/-, 12/6, 8/6, 6/6
Dress Circle 12/6, 8/6, 6/6 : Upper Circle 3/6 : Gallery 2/-
Box Office open from 10 a.m.

THEATRE WORKSHOP
presents

Oh What a Lovely War

a musical entertainment written by
CHARLES CHILTON
and The Members of the Cast
(Military Adviser : RAYMOND FLETCHER)

on the basis of factual data in official records, war memoirs,
personal recollections and commentaries including those of :—

The Imperial War Museum	Engelbrecht and Hanighen
Kaiser Wilhelm II	Siegfried Sassoon
General Erich Ludendorff	Sir Philip Gibbs
Field Marshal Graf von Schlieffen	Edmund Blunden
Marshal Joffre	Leon Wolff
Field Marshal Earl Haig	Captain Liddell Hart
Field Marshal Sir John French	Barbara Tuchman
General Sir Henry Wilson	Herman Kahn
Rt. Hon. David Lloyd George	The Times
Philip Noel-Baker	The Daily Express

We are especially indebted for personal help to :—
Sgt. Dearsley (Royal Fusiliers)
Dorothy Woodman
Bert Sweet (ex-Gunner, 186 R.F.A., Deptford Gun Brigade) and
    many other ex-members of the armies of both sides in the
    1914-18 war
And above all, to the unknown British soldier-composers of the
    Western Front

First Public Performance Tuesday, March 19th, 1963

TOP LEFT Charles in his home observatory
TOP RIGHT *Oh What a Lovely War* programme – no mention of Joan Littlewood
BOTTOM Receiving the MBE: Charles with Mary and Penny, 1972

TOP Signing books for fans, 2011
BOTTOM Charles at the hardback launch of *Auntie's Charlie* and *Journey Into Space*

seven years before being able to petition for a divorce on grounds of separation. Added to this was the BBC's attitude to divorce, which was still deeply affected by Reith who had sacked one of his most loyal associates because he divorced his wife.

In the few weeks before I went off to join the RAF, Pen and I spent many happy and unhappy hours together. We had lovely days when we visited places such as Stratford and Worcester, but sad times when we watched the fires of Coventry burning, and when I heard that my great friend Jimmy Gatt had been killed in action.

Eventually the dreaded day arrived and I left the BBC and Pen (who went into the BBC Italian service) to start a new life in the RAF.

Chapter Twelve
In the RAF
↗

On 12 February 1941 I left Evesham for Blackpool. I had handed over the Radio Rhythm Club to Harry Parry to run while I was away. Once again the BBC was very kind to me. Throughout the war I received my usual salary, less what I received from the RAF. Soon after I got to Blackpool I was informed that from April my salary would rise from £265 to £285 per annum.

During the war Pen and I wrote to each other every day, except when I was on leave. Excerpts from my letters illustrate my life in the RAF.

12 February 1941
1220509 AC/2 Charles Chilton
33 White Gate Drive, Blackpool, Lancs

I'm settled (more or less) in a billet now. There are twenty of us here, half in uniform. Four of us shared a compartment from Crewe and we all got out at Blackpool. The other three have been in the RAF for some time now and they spent most of the time telling me what I was in for.

At the billeting office I was given a slip of paper with the above address on it and told to wait with some others in the street until an AC (Aircraftman) took us to the place. We waited in the dark for about a quarter of an hour and then, as nobody came anywhere near us, we set out to find the place ourselves. After lots of walking and arguing we found it.

I feel very hungry. One of the slips of paper entitled me to 'TEA' from my landlady. It has arrived. One lump and two biscuits. I really must go to the centre of the town and get a real meal. I have to report at 8 a.m. tomorrow at the Empress Ballroom and I bet it's not for a swing session.

Blackpool 21 Feb. 1941

How are things at the office? I miss everything so much and there is so much to remind me of it all. What makes me work-sick more than anything else is for me to hear the programmes coming over, presented by the old familiar voices, and know they are apart from me now.

Judging from the reports of airmen who have been to other places this is a good billet. Three men who came here last week were, until then, billeted elsewhere. The house was damp. The wallpaper wouldn't stay on the walls, the bedclothes were filthy and food scarce. The landlord turned off the electric current at 10.30 p.m. and allowed no talking after that time. He even listened outside the bedroom doors to hear if they were whispering about him in particular, and of course they were!

The landlady's daughter prepares our meals for us but she is not in good favour with the boys here for she walks out with a Polish officer! The men hate them. No one salutes a Polish officer although we are supposed to.

As a wireless operator I had to learn to send and receive the Morse code.

Blackpool 19 March, 1941

The greatest thing today was the 5 wpm Morse test. We paraded at 8.20 a.m. and did a little drill. We were all quite excited and anxious – me in particular. I cannot say I'm extremely keen on being in the RAF but now I am here I want to make a good job of it if I can. The test was not until eleven and at 9 a.m. we marched down to the recreation ground and changed into our PT kit. We ran about a mile or so, played games and forgot about the test. I'm having more exercise now than I've had since I ran about the streets of King's Cross some nine or ten years ago. We had PT twice yesterday…

We finished PT at 10 a.m. and we dressed and marched down to the front. We were dismissed until 10.55. Tom and I went into Woolworths [sic] and had a coffee and a salad sandwich. At five to eleven we were outside the Burton Dance Hall with the rest of the squad waiting to go into the test room. The suspense was terrible. The test was supposed to be at eleven but we were still outside on the street – waiting.

At last we went in. The test room was above Burton's shop and in peace time is a dance hall. There were tables and headphones enough for about 600 men. We seated ourselves and filled in the forms provided. The sender talked to us through a microphone to our headphones. He told us not to be nervous, to concentrate hard and not to use a propelling pencil. The test began. My fingers perspired so much I thought the pencil would slip through them. The letters seemed to come much slower than I expected and I had lots of time to think about each one. I put each one down deliberately and carefully and as neatly as I could. The test was over in five minutes and, as far as I know, I didn't make a mistake.

During the rest of my time at Blackpool I took many more Morse tests, each one faster than the last. On 9 May I passed the 12 wpm.

I mean to practice very strict economy now and I had told myself that I must resist the temptation to buy books so often. After the test, though, I somehow found myself in Boots' book department. Of course I had no intention of buying books but merely wanted to see what was new. I came across a very good poetry anthology called *The English Galaxy of Shorter Poems*. I stood reading it for a long time. I had no intention of buying it of course. Anyway I left Boots eventually and went (after a lovely hot bath at the baths) down to the Palatine for my dinner. I read the anthology while I ate.

After finishing my training at Blackpool I was sent to the RAF college at Cranwell to be trained as a Wireless Operator/Air Gunner. During the years between the wars an organisation called the Peace Pledge Union, founded by Dick Shepherd, canon of St Paul's Cathedral, had worked very hard at trying to enlist members of the public. Both Pen and I remember signing the pledge while at school. Later I seriously thought of becoming a conscientious objector, but the enormous horrors of the Hitler regime convinced me that the war had to be fought. (At this time we knew about the persecution of Jews, gypsies and negroes, but not the full extent of the horror.)

Cranwell September 4, 1941
I know how you must feel about taking a part in killing people whether directly or indirectly. I know it only too well. I felt very strongly about it once. I still do and loathe the things I'm training for more than I can say. Learning about wireless and flying about in the sky is lovely, but when I think of the real reason why I'm doing all this I shudder, not because I'm afraid but because I shall, when my training has finished, almost certainly take a very major part in doing to German cities and people what I've seen done to London.

I still managed to get down to London occasionally to work with the Radio Rhythm Club Sextet.

Cranwell, 8 Sept. 1941
Sunday was for me a good day. From 9.30 until 1.30 we rehearsed and recorded a Sextet show for reproduction on 19 September. Then from 2.00 until 5.00 p.m. we were at the Palladium. The Sextet went on about 3.30. They got a very loud and long ovation as soon as the signature tune was heard and they were certainly a great success.

I had done a little guitar playing before the war, first with our BBC Boys' Band and later with my friend Joss Froggart who had also played in our group. But now I felt I wanted to take it up more seriously.

On one of my weekend leaves I went to A. P. Sharpe's shop in Charing Cross Road and bought a new guitar for ten pounds. The result was that I found myself playing with a dance band on the camp run by Ozzie Noble, a professional drummer who was an instructor at Cranwell. He was always trying to find musicians among those who passed through the camp and contacted me.

Cranwell Nov. 5 1941

Last night, Pennino, I had the best time I've ever had as far as music goes since I began playing here. I told you that the corny sax players were on leave – well last night when most of the boys from the swing band (Nobles's) took their places we were eleven strong. There was a full brass section, three saxes and five piece rhythm. Another guitar player came along. He reckoned he'd played with Grappelly [sic] and [Django] Rheinhardt but when I got talking to him about Steph he didn't know much about him. Anyhow in spite of the impression he tried to make he's a good player – as a technician he's miles above me but he didn't seem able to get any guts out of his instrument. It went 'chink chink' and was all top notes. I like to hear a strong bass effect. Anyhow between us we supplied a strong rhythm section. Everyone was on form and it sounded wonderful. When we started it sounded so good that I laughed out loud. I couldn't help it. And did we swing! Actually we played from the dots [reading music, not improvising] most of the evening but I enjoyed it just the same. At the end of it we were all paid 7/6d. That was a pleasant surprise – 7/6d for doing something I like a hell of a lot.

Ozzie's band played not only for dances at Cranwell but for all sorts of organisations around Lincolnshire. So we were kept pretty busy.

Cranwell, May 23 1942

Last night I played at the officers' mess… It was a dull job – the only thing I got out of it was an insight into the way that officers live.

Compared with our standard of living (AC/2s [second-class aircraftsmen; the lowest possible rank]) they live a life of extreme luxury. Every possible thing is done to make them comfortable. They have a very grand mess and are waited on by batmen. Before the dance began the band was given a supper of fried fish, meat pies, cake and beer. We too were waited on and could have as much as we felt we needed. Cigarettes were also supplied. Things I do notice about officers and their dances is that 1) they cannot dance and 2) they haven't any attractive women, either as wives or girl friends.

May 24 1942

Our C/O is the biggest snob I know. He was at the officer's dance last Friday and although I spoke to an officer he knew while I was there (one whom I had instructed in the air) the C/O would not acknowledge my presence with even a nod or a smile, let alone a 'good evening'.

So my life at Cranwell became pretty busy. For six or more hours a day I was flying as a radio operator. Many evenings were spent playing the guitar or organising entertainment of various kinds on the camp. I even started a Cranwell Rhythm Club. Besides all this I was writing programmes for the BBC, programmes such as *The Story of New Orleans*.

18 Feb. 1942

I'm progressing slowly with my material on New Orleans. I've learned more about American history than I knew. I think it will make an interesting programme. ... Early songs are going to be difficult to get hold of though, particularly as they must be French or (and) Spanish. I expect we'll get round it with Cielito Lindo or something like that. We must use some Mark Twain in it too. He describes the city as it was in the middle 19th century.

There are so many programmes I want to do dear Pennino and that I'm sure I could if I were not in the RAF and had the time I had before the war.

Meanwhile, a F/Lt Richardson, who had read about me in the *Radio Times*, had approached me.

'As you know only too well, Chilton, we do a very responsible job here. Without us there would be no wireless operators flying. The men who train them are as important as those that are trained.'

I agreed with him.

'We are No. 1 Signals School,' he said, 'and the cream of wireless operators and mechanics, whether they fly or not, pass out of here.'

I knew what was coming next.

'Is there any chance of our being represented on the BBC?'

I told him I would see what could be done. I at once thought of *Radio Gram* on Wednesday, but reckoned it might be a bit better than that. Anyhow, before very long No. 1 Signals School was represented on the air.

When we'd finished talking, all he said was, 'How would you like to stay on this camp?'

This was a prelude to the question of my work at Cranwell. I had been posted as radio operator/air gunner, but when the time came for me to go on the gunnery course, so many men were being sent to us for training that there were not enough instructors to go round. So I became an instructor, to teach radio operators to communicate with the group and other radio operators in the air, and to help the pilot to find his way, at first only on the ground but very soon in the air with the rank of corporal. Our work entailed taking groups of four or eight trainees up in the old De Havilland Dominie planes that were used for instruction. We taught the new recruits radio operating and direction finding, taking each group up for about an hour; then landing and going up with another lot. In all we did some six or eight flights each day.

24 September 1942

Do you remember my telling you about the pilot who stunted over a castle and of the poor bloke that messed himself when he did it? Well for that the pilot was grounded for fourteen days. He came back again this week. I've had him as my pilot every day for two or three trips each day... Before we start on any trip he tells me to tell any pupil that 'has his heart in his trousers' to get out. I tell them but none of them do. Yesterday I had four chaps who had never flown before. Over the castle we did a couple of steep banks and a small dive. It wasn't much at all. I went to carry on with a pupil where I'd left off and found him looking very pale and with sweat on his upper lip. I gave him the bucket and told him to use that and not the floor if he were sick and sat him in the seat behind me. The pilot looked round and said 'Anybody sick?' I told him no. Then he climbed way far above the clouds until we couldn't see the ground at all, and did some switchback stuff. That did it for the poor chap behind me. I told the pilot that a pupil had been sick and that seemed to satisfy him. 'I'll go down then,' he said. Going down didn't relieve the chap behind me in the least. We passed through some thick grey cloud and struck some lumpy weather. Visibility, even when we came below the clouds, was nil, or almost nil, and the plane rocked and swayed in a high wind. And then we hit an air pocket – the deepest dive I've ever been in. We just dropped a hell of a way without any sort of warning. I literally stood up in my seat and my head hit the ceiling. There was a crash and my accumulator came out all over the floor. The bloke behind me moaned and shut his eyes and tried to forget everything. Nearer the ground it was a bit smoother but still lumpy, visibility was poor and it was hard to distinguish any landmarks at all. Soon however we saw some and made for home – we landed some fifteen minutes later.

On another occasion I was very scared when one of my pupils was sick and vomited up what appeared to be a great deal of blood. I told the pilot and immediately we headed for home. We rushed him to the first-aid station, only to be told about five minutes later that it was all right: he had eaten a lot of beetroot for dinner.

Cranwell 27th March 1942

Sgt Marks came back today and I did all my trips with him and, as I often do, I spent a fair amount of time in the cockpit with him. He's one of the best pilots we have here and the nicest. He seems such a gentle sort of chap. I often wonder why he ever became a pilot at all – he doesn't seem the type.

He loves the clouds. He goes just over the tops of them and sings at the top of his voice. Occasionally he turns round and says 'Lovely isn't it?' I agree wholeheartedly.

As Leslie would say, I have a 'thing' about clouds. Until recently I have surveyed clouds with the eye of any ordinary person. Some clouds are white, some are grey, some are even darker. But I have since discovered that there are all kinds and manner of clouds and that they all have character.

The best type of cloud is the wispy white one that appears on a warm day. These clouds do not like a lot of company and they prefer to roam around by themselves. Closely allied to this type of cloud is the white-grey. These are a bit more fond of company than the white ones and travel much closer together. They are the billowing type and are not at all level on the top as the white clouds are. They look more like great hills.

The grey black clouds roam about en mass. They push themselves together very thickly and do their best to blind the pilots and keep them so. These clouds, although they like each other's company, hate all other clouds that are not like themselves. They keep away from them as much as possible and to do that they come down near to the earth, very near. Five hundred feet or less. They pack themselves up and shut out the sun so that people shiver and put their macs on. The friends of these clouds, the mists, go up to meet them and they too do their best to blind the poor pilots. Visibility drops and the planes are grounded for we haven't a great deal of choice against such powerful enemies. Sometimes these clouds bring lightning with them just to make things more uncomfortable. This lightning plays about with the aircraft's radio and, if it were not for special devices in the aircraft, would strike it and set it on fire. Apart from the grey-blacks, clouds are very beautiful things. I love them and love flying above them and in and out of them.

Sometimes when I was up with a sympathetic pilot like Sergeant Marks we would make a few detours on our way home and fly over places we knew and liked. My Uncle George, who had once lived in the house in Sandwich Street, had married and now lived in Scunthorpe with his wife Jean. Sometimes if I had a free Sunday I would take a bus to Scunthorpe and go to see them. I told Aunt Jean that on a certain day I would try to fly over their house and hoped she would be able to see my plane and me. I told her to look out for a bi-plane circling round the house and take a tablecloth out into her garden and wave it if she saw us. On the appointed day we found the house and started circling around it. Almost immediately there was a response. In the garden of nearly every house in the neighbourhood there was a flutter of waving tablecloths. Aunt Jean had told all her friends to keep watch.

Direction finding was, of course, one of the principal jobs of the radio operator. A story went round about a British bomber returning from a night-time raid on Germany. It had received some direct hits and was behaving badly. The weather was atrocious. The pilot was anxious to land.

'Where are we?' he asked the radio operator.

'Not sure, Sir, but I think we're still over Germany.'

The plane gave another lurch.

'Hold on – there's nothing for it. We'll have to make a forced landing.'

They landed safely in a field and proceeded to carry out all the instructions they had received about landing in enemy territory. They burnt the aircraft so that it would not fall into enemy hands and went to hide in some nearby woods. In the morning they saw a farmer working in the field and in halting German told him they were the crew of a British aircraft and asked for his help.

The farmer looked at them and said in broad English, 'Where do you think you are, mate? You're on my farm in Essex.'

The story doesn't relate what the Air Ministry said when it heard the story of the burnt aircraft.

I had one rather scary experience while flying at Cranwell. The pilot called me to his cabin.

'Look at that!' he said, pointing out of the window.

I saw a plane, not a British one but a German fighter. It was hot on our tail. There was nothing we could do as we had no means of firing at it, and our old-fashioned Dominie would never be able to manoeuvre out of range. The enemy aircraft drew nearer until eventually we could see the pilot. He was a young man with a big smile on his face. He seemed to be making straight for us but at the last moment he straightened out, and, giving us a cheery wave of his hand, sped off until he was out of sight.

Cranwell, April 1943

We are doing more flying than ever. The pupils not only have to do a D/F [direction finding] exercise in the air but W/T [wireless telegraphy] as well which means we now have two pupils at once. One on the D/F set and the other on the W/T. It takes all the time one has to watch them both and tell them things. In fact one's attention is divided so much that neither pupil is really informed or taught much at all. None of the instructors like this idea at all (including me) and think it stupid. It's the idea of the new C/O and all new ideas from him are orders...

The C/O, of course, has never been in a Dominie, has never instructed any pupils on W/T or D/F and, as far as I know, has done no flying beyond a pleasure trip or two. If I could, I'd make him take a trip and watch how he'd get on with it and then, as he's standing in between the pupils, have Zack do some of his wildest of stunts until the pressure forced him to his knees as it did me today. It's a bad thing to stand up under such conditions but Zack took me by surprise so I was forced down and was unable to move before I could get to a seat.

At the end of 1942 I took back the running of the Radio Rhythm Club from Parry who was not making a satisfactory job of it. This entailed a lot more work for me as a letter of 6 December shows.

I devoted all the evening to work on the RRC. I planned up to the first week in April. Parry is due to appear only once a month instead of twice. I have also scheduled Tom Bromley to assist in the 'Making Your Own Swing Music' series. I've also put down Cyril Blake and Lauderic Caton to do the Negro Spirituals and Folk Songs. I shall record those when I'm on leave. My next leave will enable me to take part in two RRC shows live. On 2lst January I shall produce a Jazz Biography and on the 28th the first of the 'Making your Own Swing Music' show.

By this time what with flying all day, playing in the band or organising entertainments at night, and trying to research and write programmes for the BBC in between, I was exhausted. I began to suffer from the bends due to being in the air for so many hours. This led to my being grounded, which I hated.

Back in London, Harry Alan Towers, a scriptwriter that I had used occasionally, was now in charge of the Overseas Radio Broadcasting Service (ORBS) which recorded programmes for the benefit of the Forces serving overseas. When on leave I asked Harry whether he could apply for me to join him in London at ORBS, which he did. So for a few months I was based in London where I rented a small flat and concentrated on my favourite work of writing and broadcasting programmes. One of the other servicemen in the ORBS was Able-Seaman David Jacobs. We became close friends.

But this happy state of affairs did not last for long. At the end of 1944 rumours were going around of overseas posting.

'Don't worry,' said David, 'they'll never send us. We're too valuable for them here.'

I wasn't so sure, and said so.

'Bet you ten bob they don't send you,' said David.

On 17 March 1945, however, I found myself in Morecambe awaiting posting overseas.

During my walk around town I dropped into one of the many cafés on the front. Only one other airman was in there and at first I took no notice of him, but when I had got my coffee and had a good look at him I saw that it was Tito Burns. I had met him at Lauderic's Club a few months previously, and this was the first time I had seen him since he had appeared on RRC in 1940. And to meet him here! I nearly dropped my coffee in surprise.

A few days later I found myself aboard the RMS *Mauritania*, a passenger liner now being used as a troop ship. To my surprise and delight, Tito was on the same ship. I enjoyed the voyage, though it was rather scary knowing that most of the way we had no destroyer protection should we be attacked by U-boats. The Mauritania was a fast ship, which helped.

I had gathered from Harry Alan Towers that he was trying to arrange for me to join a BBC ORBS station at Cairo, but our ship never stopped there and sailed straight on down the Suez Canal.

Meanwhile on board, Tito and I provided much entertainment for the troops. We formed a dance band and did crazy variety shows in which I did my own Max Miller type of act, told a few jokes and sang the 'Dustbin Song'. I also did a dance of my own invention that raised a big laugh especially the tricky bits.

After eleven days we arrived at Bombay. From there I went to Mauripur, then in India but later in Pakistan. As I was no longer flying I had been reduced in rank to AC/2 and assigned for work as a ground wireless operator. I found this very difficult, as I had not done this work for ages.

Mauripur 2nd May 1945

As I expected nothing has happened as Harry Towers said it would. I asked him to let me have a letter to help my case for joining McNabb [an army officer in charge of Radio Seac in Ceylon]. I'm afraid I'm not at all happy. I'm quite incapable of carrying out the work allotted to me as a W/Op. I've spoken to the Warrant Officer about it all and he was very kind and sympathetic but says that nothing can be done except through official channels and I must wait and see what happens.

In the meantime I tried to find out as much as I could about Indian culture, its history, how the people lived and worked, their language and their music.

All the Indians here, like the bearers in our billet, the *cha walla* and the *dhobi walla* take an acute interest in my guitar. They call it a sitta [sic] – that's because they have an instrument of their own that looks very like mine of that name. An acute interest is aroused whenever my guitar is noticed. I'm always asked to play it. When I first came here and lived in the tent the bearer asked me to play. I did. Just to see what his reaction was. Within a few minutes there were four of them all sitting cross-legged round my bed listening, it seemed, with great rapture. All I did was play a few chords. Then I sang a song and they joined in. But they didn't sing the song I was singing – they sang one of their own – not in the same key either – with all its glissandos, quartertones and what have you. I thought maybe they wanted to sing one of their songs to me so I stopped playing. They stopped singing and wanted to know why I had stopped. I carried on. I played four different tunes (the chords to them anyway) in four different tempos and four different keys, but that didn't disturb the performers, not in the least. They went gaily on and were obviously enjoying themselves. When at last they finished they told me that they had been singing to their ancestors.

I also went canoeing and fishing. Three of us hitched a lift into town and found our way to where the *bunder* boats are moored. A *bunder* boat is a boat with one large triangular sail supported by a mast that slopes forward. Fishermen used them mostly for local sailing.

When we arrived at the mooring place the Captain came out to meet us and asked if we'd like a fishing trip. He would supply the fishing tackle, bait, tea and the necessary utensils to cook the fish. Having set the price, we boarded, unfurled the sail and were away. I can't tell you what a lovely thrill it was to be skimming over the water with the huge white sail billowing out in the wind. The biggest thrill of all were [sic] the porpoises. They played in twos and threes, jumping out of the water and chasing each other and having no end of fun…

After a time we came to suitable fishing grounds and dropped anchor. We each took a line and baited it with large shrimps and dropped them over the side. A tiny little boy sat with me with his line too. A minute or two later he gave his line a jerk and up came a fish. It was a little silvery thing about six inches long with yellow-brown fins. And just at the same time I felt a jerk on my line too. I pulled up but found the bait had gone and I had nothing but a bare hook.

After about an hour the four of us had only one little fish between us and in the little boy's tin there were at least a dozen. Then Ali came to the rescue and showed us how. It is important that you give your line a jerk the moment a fish nibbles at the bait so that the hook is forced into its mouth before he has time to get away. We tried again and were more successful. I caught more than half a dozen in a very short time – so did the others. We thought that was enough for a meal. We unfurled the sail and were away again for a spot where we could swim. While we made for it a charcoal fire was lighted in a little bucket and the water put on for tea.

It didn't take us long to stop for a swim and how lovely it was. We ran along the hot golden beach and took a header into the first big wave that came our way. The water was lovely and cool but not a bit cold. When we got back to the boat we found the fish all beautifully cooked (fried in oil) and all ready for us. Tea was made, piping hot and sweet (as it usually is out here). I did enjoy that meal. When we'd eaten we hoisted sail again and made for home...

Mauripur, May 18th 1945

VE day was received by the boys with mixed feelings. Everybody, of course, was glad that the war in Europe was over, particularly those of us who had relatives and friends in London and round about. However the end of the war in Europe can make little difference to us out here unless, of course, as for some, it is time to go home. For those of us who have still a long time to go, things will go on just the same except that we can now look forward to more concentrated action against the Japanese and a reasonably quick finish to that war.

Although we all knew about the end of the war with Germany already, we had a special parade for the C/O to tell us about it and to tell us that we were to have two days holiday and a special victory lunch on another day with a day off to follow.

I was unable to have any time off at all as it is important that the trade I'm in works all the time and stops for nothing. [I was now a ground-based, rather than an air-based, radio operator.] The best day of all was Monday and I did see something of the celebrations then. On that day all the cinemas in town were open free to the forces and free food was very plentiful and very good. I had the evening off and was able to play with the band. We went up to town by *ghari* [sic] before it was dark. On the way we could see the glow of bonfires and the bursting of fireworks. As we approached the town we passed houses and public buildings all decked out in flowers and flags of the Allies. Horse-drawn *gharis* [sic] too were all decorated with flowers. Large buildings were lit up in coloured electric light, many of them spelling out 'V.E.'. There was lots of music and dancing, both Eastern and Western, to be seen and heard everywhere. All the inhabitants were dressed in their best clothes (those that had them) and the women looked specially nice in lovely saris of all colours with gold or silver edging. The children seemed to enjoy it most.

We, the band, played our part at the Indian General Hospital where there was a free entertainment of dancing and eating. The hall we played in was very nice and cool. It had lovely murals all round the walls of scenes of Indian life.

During the interval we were fed. We had the choice of English or Indian food. I went to the Indian table and consequently was alone, apart from the inhabitants of the town of course. Most of them could speak English and they were very kind to me when I went up for Indian food. They all wanted to recommend what they thought was best and it was difficult for me to refuse all that they were offering me. First I had some rice boiled and then cooked in butter with some little curried meat balls. I followed that with some little pastries with curried meat inside but I couldn't get through more than one of these as they burnt my mouth so much. Of course all the while I was eating everyone was interested in my reactions to the food and were all lining up more and more plates of things I particularly liked. One dear old lady in a blue and white sari suggested that I should try some 'juleebe' [jalabi] (that's how they are pronounced – not spelt). They consisted of some pastry rather like spaghetti or noodles that was rolled spirally and then allowed to soak for a few moments in hot syrop [sic]. I can't tell you how lovely they were.

Mauripur May 27

This afternoon the radio was on and I heard an announcement that jolted me rather. It made me feel rather sad and I couldn't read any more. The announcement was that Radio Seac [South East Asia Command] has just opened and a special programme was given by the AEF [Allied Expeditionary Force] in its honour. Glenn Miller's band provided half an hour of music. A special announcement was made wishing Radio Seac every success. What made me feel so depressed was that I was not connected with it in any way whatever. In my billet is my little library of reference books [for possible programmes] which I thought I would be using almost as soon as I got here but there they are lying in my trunk, not serving any purpose at all but to make my kit all the heavier...

The BBC announcer was Margaret Hubble. Hearing her reminded me of Evesham and of the lovely times you and I knew there. In those days Margaret had no idea she would ever become an announcer and I had no idea that I would one day be thousands of miles from home, missing all the radio business so much, listening to her making an announcement that was to depress me.

But at last at the beginning of June 1945 came the news that I was waiting for so anxiously. I was to report to Radio Seac in Ceylon. Getting there was unexpectedly difficult. Each day I would turn up hoping to board a plane, but each day I was turned away because all the seats had been reserved for officers flying out to Burma and the Far East. The war in Europe had ended but the fight against the Japanese had not.

In the end I went to the station commander and asked whether I could go by train.

'By train?' he said, 'But that would take ages.'

I pointed out that I had already been waiting ages for a flight and in the end he agreed. Because of the nature of the job (writing, producing and announcing programmes) in Colombo, I was promoted to sergeant and set off on the longest train journey I have ever made. It took ten days. First I had to go north from Mauripur to Karachi, and then to Delhi. From Delhi we started going south, stopping at various places along the eastern coast. The trains were invariably packed to the limit with Indians hanging on to the windows and sitting on the roof (luckily there are no tunnels in that part of India), but I was allotted a carriage to myself. Occasionally some other British servicemen who were going on short journeys joined me (at my invitation, as they had no special passes like me and would have had to join the Indian passengers otherwise).

We slept one on each side of the seats and two on the luggage racks. Most of the time, however, I was on my own and quite comfortable. At the various stations we stopped at we would be surrounded by beggars. We had to close the doors and windows to keep them at bay. Then a *cha wallah* would come by and shoo them off. We drank tea by the gallon. Food was provided by bearers who had special licences to serve food to servicemen.

Eventually we arrived at the southern tip of India and crossed over the sea to Ceylon. Then there was another all-night train journey to Radio Seac's base in Columbo. When we arrived, I phoned the camp.

'Who's calling?' somebody asked.

'Sergeant Chilton.'

'Sergeant Chilton – it can't be.'

'Why not?'

'You're dead.'

'No I'm not. I'm waiting at the station hoping somebody will pick me up.'

It turned out that one of the planes carrying high-ranking officers to the Far East had crashed and everyone had been killed. My name was on the list of passengers but of course I'd never got on.

'All right,' said the voice again. 'I'll send somebody to pick you up.'

Shortly afterwards a jeep pulled up and out stepped David Jacobs. 'Hello Charlie,' he said. 'Here's your ten bob!'

David, of course, being in the Navy, had arrived in Ceylon by air. I, being in the RAF, had arrived by train and boat.

Radio Seac 17 July 1945

I'm here at last and it looks as though I'm going to spend my time abroad in the best possible way. I had a long talk with the C/O Major McNabb and it seems that I shall be given special programmes to do and will also take my place as an announcer. Duty announcer means being in the studio and doing all announcements for about 3 hours at a time. But when I'm not on announcing duty I'll be writing programmes.

We use a lot of ORBS stuff – all the programmes I did in London have been used out here but they want me to do original stuff too.

My first living quarters were in a little *basha* (a native-built hut) outside the main station buildings. Pete, a native boy who spoke fairly good English, looked after me. He brought me tea in the morning, cleaned the hut, washed my clothes and did everything he could to make me comfortable.

The area abounded in wildlife as we were on the edge of a forest. There were birds, animals and insects. Mosquito nets were a must. I awoke one morning to see the door of the hut opening as a dragon appeared at the entrance. It was a big, long scaly creature with a tongue that darted threateningly in and out of its mouth. I yelled for Pete. He came running.

'Don't come in,' I cried. 'There's a monster in here.'

He took no notice, pushed open the door and gave the dragon a kick with his bare foot.

'Go on, get out!'

As it disappeared through the door its tail dropped off and lay squirming on the floor. It was a completely harmless iguana that feasted on flies and other insects in the area.

A few days later I found a black hairy spider on my bed in my hut and knocked it away with my hand. In the morning I told Pete about it. If his skin had been white he would have gone pale.

'Where is it now?'

'I don't know. It went on the floor.'

We looked but couldn't find anything. Pete told me it was a black widow, one of the most deadly spiders in the world. That night I examined my bed very thoroughly before getting in it and made sure the mosquito net was firmly in place. I didn't sleep very well. Later I learned that a bloke in the hut adjoining mine had seen it and squashed it by overturning his wardrobe on it.

One evening I was walking back from the canteen to my hut and jumped over a coil of rope lying on the ground. As I landed the end of the rope shot up in the air with a hissing noise and turned into the unmistakable shape of a hooded cobra. I ran for my life. This must have frightened the cobra because it slid under the NAAFI building.

There was one other rather disconcerting thing about living in my little hut. Each day as I walked to the mess and back I noticed there was always a strong smell of burning in the air. I discovered that nearby was the place where the local people burnt their loved ones after they'd died: it was an open-air crematorium.

In spite of these adventures I enjoyed living in my little hut, which I did until the quarters being prepared for us in the main building of the station were ready. There we each had our own room and were looked after handsomely by bearers, mostly Sikh soldiers from northern India, who cleaned our rooms, washed our clothes, and even polished our shoes.

Radio Seac July 1945

The studios in Turret Road are lovely. They are in a beautiful white and green house and when they are completed will give us the possibility of doing all kinds of broadcasts. At the moment we are putting out recordings – ORBS, USA stuff and commercials.

Apart from David and me, most of the other announcers on the station were commissioned officers, but in the studio all differences of rank were forgotten. MacDonald Hobley, who became a BBC announcer after the war, worked with us.

David and I shared an office. On my desk was a placard reading 'Sergeant Chilton'. On his desk was a placard reading 'Admiral Jacobs'. This was fine until Admiral Mountbatten, who was responsible for founding Radio Seac, made an official visit to see how things were going. He came into our office and eyed the placards on the desks.

'Who's the admiral?' he asked.

'I am,' said David.

Mountbatten looked at him. 'I don't think you'll ever make it,' he said.

Radio Seac 3 August 1945

On Wednesday morning I was asked to write a script for what has been the biggest programme attempted here yet – a 45 minute show for hospitals. It was to include various features and have a popular appeal. That was it. So I started thinking about it on Wednesday evening, worked at it all day Thursday, finishing typing it in time to get to bed about 1 a.m. this morning.

I wrote a Hospital Magazine and in it put Paul, David, Peter, myself and Marjorie as editor. It retained the magazine atmosphere with features on music, comedy, the theatre, a quiz and so on. Effects were used, telephones, gongs and whatnots to produce the atmosphere of an office and turning of papers etc.

My own feature (in which I appeared) was London Calling with emphasis on cockneys (pointing out great cockneys like Lamb, Dr. Johnson and the Music Hall artists) and finishing with a complete act of Max Miller from the Holborn Empire. I called a rehearsal for two hours this morning (I was also producer) and knocked things into shape. The show went out at 4.45 and, from the reports we heard, was a success.

Monday 6th August 1945

I'm pleased about the election results – very pleased indeed. I feel now that we shall make a little more progress in the way of giving as much as possible of the social and economic things of life to everybody. I think too that we shall do far better for our people by electing a government with men in it that have a scientific and modern approach to problems. I hope though that when the changes come they do not produce too much muddle so that people turn against them. Most of the boys here have had a big drinking evening as a result of the election. We have only one Tory in our (Sergeants') mess. Most people at the station seem to be pleased about the result. One or two said they were unconcerned but, I rather think, were actually covering up the fact that things went contrary to what they hoped.

Wednesday 15 August 1945

We're having a party here to celebrate the Japanese acceptance of the Potsdam terms. What wonderful news that is. Of course the surrender hasn't been signed yet but it looks as though the Japanese war is definitely over...

Thursday 16 August 1945

Everyone is celebrating VJ day here. The public buildings in the towns are decorated with the flags of the Allies. The town hall is floodlit with red, white and blue lights. All the cinemas are open free to servicemen as they were in Karachi and, as in Karachi, I'm working all the time. But this time I don't mind in the least. At our mess we are not holding a celebration until Saturday. We're having a dinner and dance.

Sunday 19 August 1945

I'm in the studio now. We have just gone over to London for the Thanksgiving Service at St. Pauls. It's 3.30 in London and according to the commentator is a lovely sunny day.

As usual everyone drank too much. MacDonald Hobley was the duty announcer on this famous occasion and certainly not sober.

'Ladies and gentlemen,' he announced, 'we are now going over to London to hear the balls of St Pells.'

17 November 1945

You can guess how surprised I was when Tito Burns phoned up. He arrived in Colombo last Saturday. He did a tour as WOP/AG [wireless operator/air gunner] against the Japs and lost most of his crew, two of them boys on the boat who did shows with us. Poor old Tito didn't get away scot free either. He got into a tussle with a Jap fighter and shot him down but got a couple of bullets in his thigh. He has the scars but they are quite neat as they went straight through his thigh muscles and didn't touch the bone. But they are quite high up and he lost a lot of blood. His first words to the nurse when he woke up in hospital were 'Will I be able to get married?' He will, but it was a close thing.

I am trying to get Tito on the station. I'll be able to form a band round him and will probably play guitar in it myself. I got a very good guitar from Army Welfare today and will probably use that.

From December onwards there was much talk of when we would be released and be on our way home. I was asked whether I would like to try for a commission and stay on at the station in peacetime. I did consider this, but not for very long, and decided that I would rather return to the BBC. Meanwhile Tito was assigned to the station and we worked together to form a band.

12 December 1945

John, Tito, Jimmy and myself went down to a club called the Fawn. It's a very nice place, very modern with a good floor and good food. We went down to rehearse the band there and we played for half an hour. We had to borrow the other band's bass and drums but they were quite good. The crowd liked us. As a result we are going to do an O/B [outside broadcast] from the Fawn every Sunday. After the show we were introduced to the manageress. Her name was Mrs. Bradley. Her daughter, Yvonne, a young girl of 18, is a very good dancer and has a good microphone voice so we'll use her in some of our Seac shows. She took me round their house and showed me all her animals. Five dogs, four cats, a parrot and a monkey!

14th December 1945

The committee at the Fawn want us to play there for four days over Christmas and on New Year's night. I will probably be here for Christmas but not for New Year. John (F/L Hooper, our pianist) and I are both due at Warli on the same day for we are both due for release. We have our air passage booked to Bombay now but we are waiting for it to be confirmed.

Christmas Day 1945, 4 a.m.

It's not really Christmas day, it's Boxing day but this is the first chance I've had of writing to you for I've only just got back from the Fawn (where we did a Christmas broadcast).

The unit is in a hell of a state because David has been taken to hospital with mastoids and Robbo is sailing for home on Friday and has had to leave all his work to get cleared and packed. And that has meant my doing so much work and rushing round in such a panic that I haven't been able to spare a moment until now.

I had to reorganise the broadcast party, write the Pantomime and do lots of other things to do with broadcasting and in between time keep running up to Ridgeway to get as much as possible done up there with my documents etc. I haven't done it all yet. After all it's Christmas and the boys needn't work. It's very good of them to do so much to help me get away. By the way you will be amused to hear that on Christmas morning the boy brought me my tea in bed quite early, tidied up, swept the floor and woke me up with outstretched hand saying: 'Happy Christmas present, sahib!'

Tomorrow I shall know about my air passage.

Sunday 30 December 1945

Here I am in Bombay again on my way home to you, my darling. I don't know when I shall leave here but there is talk of a boat sailing on the 11th. I can hardly believe that I'll be with you again soon. I might be on the sea and on my way by the time you get this.

Bombay 13 Jan. 1946

Good news for you today. I'm on the Capetown Castle with John. When we paraded this morning we were told that there was 'a boat' in. All groups up to 28 were told to report to the theatre to be issued with berthing tickets for the boat. Only a limited number of men can go it seems and when that number is detailed there will be no more going aboard until the next boat arrives. As my group is 32 I thought I'd had it but this afternoon at 1.30 there was a special parade and all groups up to 32 had to go to the theatre. We were told that the list would have been read out by 5 o'clock. 3000 tickets were available.

It took a long time to read through the list and as fast as men were called out, taking their tickets and leaving, new ones were coming in their place from outside. I didn't hold out much hope for myself and when at 4.45 my name had not been called I began to give up hope. However at about this time I was called, my number being 2704. The general opinion is that the boat will be leaving on Friday (the 18th) but it may be Saturday or even Sunday. The 'Castle' does the trip home in about sixteen days... I should be home about the 10 February.

And so my war ended. We arrived at Southampton on 10 February, were sent up by train to Hednesford in Staffordshire where we were officially released and given our civilian clothes. Forty-eight hours later I caught the train to Euston, made my way to Pen's flat, rang the bell and caught her in my arms as she raced down the stairs to meet me.

CHAPTER THIRTEEN
BACK TO THE BBC

When I arrived back at the BBC in 1946, I found many things had changed. My job in the Gramophone Department had been taken over by Pat Osborne, who had become a producer and was responsible for the popular programme *Housewives' Choice*. I was assigned as a producer, 'the fellow who holds the stopwatch', responsible for getting the programme on the air, to what was then called 'Variety' and later became the 'Light Entertainment' Department. I stayed there until my retirement in 1977.

At this point, Pen and I had many things to sort out. For instance, where should we live? There was also the question of how I was to get divorced. Pen's parents were adamantly against our 'living in sin', and her father went to see our lawyer to ask what could be done. Later, our lawyer told us that when Pen's father arrived at his office he was carrying a parcel that he dropped on the floor. Inside was a fierce-looking chopper. For a moment the lawyer thought an enraged father might attack him. Pen's father explained that he had just been to the Army and Navy store to buy some things for his garden.

In 1946 Bess was persuaded to start divorce proceedings. We got as far as the Decree Nisi when quite suddenly she died.

Pen and I were married at Kensington Registry Office on 15 February 1947. As we came out of the registry office, to our great surprise we were greeted by Tito Burns' musical group who were waiting to serenade us. We went back to Pen's flat for a small family party and left afterwards, not on a honeymoon but to go to a house in Bromley in Kent. In those days, housing of any kind was exceptionally difficult to find because of the extensive amount of war damage that had occurred. So when the husband of a great friend of ours offered to rent us a house (as long as his mother-in-law could have a room in it) we jumped at the chance.

Empty houses were almost always taken over by squatters, which is why we had to move into it immediately after our friends had moved out. In fact I had had to be there the night before we got married, otherwise it would have been unoccupied. I have never been so cold as I was that night. The winter of 1946–47 was one of the coldest on record; power cuts were frequent, coal was scarce, and there was no central heating. When she heard about this, Pen's mother said that it was the first time in her life she had felt sorry for me. We moved in on our wedding day, and in spite of all the difficulties began to enjoy life together in our new home.

Pen gave up her job in the Italian Service of the BBC, partly because the service was being cut down because the war had ended, but mainly so that she could help research my BBC programmes, which she did throughout my career.

I was now based at the BBC's premises at the Aeolian Hall in New Bond Street. My boss was Michael Standing, head of the Light Entertainment Department. At first I felt like a new boy, starting out all over again in a BBC that had changed a lot during the war.

Some of the first things I did were taking over the production of programmes that were already on the air. One of these was *Rocky Mountain Rhythm*, featuring Big Bill Campbell. Big Bill took his show, which he both produced and directed, around the country doing live performances at many of the variety theatres. In order to do the broadcasts I had to go wherever the show was playing and put it on the air from the nearest BBC studio. It was a terrible show. Once, in Glasgow, a man much the worse for drink was at the box office trying to get a ticket. The girl at the box office wouldn't sell him one.

'You're drunk,' she said.

'I know I'm drunk,' roared the man. 'Do you think I'd come to see Big Bill Campbell if I was sober?'

Bill was a Canadian and often talked about his ranch in that country.

'What sort of cattle do you breed, Bill? White-faced Herefords?' I asked him once.

'Cattle?' he answered. 'Not likely – I rear chickens!'

The first show of my own, the idea for which I put up to the programme planners who liked it and said get on with it, was entitled *Accordion Club*. It started on 7 December 1946 and continued for six Saturdays. It featured Tito Burns and his Sextet with Irene King as vocalist and 'The Four Ramblers' (four boys and a guitar) who came from Ireland. The MC was Roy Plomley. It was a great success and was given a second airing of ten weeks starting 24 April 1947.

Next came a programme that was influenced by my working with Alistair Cooke before the war. It was called *Song Bag* and presented Anglo-American ballads and folk songs dating from the seventeenth century to modern times. In it I explained the origin and development of each song before it was sung.

Joel Chandler Harris published his first volume of *Uncle Remus* tales in 1880. In these books Uncle Remus is a Negro slave who knows many African folk tales and songs that he used to tell and sing to a little boy who visits him in his cabin. As a boy the author had worked side by side with Negroes on the Georgia plantations and there was scarcely a Negro myth, legend, custom or peculiarity he did not know. His writings, therefore, form an authoritative foundation for the scientific study of Negro folklore. His first volume of stories, as told by Uncle Remus, contained thirty-four plantation folk tales, nine Negro songs and twenty-one sayings and proverbs. Their chief figures are animals empowered with human characteristics, such as Brer Wolf, Brer Fox and Brer Rabbit, and the dialect in which they are told is authentic and so accurately reproduced as to be worthy of study in itself.

It was with these characters that I embarked on my first more ambitious radio programme that included actors, singers and a choir on 3 August 1947. It was called *Cabin in the Cotton*. Edric Connor, a West Indian actor and singer, played Uncle Remus. He recalled that when he was very young he used to slip out of his bedroom window to visit an old Negro who, with the aid of a guitar, taught him many songs and stories, just as Uncle Remus taught the little boy in the Joel Chandler Harris books.

In our case the little boy was in fact a girl of fourteen called Petula Clark, who visited Uncle Remus week by week to hear his stories and his friends singing. They included Benny Lee as Brer Rabbit. My main difficulty was to find a choir who could sing the Negro songs required for the show. I had heard about a choir formed during the war by George Mitchell. After the war they had done a few sessions for *Variety Bandbox*, but George had decided that it wasn't worth continuing with the choir and had disbanded it. I rang him and told him what I needed. After much discussion I persuaded him to give it a try. He reformed the choir and started work on the songs I needed. The result was excellent and led to my using the George Mitchell Choir for many of my future programmes.

We all became very close during this show. I remember once that there was rabbit on offer in the BBC canteen – no one in the cast would eat it. On the last night of the show many were in tears.

Another programme about this time was *To Town on Two Pianos* which I took over from Pat Dixon. The two pianists were George Shearing and Arthur Young. Stéphane Grappelli played his violin, Elisabeth Welch sang and Roy Plomley presented the programme. Arthur Young was somewhat of a problem as people to whom he owed money were always pursuing him. Sometimes his creditors would wait outside his house. On one occasion he was very late in coming to the studio and we had to start without him. Suddenly the door opened and in rushed Arthur, dressed as a woman. It was the only way he could avoid the creditors. He went straight to his piano and started playing, still in his woman's outfit.

Stéphane Grappelli was also sometimes a problem. I had used him in the Radio Rhythm Club when he was living in London, having escaped from France during the war. His playing was spectacular but his womanising almost as remarkable. During our show when Elisabeth was singing he would try to embrace her, fondle her breasts and generally embarrass her. She would give him as good as he deserved. She would take hold of his violin and threaten to hit him over the head with it. That would bring Stéphane literally to his knees, pleading with her to stop; the violin was a Stradivarius.

Another of these early programmes, when I was finding my feet and learning to cope with song publishers, agents, and up-and-coming artists, was called *Bowery Bar*, and was set in an American-style barber's shop with a sawdust and spittoon atmosphere. It featured the songs of 1900 to 1914 with music by Nat Temple with a special nine-piece orchestra (no saxes) and Johnny Johnston of the Keynotes leading a singing sextet. The accent was on simple harmony, with songs such as 'Don't Go in the Lion's Cage Tonight Mother' or 'I Want to Play in Your Yard'. The scriptwriter was a young man who had visited me at my home in Bromley, hoping to get some work: Spike Milligan.

The singers and actors were Len Young and Hattie Jacques. Len Young had some problems. On the very first night when the red light was about to be turned on for transmission he was nowhere to be found. A frantic search was made and he was eventually found in the gents' loo, having locked himself in and refusing to come out because he had never broadcast before and was in the throes of intense stage fright. Spike came to the rescue.

'I'll read his part,' he said.

And he did, most successfully. In future he took part in most of the shows as well as writing the script.

At the end of the show we had to switch to an announcer who read the credits. That night it was that veteran announcer Stuart Hibberd.

'Ladies and gentlemen,' he announced, 'you have been listening to *The Bowery Bar* with Hattie Jacques and Yong Lin.'

We gasped. When I told Hibberd what he had said he was most apologetic.

'I'm so dreadfully sorry,' he said.

The next time the show was on the air Hibberd was once again the duty announcer. We couldn't believe our ears when the announcement came:

'You have been listening to *The Bowery Bar* with Hattie Jacques and Ling Yon'!

We gave up and Len Young became Yon Lin, the Chinese entertainer, for the rest of the series.

Chapter Fourteen
Riding the Range

O n 18 January 1949, I inaugurated the first of my serial programmes that ran for many weeks. Initially I thought of the idea, which I put to Mike Standing, who in turn put it to the programme planners. They liked my idea and left me to think the whole thing up, write, produce and direct the programme.

What I wrote was a western called *Riders of the Range*. My introduction to the American west had been through the cowboy films I had seen as a child and my interest in American folk song that had been inspired by Alistair Cooke. I told Michael Standing I thought I could write a more convincing series about the West than Big Bill Campbell. He told me to go ahead and submit a trial programme. I wanted to write a programme that would give a true picture of the cowboy, his cows, his songs, and his life on the range, and not to show him as the romantic so often depicted on screen. The first series was entitled *The Chisholm Trail* and told the story of the first cattle drive from Texas to Wichita in Kansas. In the billing it was described as a 'Musical Drama of the West'.

I started to read all I could about the trail. I consulted the Royal Geographic Society who presented me with a map that I hung on the wall of my office, showing the boundaries of Indian reservations in the United States as they existed in 1875. This helped me to visualise the historic thousand-mile cattle drive. I read everything I could find about cowboys, long-horned cattle, Indians, the hazards of the cattle drive, the stage routes and the songs that the cowboys sang.

Pen hunted in second-hand bookshops for first-hand accounts of life in the West during the 1860s and 1870s. The books of John and Alan Lomax, Frank Dobie, Burl Ives and many others provided me with folk songs of the West (many of which had originated in Britain). I read the works of Mark Twain, Brett Harte and many others.

Our ranch was the 6T6, based in Texas. Our ranch owner was Cal McCord (played by Macdonald Parke). Mary, his daughter, was played by Carole Carr; Jeff Arnold, the hero and a Texas Ranger, by Paul Carpenter; and Luke, the old cowhand, by Charles Irwin. Music was by the Four Ramblers and the Sons of the Saddle, led by Jack Fallon. One of the Four Ramblers later went solo and became a star. His name was Val Doonican.

Perhaps the most unusual member of our cast was Rustler, the dog. He was a real live police dog, trained by Trevor Hill, an ex-stunt actor who specialised in training animal stars. He controlled Rustler by means of hand signals that made him bark, whine, or growl at appropriate moments, and he never missed his cue. We only had one problem with him, when an effects man came into the studio carrying some guns. At the sight of them Rustler, who had been attached to the studio piano, sprang to his feet, growling and barking. Next thing we saw was a scared effects man rushing towards the door with a piano chasing after him.

As the story progressed the fan mail rolled in. Some listeners seemed to think that the ranch actually existed and wrote letters addressed to the 6T6 Ranch, Texas. They would eventually arrive in my office. Luke, the old timer, received the most fan mail – and more than fan mail. At one point in the script Luke mentioned something about the canned pork and beans that he was eating. All the following week tins of pork and beans arrived at the BBC addressed to Old Luke, 6T6

Ranch, Texas. Worse was when he lost his false teeth on the trail and dozens of dentures arrived for him in the post.

Some of the essential effects for the programme were difficult to find. In particular I was horrified to find that the sound effects department had no howling coyotes (essential for when the herd was bedded down at night and the cowboys were relaxing around the camp fire). All the effects department could come up with was a record of a laughing hyena. The BBC had no objection to rushing the hyenas into the breach for a scene laid around a campfire outside Eagle Pass, but I put my foot down. I knew that if I compromised by sticking hyenas in Texas, the next thing would be elephants watering in the Rio Grande and kangaroos grazing in Wyoming.

Then I discovered there were two coyotes in the London Zoo. A BBC sound engineer hurriedly set up a tape recorder outside the cage. Every night for a week they waited for the desert prowlers to sound off. Nothing happened. Suddenly the truth dawned. Coyotes bay at nothing but the moon, which is rarely visible over damp and foggy London. These coyotes had grown weary, disillusioned and permanently silent. Eventually the BBC managed to record a noise made by a she-wolf at Glasgow Zoo. For the rest of the series the wolf stood in as a coyote and nobody noticed the difference.

In the third series in April 1950 we told the story of Billy the Kid. Two stories come to mind relating to this series. The first concerned a scene in which I had the 6T6 outfit marooned in a canyon, fearing an attack by Indians. The cowboys were saved by a herd of wild horses careering down the sides of the canyon. Reed de Rouen, as one of the cowboys, was supposed to say, 'It's all right, boys, here comes a herd of horses.' What we actually heard was: 'It's all right boys, here comes a horde of hearses'!

The second story was about Billy the Kid himself. The line was supposed to read, 'Billy the Kid's been seen in Corydon' (a small Texas town). It came out as, 'Billy the Kid's been seen in Croydon'. In those days the show went out live.

From the beginning I had been encouraged by letters – some of them from ex-cowboys – that asked which ranches I had worked on when I'd been in the West. In fact I had never been to the United States; I had never even ridden a horse. I wondered what Americans would think of *Riders of the Range*. Would they laugh? Had I really got my facts right?

Then came one of the highlights of my broadcasting career. In April 1950 I received a letter from Barney Hockstad, Marshal of Tombstone, Arizona, said to have been the toughest frontier town in American history. He said the work I was doing to present the true story of the West had come to Tombstone's notice and that he would be pleased if I would accept the Honorary Deputy Marshalship of the town. Also included was an invitation to be the guest of honour at Tombstone's 'Helldorado'.

How was I to get there? Luckily for me the Reverend Marcus Morris was in the throes of starting his new comic magazine *Eagle*. He came to my office soon after I received the invitation to Tombstone and offered to finance my trip in return for three articles I would write for his magazine. He also said he would like to feature a *Riders of the Range* story in strip-cartoon form in his publication.

Tombstone is situated in the heart of what was fierce Apache country. Apaches were the last Indians to be subjugated by the United States Army in 1886. In 1877 a lone prospector named Ed Schieffelin attached himself to the army fort to examine the neighbouring hills in the hope of finding gold. Each night he returned to the fort.

'Found anything yet?' the soldiers would ask him.

'Not yet,' Ed replied, 'but I will one day.'

'All you'll ever find in these parts,' the soldiers said, 'will be your tombstone.'

One day Schieffelin found a piece of rock with a bright glint in it. It turned out to be silver. Remembering what the soldiers had told him, he named his claim 'The Tombstone Mine', little knowing that he had laid the foundation stone of the toughest, roughest, wildest, rip-roaringest town in Western history.

The town of Tombstone was laid out about a mile from his original camp. By 1881 there were some 7,000 people living in it. Prospectors, gamblers, saloon proprietors and all the flotsam and jetsam of the South West flocked in to try their luck. Tombstone was the scene of the famous fight in the OK Corral between Wyatt Earp and the Clanton brothers. Its Bird Cage theatre, which opened in 1881, was now a museum. Amidst the faro, roulette and chuck-a-luck tables, many died with their boots on and were carried to their last resting place up on Boot Hill. The population of Boot Hill increased with that of the town. Little crosses mark out the burial place of outlaws, gunmen, miners and peaceful citizens who died violent or natural deaths during Tombstone's most turbulent days. Some crosses bear the legend 'Unknown', with the name of the victim's killer neatly inscribed below. Other headstones show where justice had the last word: 'Dan Dowd, Red Sample, Tex Howard, Bill Delaney, Dan Kelly, legally hanged, March 8th 1884.' The saddest headstone reads 'Hanged by Mistake'.

Every year, during the weekend nearest to 26 October, the date on which the OK Corral Fight took place, Tombstone holds its 'Helldorado'. The whole town takes on the appearance of the days of the 1880s. Men and women dress in period and cowboy costume, and Wyatt Earp, Billy Clanton, Doc Holliday and many other old-time characters walk the streets again.

This was the place I had been invited to visit as guest of honour. The story I tell below is based on diary entries I wrote at the time.

On 22 September 1950 I set sail for America on the SS *Washington*. Five days later the Statue of Liberty loomed up out of the mist. To the American citizens aboard, sighting the statue was a great thrill: it was a sign that they were really home. As an alien, it was also a great thrill to see the world's most famous landmark for the first time. She looked very fine:

a colossus towering high above the water gazing across New York Bay.

We steamed slowly up the Hudson until the towboats (never tugs in New York) came out to tow us to the pier. We tied up amid the shouts and cheers of the people on shore and the strains of the ship's band playing 'The Sidewalks of New York', 'The Bowery' and other songs about the great American city. The formalities of emigration and customs over, I stepped out onto American soil. A porter took my luggage (baggage) and escorted me to a taxi.

On Friday 29 September I left New York at the start of a fantastic ride by Greyhound bus, stopping at many of the places I'd read about in my research. We travelled to St Louis, the place where so many pioneers set off in their covered wagons to the West; then the Mississippi river and Mark Twain's home town of Hannibal. Later we arrived at Kansas City where there were men walking about in Stetson hats and riding boots; then further across the barren, bleak plains in Colorado where I imagined how tough it must have been for the pioneers travelling by ox cart and wagon. Eventually we arrived at the foothills of the Rockies, which were a real joy to see, with Santa Fe in New Mexico, Flagstaff and the Grand Canyon. Finally, on 15 October, we arrived at Los Angeles in California.

I set out on the last lap of my journey to Tombstone by boarding the Tucson bus from Los Angeles on Tuesday 17 October at 7.30pm. I settled down in my reclining seat in preparation for the seventeen-hour ride. It took us all of nine hours just to reach the Arizona state line, passing through orange, peach and date groves and little Spanish-styled towns. It was 3.45am the following day before we reached Yuma in Arizona and 7am before we stopped in Dateland for breakfast. We were really in Arizona now – right in the heart of its mighty desert. Giant cactuses, those tall sentinels of the wasteland, were growing everywhere. So were the squat, tubby-barrel cactus, the water preservers of the desert that have saved the life of many a thirsty cowboy or miner. Sagebrush, mesquite and Spanish yucca, with its tall flowers and sharp-pointed leaves, could be seen stretching across the rolling plains as far as the eye could reach. And in the distance were the mountains, some nearly a hundred miles away, but because of the pure atmosphere seeming to be almost within walking distance.

Our bus rolled along the desert highway at a steady fifty-five miles an hour. Way ahead of us was a long range of mountains through which we had to pass before reaching Tucson. They looked very beautiful in the early morning sunlight and I found a great deal of satisfaction in just lying back in my seat and watching them. Then, quite suddenly, I noticed something very peculiar: the mountains were a most fantastic shape. The range to the west was topped with huge slabs of rock standing on their ends with other slabs placed horizontally on them, rather like the rocks at Stonehenge.

I asked the driver what mountains they were, because I was sure there could be no others anywhere in the world shaped like these. The driver laughed at my question.

'Yes mister,' he said. 'Them hills do take on mighty strange shapes at times. But you keep a-looking at 'em; you ain't seen nuthin' yet.'

I kept a-looking and there, right before my eyes, the mountains began to change their shape. The huge slabs of rock disappeared and new patterns emerged. Great trees appeared in the air and hung over a mountain top. They were replaced by a huge gap in the mountain, shaped like the letter 'V'. I couldn't be sure I wasn't dreaming and the driver laughed again.

'Fact is, mister,' he said, 'what you can see ain't no mountain at all – that's a mirage.'

About midday we arrived at the town of Tucson (pronounced Too-sahn). This was as far as my bus went. I still had another eighty miles to travel, almost to the border of Mexico, before I reached my final destination. I checked my baggage, went to the station rest rooms for a clean-up and then, feeling much refreshed, phoned through to Tombstone to tell the folks there how far I had come.

I spoke to Mrs Palmer, wife of Mort Palmer, President of the Restoration Commission who, after a word of welcome, told me to watch out – a posse had left Tombstone two hours before en route to Tucson with orders to 'bring me in'. Not long after I had spoken to Mrs Palmer, Earl Billiter picked me up outside the Westerner Hotel and took me in charge. The Sheriff was notified of my capture and I was taken to Mr Billiter's office to await escort.

The Tombstone Vigilantes arrived half an hour later: four tall, sturdy-looking cowboys with big black beards and six-shooters on their hips. They placed me under arrest and took me in their car for the run to Tombstone. There was no doubt about it; now they had found me they had no intention of letting me out of their sight.

Just as a beautiful sunset was fading from the sky, the lights of Tombstone appeared in the distance and things began to hum. A group of horsemen who had been lying in wait behind some rocks suddenly came into view and, yelling at the top of their voices and firing off their six-shooters, came galloping towards us. It was a hold-up. It all happened so suddenly that my guards were taken completely by surprise – all they had time to do was stop the car and put up their hands. This was what I had been waiting for. Now, maybe, the horsemen from Tombstone were about to free me. But I was mistaken.

'Where's that dude Englishman?' yelled the leader of the hold-up gang. 'Bring him out.'

I stepped out into the road.

'Put up yer hands mister – and keep 'em up.'

I put 'em up.

'Now start walkin'.'

I walked, my former guards, now disarmed, on either side of me.

A short way down the road we were given the order to stop. I thought I could drop my hands now, but a gun exploding near my face told me I had better not try – so I shot 'em up again, quick.

Then came a yipping and yelling and the sound of horses. From behind the rocks where it had been hidden appeared a magnificent stagecoach, complete with bearded driver and shotgun guard. It pulled up close to where we were standing and we were ordered to climb in – me first. Inside the coach was Mayor John Giacomo waiting, with a big smile on his face, to welcome me to Tombstone.

The driver whipped up the horses and the stagecoach moved towards the town in real Western style, with an escort of yelling, gun-firing cowboys, and a greater part of the population who had turned out to see what the ambassador from the *Eagle* really looked like.

In and around the town we drove, past the old-time buildings, the Crystal Palace, the Bird Cage Theatre, and finally coming to a halt outside the Wagon Wheel Inn directly opposite the OK Corral, the spot where the notorious fight between the Wyatt Earp and Clanton factions took place. There I met Mr and Mrs Medigovich, whose guest I was while staying in Tombstone.

When I had unpacked my baggage I was taken up to the Loma de Plata, high upon a hill overlooking the town, and given the biggest T-bone steak I've ever had. It was delicious. Back at my room I found a huge notice over the door that read 'Welcome Chilton'. I was tired but was not allowed to sleep just yet. Just as I climbed into bed I received a salutation from six guns fired outside my window by a deputation of cowboys.

Friday 20 October was the start of the 'Helldorado'. Early in the morning, feeling a little out of place in my English clothes, I stepped out onto the sidewalk and made my way, as instructed, to Steve's store where I was to be fitted out in true Western style. I was shown to a room at the back, and there, laid out on a settee, was my brand new kit. Or rather two kits:

my cow-punching outfit and my western dress suit. The punching outfit consisted of a pair of Levi's, a blue shirt, cowboy hat, belt and a handsome pair of riding boots and spurs. The dress suit differed from the punching outfit only in pants (trousers) and shirt. These take the place of the Levi's and blue shirt for dress occasions and are made in two shades of brown with white cording on the pockets.

Donning the hat, shirt and Levi's was simple enough, but pulling the boots on was quite a different matter – in fact it was impossible. I heaved and strained, changed my socks for thin cotton ones and smothered them in talcum powder to make them slippery, but it was all no use. Steve went back into his store and returned with three more pairs of boots, all one size larger than the next. He told me to try on the largest pair first. This I did and managed to get them on with a struggle. Having got them on, the Marshal and Steve, using me as a rope, immediately went into a tug-of-war struggle of their own to get the boots off me again. The idea was to get my feet used to the feel of the larger boots and then, by working my way down through the smaller sizes, finally arrive at the pair that was supposed to fit me. With the help of lots of talcum powder and pulling and pushing, I finally fought my way into the designated pair of boots and, with my feet snugly packed into them, walked around the store to see how they felt. Surprisingly enough they felt fine and did not pinch or rub. The secret of riding-boot comfort is to have one's feet fit very snugly, almost too tight, because there are no laces or buckles to hold them on.

My dressing complete and feeling a little strange in my new high heels, the Marshal and I walked down the street to keep my next appointment – with the Judge. Judge John P. Sebring was a venerable old man who had spent the greater part of his life in the West. After inviting me into the house he 'swore me in', in the presence of his wife and the Marshal.

'Charles Chilton, raise your right hand,' he said. I did just this and, repeating the Judge's words, took the oath. I swore to support the constitution and laws of the State of Arizona and defend them against all enemies, and to discharge my duties faithfully and impartially. The oath over, the Marshal pinned the badge of office on the left breast of my shirt; a neat little golden star on which is inscribed in blue enamel the words 'Deputy Marshal, Tombstone, Arizona', together with my name.

An hour later the 'Helldorado' officially began, and the day closed with a square dance at which I was the guest of honour. Round about eleven o'clock the dance ceased for the event of the evening: the crowning of the 'Helldorado' Queen. She was a fifteen-year-old Tombstone schoolgirl called Arminda Vasques, and was introduced to the audience amid loud applause. A huge western saddle was brought on stage and placed on a wooden horse. Arminda mounted and, after making a little speech to the audience and to Arminda on behalf of the *Eagle*, I crowned her with a fine white 'ten gallon' hat. After the crowning the dancing began again, wilder and even more joyful than before.

My next adventure was to involve cow punching. Although Tombstone is a mining town, it is set right in the heart of some of the best cattle-raising country in the south-western states, and a great deal of it stretches down into Mexico. It is good, grassy country on which cattle have been fed and fattened for generations. The ORO ranch down in Mexico and the NI ranch in Arizona both invited me to try my hand at cow punching.

My day as a cowboy began at 5 o'clock in the morning when Barney Hockstad, the Marshal of Tombstone, drove me seventy miles south to the ORO outfit in Mexico. We were met at the border by the ranch supervisor, Mr Flippen, who told me what was taking place on the ORO that morning. A herd of some 1,500 head of cattle had arrived the night before from Chihuahua, a drive that had taken fifteen days. Now that they had arrived, Mr Flippen, aided by his ranch foreman, was going to select the best of the herd and keep them for breeding or fatten them for the meat market; those that he didn't buy would be driven further west in search of another buyer.

Waiting for us at the ranch was the foreman, a handsome *vaquero* (Mexican cowboy) called Chito Romero. For the next few hours he was to be my foreman too, because it had been arranged that I should be given a horse, be allowed to ride among the cattle and, if I thought I could manage it, help 'work the herd'. I told Chito I'd like nothing better, so a pair of chaps (wide leather leggings) and a fine paint horse were brought for my use.

Before I left London I thought I had better have a few riding lessons, because I had never been on a horse. But trotting round Hyde Park was very different from my experiences at the ORO ranch. The saddle was very large and heavy, had a large support at the back and a high horn in the front. It was very comfortable and made me feel secure. The stirrups were very long so that I had to ride with my legs stretched full length but with heels down and toes out just like back home. There was only a single rein, which was in two parts, so that on releasing them they both hung down to the ground. There's a good reason for that; once the rein is dropped the horse will 'stand' and will not move away from that spot until driven or led.

I mounted Old Paint. The herd was about a mile away and, while I had been donning my chaps, many other cowhands had been riding towards the cutting ground. I thought it was about time I joined them. Old Paint was facing in the opposite direction from which I wanted to go, so, giving him a light touch with my spurs, I pulled down on one rein hoping to turn him – but all he did was shoot forward at a gallop. I hadn't reckoned on that at all and reined him in. At once he came to an abrupt stop. I could start him and stop him but I couldn't turn him, and it looked more than likely that the herd and I were never going to meet. Then I remembered that cowboy horses are neck-trained. All you have to do to turn a horse is lay the rein across his neck. I pulled my right hand across my chest and laid the leather across Old Paint's mane. He turned at once and went 'splitting the breezes' towards the other cowboys.

Chito and Mr Flippen were already cutting out the cattle when I caught up with both of them in among the cows, selecting the good-looking white-faced youngsters and driving them out. In many ways cows are like sheep; if one starts running the rest are inclined to follow. So when calves were cut out it took all the rest of the outfit's time to keep the rest from following – and to keep those that had been cut out from returning. That was my job, along with the rest of the *vaqueros* – to keep the main herd bunched up and to turn back those cows that had ideas about getting away.

I got my first opportunity to do my stuff almost immediately. An old cow came charging out of the herd and straight towards where Old Paint was standing with me on his back. As it approached us it swerved to the left hoping to dodge round us and get away. I kicked my heels into my horse's side and got after that cow – as I kicked I pulled my rein over and braced myself for the take-off. Old Paint didn't need any encouragement. He was after that cow like a streak of lightning – dodging and twisting in that cow's path in an effort to turn her back. She went back and, once safely where she belonged, I reined and waited for the next. I was feeling very pleased with myself. Then it occurred to me that I had hardly guided Old Paint in the dodging and twisting at all; he had sorted all that out for himself. Like all the horses in the ORO outfit, Old Paint knew exactly what to do and did it.

Soon the cutting out was called to a halt while the cowhands rested. Setting a few of them to keep guard on the two herds, Mr Flippen told Chito to line up all the rest for a photograph for the *Eagle*. This they did very willingly – giving me the place of honour right at the end of the line.

A few minutes later I was back in the car and heading for the border and the USA. The NI ranch, owned by Mr Ralph Cowan, was the biggest in the district of Tombstone, about thirty miles from the town, and I was taken there across the desert in a truck driven by old-timer Fred Bennett, one of the oldest and most respected cow punchers in those parts. Mr Bennett came to Arizona from Texas in 1896 and still wore the same hat he had bought in Tombstone in 1897. Fred had a little ranch of his own near the NI. Aged seventy-five he could still ride and rope with the best of them, and probably knew more about the ways of cows and the country they live in than almost anybody.

Cochise County is fine cattle country and, if the weather is good, a cow will fatten up quicker here than anywhere else. There isn't much grass about, but that doesn't matter as a cow will eat almost anything: cactus leaves, prickly pear or even *cholla*, the prickliest plant you ever saw. Even desert plants need rain and that's a commodity Arizona is short of. Of course, it does rain – in July it pours down – but, as Fred pointed out, it often rains only in patches and his ranch, being near the mountains, is the first to suffer if the rainfall is poor. From where we were on the road to the NI, we could see the spot where Fred's ranch was situated. Great patches of it were yellow and stood out in sharp contrast to the dark green vegetation through which we were driving.

'See them yeller patches, Chuck?' (All Charlies here are known as 'Chuck'.)

'Yeah,' I said, 'I see 'em.'

'Well that's part of my range and them yeller bits is where no rain ain't fallen for months. But that's how it is out here – a storm will come up and soak the countryside all around and yet leave me with my tongue hanging out. Last rainfall we had it come pretty close, but didn't quite make it – the NI got it all. Goldarn it, the wire on Ralph Cowan's side of the fence is red rusty – and on my side it's as bright and shiny as the day it was erected.'

Judging by the yellow patches I could well believe it.

The reason Fred was taking me to the NI ranch was that Mr Cowan was 'working' his cattle and Fred wasn't. Seven hundred head were being rounded up that day, mostly cows with calves, because a large number of the calves, worth a hundred dollars on the market, were going to be 'shipped'. (This was a word left over from the early days of the cattle trade, when the only way to sell a herd was to drive it to the nearest seaport and load it on to cattle boats.)

Pretty soon we saw clouds of dust rising into the air about ten miles ahead. It was the NI herd on the move. The cattle grew in number, and nearing the corrals started bellowing and bawling their heads off. This was because the calves had been separated from their mothers in the round-up and, as a cow cannot recognise her calf by sight but only by sound or smell, both calves and mothers were bellowing, hoping to find one another. Just before the corrals were reached Mr Cox had the herd brought to a stop in order to 'settle down'. What he meant was that the herd was stopped to enable the cows to find their babies, which they did in about fifteen minutes, after which the bellowing stopped. Eventually they were driven into the corrals ready to be loaded into huge trucks and then shipped to other ranches all over the South West to grow and fatten for the meat market or to be used for breeding.

When the cattle had been corralled we adjourned to the camp for chuck (food). There, under a large awning stretched out over the chuck wagon to provide a little shade, I found 'Shorty' the cook. When he heard I was English he began asking me all manner of questions about English county cricket. I was surprised to find the cook of a cow outfit interested in cricket, but it turned out that Shorty was English and had been one of the better-known amateur players in his home county of Cornwall.

That was thirty years ago but, he said, 'I can still send down a fast googly when I have the mind for it.'

The banging of a frying pan with a tin spoon told us that dinner was ready, and to 'come and get it'. We came and got it – one of the best meals I had out there in the West. There were no seats to sit on where we ate – you had the choice of squatting on one heel or standing up – most cowboys preferred the former – but what do seats matter if the food is good and you have the appetite for it?

Sunday was the biggest day of the 'Helldorado' for then, besides the re-enactment of the historic gun battles and other events of Tombstone's past, there was a big parade and barbecue.

On Sunday morning I was up before daybreak. Even at that early hour people from all over Arizona and other states were pouring into the town to see the show. I was to ride as guest of honour in the parade, so I dressed in my best cowboy clothes, my boots all shiny and my gold Deputy Marshal badge on my breast. Feeling like a million dollars and a little stiff in my new chaps, I walked to the corral, my spurs a-jingling. There, already saddled and patiently waiting, was Woody, another old paint. He had been groomed until he shone and looked just about the handsomest horse I had ever seen. He must have thought I was the handsomest cowboy he had ever seen for when I walked up to him and patted his neck by way of saying good morning, he nickered and put his nose on my shoulder. Bud and Henry, who were to be my escort, were already mounted on their frisky ponies so I mounted Woody and off we rode to take our place in the line.

Heading the parade was the Tombstone band. Behind the band was Arminda, the 'Helldorado' Queen whom I had crowned at the square dance on Friday. Behind Arminda were her ladies-in-waiting and then me – with Bud and Henry riding just behind.

With all the excitement Woody wasn't too happy – he kept shaking his head in protest and trying to break out of line. When the band raised their instruments and Woody saw them flash in the bright sunshine he decided he'd had enough of parades and backed away. Before I had time to check him he had left his place in the line and was on his way back to the corral. We'd mounted the sidewalk before I could bring him to a standstill, and by the time I got him back to our appointed position the parade was ready to move off. The drums rolled and the music began. Woody pricked up his ears, I pricked his flanks with my spurs and we began to move. The crowd started to cheer and Woody, thinking they were cheering him, held his head high and followed the band as proudly as any circus horse ever did.

The parade was more than a mile long and all aspects of Tombstone's history and life were represented in the colourful pageant. There were prospectors with mules, picks, shovels and corn-cob pipes; Arizona sheriffs in brilliant scarlet uniforms mounted on beautiful palomino horses; old-time fire engines; and the American Legion. There was also an American flag that had flown over Fort Huachuca during the wars with the Apaches and was so large it took twenty men to carry it. Then there were cowboys, the old stagecoach and covered wagons carrying whole families dressed in period costume. All this made a tremendous spectacle on this brilliant Sunday morning.

Chief White Mountain Lion, an Osage Indian, had travelled all the way from Oklahoma. Mounted on a beautiful paint pony, he was probably the most colourfully dressed man in Tombstone that day. On his head he wore a war bonnet of white eagle feathers, the tips of which had been dyed a brilliant indigo and fastened into a headband of beads woven in Indian designs. His jacket, too, was covered with beadwork as were his leggings and his moccasins. His brown face was painted with red, white and black stripes that extended across his cheeks and down to his chin. In his right hand he carried a spear decorated with feathers representing scalps.

By noon the parade was over, and all of us who had taken part in it rode over to the corral to attend the barbecue. The day before, a large beef steer from the NI ranch had been killed in preparation for the feast. A huge pit had been dug in the ground and a fire of scented mesquite and brushwood had been burned in it until the pit was filled with a great mass of glowing embers. Over this was stretched the largest grill I have ever seen, on which was placed the beef which filled the air with an appetising aroma as it was cooked to perfection. To this were added beans, sweet potatoes and other tasty vegetables guaranteed to whet any appetite, the whole to be washed down by the sweetest black coffee I have ever tasted.

There were lots of tables at which we could sit and eat, but most of us squatted down on one heel, holding our plates in one hand and, with the aid of a fork, eating with the other.

I joined a group of cowboys and squatted down with them. Not long afterwards we were joined by Chief White Mountain Lion and his medicine man. Then I learned that one of the purposes of White Mountain Lion's visit to Tombstone was to make me a member of the Osages.

'When sun is one hand from top of mountains, Chief White Mountain Lion will welcome Englishman into his tribe.'

The ceremony began just before sunset in the main street of Tombstone and finished just as the sun disappeared behind the mountaintop and darkness began to fall.

The Chief walked into the middle of the road and pointed his spear in the direction of the four winds, the Indian way of indicating north, south, east and west. He recited a prayer in the dialect of his tribe and then stretched out a deerskin upon the ground and invited me to sit on it. He touched each of my shoulders with the blade of his spear and began to dance round me in a shuffling gait with his body bent forward in imitation of a mountain lion.

The dance stopped suddenly, and I was ordered to stand up and to hold my hands behind my back as though I were tied to a stake.

'I am now going to re-enact a torture,' the Chief whispered. 'Stand still and you won't get hurt.'

By this time the crowd who were watching the ceremony were getting really interested, as they weren't quite sure what would happen next. The drum beat louder and faster. The Chief drew a long knife from a sheath at his side and, spear in one hand and knife in the other, began dancing round me again, waving both weapons a little too close to my face for comfort.

Quite suddenly, when he was close behind me, I felt a tug at my hair and the blunt side of the knife marked out a circle on the top of my head. The Chief gave a wild yell, the drum beat even louder, and my scalp was gone – at least it felt as though it had and I had to put my hand up to my head to make sure my hair was still there.

Still the dance went on, the knife now thrown aside and the spear thrust close to my throat. Finally, with a blood-curdling scream, the Chief lunged at my heart with his spear, turning it at the last moment so that the blade went between my arm and my side. This was the final thrust and, had this been the real thing, would have been the end of me.

The Chief then made a speech to the crowd and told them how his tribe, although enemies of the British in the days of the wars, always had a great admiration for the stubbornness and courage with which the white man fought. In particular his tribe had admired the way in which the British soldiers, when fighting the French and their allies the Osages, made skilful use of long knives or bayonets.

Then, placing a necklace of beads and mother-of-pearl around my neck, the Chief announced what my new Indian name was to be: *Manh-heh Has-jah Ta-tan-kah* – 'Big Long Knife' or 'Long Knife'.

It was round about midnight when I said goodbye to my new-found brother and changed into my working outfit in preparation for a ride across the prairie to a rendezvous where I was to meet many of the old-time ranchers and cowhands for a chuck wagon supper.

Way out in the desert under the stars, and with the moon rising over the Dragoon Mountains, I found the camp. The horses that had drawn the chuck wagon through the thorny cactus were tethered nearby, and the meal was already being prepared. There were many people I'd already met who were there to greet me. As we sat round the fire eating our chuck we talked of the days when the cow punchers had gone up the trail with herds of cattle and of the ropers, branders, cutters and other tophands they'd known in the past.

The hours passed very quickly in very pleasant surroundings, and it was with great regret that I watched the embers of the fire die down and realised that it was time to put out my bed roll and go to sleep. The 'Helldorado' was over and my visit was drawing to a close.

I left Tombstone in the early hours of the morning when, escorted by two carloads of people, I made the forty-mile journey to Bisbee railroad junction (still in Arizona) where I was to catch the train to Chicago and New York.

When the train pulled in at the station the time had come to say goodbye. I was really sorry to leave and, I'm glad to say, the folks of Tombstone were really sorry to see me go. I climbed aboard the train and made my way to the reclining seat that was to be my bed for the next three days. Almost before I reached it the train began to move as I was the only passenger who had boarded at that tiny junction and the train had to be stopped specially for me.

I waved my hat and shouted goodbye and in return there was a chorus of yippees and yells which was still ringing in my ears long after the train had left the junction. When I woke the next morning I was in Texas and Tombstone was two hundred miles away.

It took nearly two weeks to travel from Tombstone to London. After a seven-day journey across the Atlantic, I arrived at Waterloo station to find Marcus Morris, a group of *Eaglers* and the cast of *Riders of the Range* waiting to greet me.

The *Eagle* published three articles about my trip and in the December of 1950 published the first strip cartoon of *Riders of the Range*. This meant my writing a weekly episode of an entirely new story, which was passed to the artist to illustrate. The first artists chosen were not always satisfactory but at the beginning of 1951 I met Frank Humphris, an artist whose work I had seen and admired in other strip cartoons and who was to illustrate *Riders of the Range* for the rest of its existence. It was not all easy going. I sometimes made Frank's life extremely difficult by being late with my copy – on one occasion dictating a complete episode over the telephone. I was on holiday in Italy at the time, while he was in Kingston. These difficulties in no way marred his work, which was magnificent.

I like to think it was *Riders of the Range* that set off Frank's deep and academic interest in American Western history. He was always ringing me up and asking searching questions about my characters, plots and locations. I lent him many books, for by this time I had collected a library on Western matters, which inspired him to build up quite an extensive library of his own, especially books on all aspects of Indian history and culture. Indians were his passion.

He insisted that his version of *Riders of the Range* should be accurate in all details: clothing, ornament, location and story. To this purpose he assembled a collection of Western artefacts upon which he could base his illustrations. These included a large variety of Western guns, a fine Western (Mexican) saddle, Indian beadwork, blankets, weapons and as many period photographs of Indian life as he could lay hands on. Portraits of famous Indian chiefs, painted in oils, became his forte. It was therefore not surprising that his illustration of 'Custer's Last Stand' that took up a complete page of *Eagle* was hailed as the most authentic illustrated account of the event yet seen in any comic strip magazine.

When it came to the history of the Western plains of America, Frank was a walking encyclopaedia. An exhibition of his work was mounted in Billings, Montana. The accuracy and authenticity of his historic paintings was acknowledged and acclaimed by all who saw them. The folks of Bexar County, Texas, honoured him by making him an honorary deputy sheriff. This was one of the highlights of Frank's career and, as one admirer commented, 'he wore his badge with pride'.

For five years, from 1949 to 1953, I wrote and produced *Riders of the Range* for the BBC. Each series consisted of twelve or thirteen episodes, so life was pretty busy.

CHAPTER FIFTEEN
1949-1953:
LIGHT ENTERTAINMENT
DEPARTMENT

My office at the BBC was on the top floor of the Aeolian Hall in New Bond Street, premises that the BBC had acquired from the Aeolian Piano Company which had shut down during the war. To demonstrate its pianos, both ordinary and pianola, the piano company had built two concert halls, one large and one small, which were turned into studios when the building was bought by the BBC.

There was a huge, old-fashioned lift in the building (used to transport grand pianos) that moved very slowly and was usually operated by a liftman. When I was very busy and working late at the office after everyone else had gone home, there was only the commissionaire on duty at his desk in the entrance hall. I then operated the lift myself. One night I finished work at about ten o'clock and took the lift for the ground floor. The commissionaire hadn't realised that I was still in the building. At that time I had acquired a Sherlock Holmes-type coat with sleeves that opened like wings when I stretched out my arms. When the lift arrived at the ground floor the door opened and I stepped out, raising my arms. The commissionaire took to his heels and ran. He must have thought I was Dracula.

At this time I was writing and producing many programmes in between episodes of *Riders of the Range* for both radio and the *Eagle*. Square dancing had become very popular in Britain after Princess Elizabeth and the Duke of Edinburgh had taken an enthusiastic part in a dance during their tour of Canada in 1951. I knew a little about this mode of dancing as I had taken part in a square dance during my time in Tombstone. Thus when the BBC wanted to reflect listener interest I started a programme called *Square Dance Revels*.

The programme went on once a fortnight and was broadcast from different towns throughout Britain. I learned to be a 'caller' and even wrote a book about square dancing, illustrated with diagrams showing the dance steps to be taken, the 'calls' (such as 'swing your partners'), and the words of some of the songs used. When we went on tour I wore my cowboy outfit given me at Tombstone.

Another programme I wrote during this period was *The Days of '49*, a documentary history commemorating the centenary of the Californian Gold Rush. It was illustrated not only by the diaries, letters and newspaper reports of the forty-niners but also by the songs they sang such as 'Oh! Susannah', 'On the Banks of the Sacramento' and 'Sweet Betsy from Pike'. Like so many songs of the western pioneers, this last song was sung to the tune of an English music hall song, 'Villikins and his Dinah'. Pen worked very hard to produce a map providing details of the various routes taken by the pioneers to reach California, and the programme received much praise from the reviewers.

Once again, the George Mitchell choir sang the songs; they were becoming a fixture in my programmes. George and I became good friends and I learnt a lot about his early life and his love of music. When he was only four years old his grandfather took him to a choral concert that he was conducting in his native town of Falkirk in Scotland.

In 1928 George and his family moved south. He was articled to an accountant in the city because his other main talent was mathematics. He could add up numbers in the telephone directory as fast as you could read them. He found an outlet for his music by forming a dance band with himself at the piano. When the war came, George went into the Army Pay Corps. He was posted to Finsbury Circus in the middle of London and remained there for the duration.

It was then that George's first and real ambition began to be realised. He helped out with the camp entertainments. He played, he produced, but fortunately did not sing because he had a terrible voice. Instead he coached others. He found that average voices improved beyond all expectation if, instead of singing solo, they sang in groups. The twos and threes grew to a dozen. Almost before he knew it Sergeant Mitchell had a choir on his hands that gave concerts at army camps and for charities all over the place.

When the war came to an end the choir just melted away.

'So back I went to Civvy Street and accountancy,' said George. 'Then there was this fellow at the BBC (Charles Chilton) who wanted a choir to sing spirituals and other plantation type songs in a show called *Cabin in the Cotton*. I accepted his offer to reform the old army choir and have them sing on the show. But as soon as I got down to work I regretted it. This was the first time I'd appeared in anything where I didn't select my own numbers. But now I was expected to sing what I was told. Six new numbers every week, all to be arranged, rehearsed and learned and only the evenings in which to do it. All the choir were working at other jobs during the day. So was I. It was beyond me. I rang up the producer and told him so. But he was very persuasive. I went to his office to resign and came away with two extra numbers to arrange and rehearse by the following Sunday.'

Pat Dixon was a great producer. He was a great instigator of programmes – that is, he started them off but seemed to lose interest in them after a while and would want to start something else. I worked with him on *Gentlemen Be Seated*, the story of the rise and fall of the black-faced Minstrel Shows.

I wrote the series and he and I jointly produced it. In the programme I told of how the minstrel show developed from a homely entertainment on the plantations of the southern states of America to a fashionable form of variety patronised by Queen Victoria.

We had a last-minute panic on the first show as Stanley Black was ill. As a result an American, Van Phillips, was brought in to conduct the orchestra.

I also met the American Negro folk singer Josh White. On Good Friday 1951 I compiled and produced a programme entitled *Walk Together Children – a Negro Anthology*, featuring Josh White, Benny Lee, Edric Connor and the George Mitchell Choir. The programme was so successful that the BBC asked me to compile six more. Eventually these went out under a new title *The Glory Road* beginning in May 1951. Henceforward whenever Josh came to London we recorded as many of his songs as we could, sometimes with his daughter Beverley who came with him from the States. Josh was a great putter-over of songs and a great guitarist. I am proud to be the possessor of one of his guitars that he gave to me on his last visit to England.

As well as the programmes that I wrote and produced, I was also expected to produce some of the standard programmes commissioned by the Department. To me, producing something that had been written and devised by someone else was much less interesting than being responsible for a whole show from beginning to end. In fact, most producers only produced; that is, they were responsible for putting on a new show commissioned by the head of department or one that was already in the repertoire. Being a producer meant that you had to check the script, music, effects, etc. provided by the author. You also had to book the actors, singers and musicians, and make sure they were paid and sitting in the control room to rehearse the show, and also ensure that the programme went on the air.

The Goon Show, another programme started by Pat Dixon, ended up being produced by a variety of people. I was responsible for quite a number of episodes at various times and enjoyed working with my old colleague Spike Milligan, along with Harry Secombe and Peter Sellers.

There were, of course, numerous difficulties and crises to be overcome. Much of Spike's humour was army humour. Spike had been brought up in the army; his father was a regular soldier in India where Spike was born. Spike told me he had experienced racial prejudice in reverse in India. The British used to treat the members of the indigenous population very badly, but he went to an Indian school and because he was white and everyone else was black he used to suffer.

I often had to tell Spike that some of his material would have to be cut because it did not comply with BBC policy. There were a lot of sexual jokes and innuendoes that contravened the strict instructions in the BBC's little Green Book that had been compiled by Michael Standing for the Variety Department. This caused a few arguments, but I'd tell Spike that my boss had said it had got to come out.

Spike was very eccentric. He was in the Artillery during the war, and towards the end of the war went all the way up Italy with the invasion force. He got blown up and very severely knocked about, not physically but mentally, which aggravated the frequent bouts of depression and major mental breakdowns from which he suffered. Occasionally during the *Goon Show* period he would have panic attacks originating from his experiences during the Second World War and bipolar disease that affected him mentally. He knew when they were coming and he had a special room at the top of his house where he would lock himself in. He would send telegrams to his wife to say, 'Where the hell's the tea?'

During these attacks he believed that the world was attacking him; therefore if he were told a bit of script had to come out he took this personally rather than simply as a matter of policy, and would walk off in a rage. Eventually, however, he'd come back to the studio, all cheerful, having forgotten all about the row. On his gravestone is written, 'I told you I was ill' – in Gaelic!

Spike's demands for *The Goon Show* placed an enormous burden on the effects department. By the early 1950s, the BBC had a tremendous disc library of effects, sold all over the world, but they didn't have many of the effects that Spike wanted. Quite often these effects had to be done in the studio and in front of an audience. Many were done by Spike himself at the microphone. I think, in fact, that the Goons themselves enjoyed the rehearsals of the programme more than when it went on the air. We always had a big studio audience, some of whom became regulars, turning up every week. They much enjoyed all the 'goonery' that went on: Spike inventing effects; Peter and Spike's constant banter; Harry Secombe giggling.

I well remember an occasion when I was sitting in the Control Room with Spike on one side of me and Peter on the other. We were discussing the script, but Spike and Peter were not talking to each other directly. They would address themselves to me.

'Charles, tell Spike that I refuse to say line 27.'

'Spike, Peter refuses to say line 27.'

'Well tell him to go and —— himself.'

Peter would usually walk out in a huff but by the time we were ready (more or less) to go on air he would return and both would act as though nothing had happened.

While all this was going on, Harry Secombe would be giggling away as he always did when there was controversy in the studio. He was the great peacemaker, a lovely man and a great asset to the show in so many ways.

One of Peter Sellers's passions was cars. He would buy a car in the morning, sell it, and buy another in the afternoon. One day we were told that a member of the royal family wished to come and see *The Goon Show*. Peter's car was parked outside the studio. He was told he would have to remove it before the royal visitor came. Peter refused.

'Tell him to go to hell,' he said.

The car was forcibly removed before the duke arrived. We expected explosions of anger from Peter, but to my surprise we saw him walking companionably through the studio with the royal personality, swapping dirty jokes.

Another production job I had at this time was *Educating Archie* with the ventriloquist Peter Brough. I could never see the point of a ventriloquist on radio, but the programme was popular enough. Brough based himself on the American ventriloquist Edgar Bergen whose dummy was Charlie McCarthy. What was extraordinary was that Brough treated his own puppet, Archie, as though he were a real boy. He was very fond of him and tucked him up in his box after the show just as though he was a live baby.

A programme with which I was connected at various times was *In Town Tonight*. I will always remember one of the earliest shows in which I had to interview a Londoner who sold sasparilla – a fizzy American concoction, the forerunner of Coca-Cola – in the streets. In those days all interviews had to be scripted. This man could only read if you helped him by running your finger under what he had to say. It started off all right.

'I – am – a – sasparilla – seller – in – London,' he began very slowly, 'and – I…'

Here he stopped. Frantically I pointed to the next line that was over the page.

'Go on,' I whispered.

'Take your bloody finger out of the way,' he replied.

This all went out live.

Some years later I was asked to produce a programme called *This is London*. It was to take the place of *In Town Tonight*, which, it was thought, had concentrated too much on recording famous people passing through London and not enough on real Londoners. We had a team of reporters who spent their time recording likely candidates for the programme. One day a reporter brought in a recording he had made of a taxidermist. He was very pleased with it and thought it would make a good addition to the programme. I played it to see what it was like.

'I understand you are a taxidermist,' began the reporter. 'Could you tell me something about what your work entails?'

'Certainly,' said the taxidermist. 'I spend my time stuffing animals. Some are more difficult to stuff than others. Small animals like mice present many problems, as do large animals like elephants. The hardest thing I ever had to do was to stuff a giraffe.'

By this time I and others listening to the recording were in hysterics. I had to tell the reporter that I didn't think his piece was suitable for broadcasting. He couldn't understand why.

Some time later I attended a BBC course for producers that was chaired by the then Director General, Hugh Carleton Greene, one of the more progressive director generals of the BBC. I told him the story of the taxidermist. He laughed.

'Did you put it out?'

'No I didn't.'

'Why not?'

'I thought it would offend listeners.'

'You would have been quite safe,' he said. 'Those listeners you might have offended wouldn't have understood the inferences. Those who did would have had a good laugh!'

CHAPTER SIXTEEN:
JOURNEY INTO SPACE

I
n Britain in 1952 there was much interest in, and talk about, the possibility of space travel. Astronomers and scientists were producing maps of the surface of the moon. Michael Standing, head of the Variety Department, received many scripts featuring science fiction stories, but they impressed neither him nor the programme planners. Michael called me into his office. Could I write a science fiction serial, he asked.

'Science fiction?' I replied. 'I don't know anything about it. I don't think I could. I've only ever written Westerns.'

'That's okay,' he said. 'Anyone who can write a Western can write science fiction.'

So, somewhat reluctantly, I began to think about it. Eventually I agreed to give it a try and write a trial programme. I bought an astronomical telescope and built a small observatory in my garden so that I could look at the moon and the planets and set off on my journey into space. I was determined that, like *Riders of the Range*, *Journey into Space* would be based more on scientific fact than fiction: a tale of humanity's battle against the forces of nature.

I bought a book on elementary astronomy and took out a subscription to the American magazine *Sky and Telescope*. With the help of Charles Irwin (who played Luke in *Riders of the Range*) I built a shed in which to house my telescope. I adapted my telescope to take photographs of the surface of the moon.

I became a member of the British Astronomical Association (BAA). In the mid 1950s it met in the rooms of the Royal Astronomical Society at the Royal Academy in Piccadilly. There I made contact with other members, some of whom were later to become famous in the astronomical and science fiction world: Arthur C. Clarke, for example, who was so clever that it was difficult to have a conversation with him unless you were up to his intellectual level.

A very enthusiastic member of the BAA who could not do enough to help new members and beginners in very many ways was Patrick Moore. He was a tall young man and at that time quite slim.

So my love with the heavens began. The new science fiction series the BBC hoped I would be responsible for was due for transmission in September 1953. As the time approached I began to include the science of space travel in my studies. Plenty of books were helpful here, mainly American.

I had one very valuable contact, a rocket designer, no less, who worked at the government's aerospace research centre at Farnborough. By coincidence, this man, Kenneth Gatland, contacted me, not because of space travel but because he had enjoyed my series of programmes featuring Josh White. When I found out who Kenneth Gatland was, I roped him in as technical adviser to *Journey into Space*. He solved all the difficult technical problems for me, such as speed of take-off, number of Gs that could be expected, how fast a space ship would have to travel to get to the moon, how long it would take to get there and how it would land.

I soon learnt that 'science fact' was dull. In the first four episodes of *Journey into Space* we never got off the ground as I tried to establish the background to our enterprise.

The reviews of the first four programmes were pretty damning. Jonah Barrington in the *Daily Sketch*:

> Sorry to pester space-ship writer Charles Chilton but after three instalments of *Journey into Space*, his party has travelled no farther than Bombay. May we reasonably expect that in

instalment four some attempt will be made to begin space travelling? Otherwise here's one listener who's going to give up on the serial as a bad job.

We took off for the moon in the fifth instalment.
Jonah Barrington again:

Last Monday Mr. Chilton said good-bye to his fears and got his rocket out of the earth's atmosphere and into space. And then how the whole thing came alive. For the first time in BBC history listeners were taken space travelling. Here's one listener who has seldom been so excited, so absorbed, or so completely neglectful of his TV set. If you can keep it up you have made history.

The trouble with space is that once you have got on the way, nothing really happens. You have to make it happen with odd noises, voices, music, sound effects and aliens. Once we had landed on the moon – incidentally the date of our landing was 1965, four years before Neil Armstrong and co. – I had to think up a convincing story.

The first series, *Operation Luna*, was scheduled to run for twelve weeks. It actually ran for eighteen and was followed by two further series, *The Red Planet* and *The World in Peril*. At the end of each programme I left my listeners with a cliffhanger. Usually I had no idea what was going to happen to my characters next. By the following Friday night I usually had a good idea of how the plot would develop and what the climaxes were likely to be. Sometimes I sat down with no ideas, but always when I started to write, inspiration would come to me. There would be a short synopsis of the previous programme. Then the last minute of the previous week would be played. Immediately following this, I would have to get my characters out of the cliffhanger I'd got them into the week before.

I never really planned anything in advance. I'd talk with Pen about how to get my characters out of trouble. I would start to write on Friday, or even Saturday. Pen would then type out the script (sometimes during Saturday night); I would take it with me to the office on Sunday where Sheila, my secretary at the BBC, would duplicate it; and the stencilling would be done just before the show was recorded. Sometimes I would be writing the last ten minutes of the programme while the rehearsal of the first part was being recorded.

Sometimes the cast would be rehearsing the first part of the script while the rest was being copied. Sometimes, too, the cast was even asked to help turn the old-fashioned duplicating machine that I'd installed in the studio, as there was no official service for this on Sundays. The word went round that if you wanted a part in *Journey into Space* you had to be able to operate a duplicating machine.

Pen once implored me to start writing at the beginning of the week. I did. But on Friday I tore up what I had written and started writing again. I remember one Saturday night when Pen had had to go out somewhere and I was left with Mary and David, our two elder children, then aged about four and two. They were playing happily so I settled down to write my script. I had only just started when all the lights went out. In those days power cuts were frequent and we were often left without light or power for some time. There were yells and cries from the nursery.

'Daddy, Daddy!'

I picked the children up and brought them into my study. Until the light came on again I sat at my desk, with one unhappy child on each knee, trying to write the next instalment of *Journey into Space*. Funnily enough, that episode turned out to be one of the best I ever wrote. I always wrote well under pressure.

I knew the best number for a crew of a space ship would be either three or four people. We'd need a commander, an engineer, some kind of cosmologist-cum-doctor, and an electronics communication engineer and operator. So that the listener would never have any difficulty in recognising who was speaking, I wrote for characters with widely differing accents. Andrew Faulds played Jet Morgan the commander. He was of Scottish extraction but sounded like a traditional Henty, stiff-upper-lip type: a strong leader with a good British accent – *Boy's Own* magazine stuff. Mitch, played by Bruce Beeby and later by Don Sharp, was an astronautical engineer, typical Australian tough guy, argumentative and a bit tetchy, the designer of the ship Luna, with a real outback accent. Doc, the American cosmologist, was played by Guy Kingsley Poynter, who kept a diary or talking book. His sweet, calm voice kept the peace when there were arguments.

Then there was Lemmy Barnet, the cockney radio engineer and operator. There's always been some controversy about such an uncouth character as Lemmy being included. Was he really the type that would be chosen to go on such an important expedition? In reality no, but in radio science fiction, yes. I needed somebody in the crew to represent the ignorant listener – to ask the kind of questions the listener would want to ask and to introduce some humour.

In spite of the incongruity of taking Lemmy along, he turned out to be very popular. Originally played by David Kossoff and later by Alfie Bass, Lemmy was based on me. I was a Londoner and had been a radio operator and navigator during the war. The part was a natural for both David and Alfie. Incidentally it was David Kossoff who created the name Lemmy. I was going to call him Alf, or Bert, or something like that. But David said no, he wanted him to be called Lemmy. I asked him why and whether it was a Jewish name. Well, he said, not particularly, but I love the name, and if I can choose the name of the character I'm going to play, I'd like to choose the name Lemuel. I thought that Lemuel was a bit thick and so shortened it to Lemmy. Lemuel from *Gulliver's Travels*, I suppose.

Besides these four main characters there were many other more minor ones. David Jacobs, whom I had known during the war, played nearly all of them. He could play any voice you liked, and sometimes did a whole scene talking to himself in two or even three different characters. He was also responsible for the stentorian voice announcing the programme: 'JOURNEY INTO SPACE'. David tells me that people still say to him: 'Oh go on – say "JOURNEY INTO SPACE"'.

Members of the cast of *Journey into Space* were great, but some of the things they got up to were quite alarming. This was especially true of David and Andrew. During a recording, for a joke David once poured a jug of water down the front of Andrew's trousers. In retaliation, Andrew smeared mustard on David's lip mike that he had to use very close to his lips in order to create all his strange voices. They came out even stranger. Recordings in those days were extremely hard to edit, so it was almost as if these antics had taken place on air.

One of the characters that made a lasting impression on listeners in the first series was the mysterious 'Voice', played by Deryck Guyler. He terrified Lemmy but was instrumental in saving the lives of the crew and getting their ship off the prehistoric earth and back to the moon 13,000 years in the future, which was our twentieth century. It was a kindly voice – the voice of a being of great sensitivity, and concern for the damage that humanity was doing not only to itself but to the planet on which it lived. Yet this creature was so terrifyingly ugly he was reluctant to show himself to the crew of Luna. They did get a glimpse of him but when they saw him Lemmy took to his heels and ran.

I have often wondered why I created this ugly/kindly character. I now think that my inspiration came from the badly disfigured men with whom I came in contact when I first joined the BBC. All of them had treated me most kindly, maybe because I was a war orphan, and at Christmas they even clubbed together and bought me a present: a book. In spite of the great distance in time that separated them from *Journey into Space*, it was members of the King's Roll that inspired the 'Voice'.

The effects became an important part of the show. Listeners could not see the various technical apparatus and therefore they had to have distinctive sounds. It was always my intention to make the effects as important as the actors. Instead of leaving them in the background, as was the custom with most radio productions, I brought them right up front. Effects are every bit as important as the spoken word and should be treated with the same respect. Good effects can save dozens of lines of dialogue. Most of the effects in *Journey into Space* were specially created. The space music, which frightened the life out of Lemmy, comprised recordings of the sounds produced at the National Physical Research Laboratory in Kingston, London where scientists were experimenting with thermionic valve oscillation.

My favourite effect was the air lock. In order to leave the ship an astronaut would have to enter the air lock and have all the air pumped out of it before he could finally open the main door that led out into space. Fans often talked endearingly of the air lock. Then there was the televiewer, a screen which showed the scene outside the ship picked up by a video camera. (It would make the same whirring sounds.) The working sound of the televiewer was recorded in a submarine. There were also the gyros, necessary to keep the ship stable and on course during flight – actually dynamos in a power station starting up or shutting down.

The best effects of all were musical – all original, composed by Van Phillips. We found that the incidental music so far as radio science fiction is concerned falls into only a few categories. We built up a library of mixed mood music pieces, none of them, except the opening and closing music, more than a few seconds long. Fear – spacious – funereal – tension – dramatic – sad – joyous, and so on.

The band would be in the studio early on Sunday afternoon to record the music. The music from our ever-increasing library would cover most events, but if anything new were required Van would insist that I sang the sort of thing I had in mind on the phone. He used to ring me up just as I was getting down to work on Friday night and say:

'What kind of music do you need? Sing it.'

I would hear him trying it out on the piano. Then he would say: 'Yes, got the idea of that,' and two days later it would be in the studio, ready to be rehearsed and recorded by Van's sextet of (partially) electronic instruments. In one script a line was: 'If we're not careful we'll end up in the graveyard.' In future programmes I could just say 'graveyard' or other words which described various situations in which the crew found themselves to indicate the type of music required. Gillian Reynolds, the radio critic, credited *Journey into Space* with the creation of the radiophonic workshop.

It is difficult for a generation reared on television to realise how important radio was and how much it was talked about and reviewed in the press. Lengthy articles on programmes appeared in the *Radio Times* and other journals. Comparatively few people had television sets when *Journey into Space* started, although the number was growing rapidly in the early 1950s, particularly in 1953 when the coronation of Elizabeth II took place.

A television producer I once talked to said that there was nothing in science fiction that television wasn't able to produce just as well as radio or better. I replied, 'How about a programme set in total darkness?' (I had a scene in *Journey into Space* when all the power failed and the crew sat in the rocket ship in darkness and heard knockings from outside, Lemmy saying, 'It must be the H. G. Wells lot.')

Once we were well under way it was amazing how many reviews the programme received, most of them very favourable. An exception was in a programme called *The Critics*, in which various, rather stuffy, reviewers aired their views.

'Did you hear what they said?' asked one critic. 'Increase your speed by one thousand miles an hour! Whoever heard of anyone going at a thousand miles an hour, let alone increasing it by that much?!'

Paul Ferris of the *Observer* wrote on 5 December 1954:

> I take back anything I ever said about *Journey into Space*. I still think Lemmy sounds too inept to be a member of the Mars Expedition but otherwise the fact is that every Monday has me waiting impatiently for my ration. This series is signally easy to listen to, thirty minutes a week of smug entertainment at the expense of benighted space wanderers. Mrs. Dale's doings, even the rural dilemmas of the Archers, are too near home. On a blowing winter evening, a good adventure on Mars is the cosiest of the lot.

By Episode 10, *Journey into Space* numbered between five and six million weekly listeners. This was the last time that more people tuned into a radio programme than watched television.

The programme did seem to have a remarkable hold. The second series, which started on 6 September 1954, entitled *The Red Planet*, originally went out on Mondays at 7.30 with a repeat on Sundays at 6.00. When the BBC moved the repeat from 6 o'clock to 7 o'clock, an order of nuns wrote and complained to the BBC that the new transmission time clashed with the hour of their Evensong and could it be changed back, please.

During the run of the first series I received an official invitation from the British Interplanetary Society to attend their annual convention at London University. This puzzled me. I had had no contact with their society. In any case their meeting was on a Monday, which made it impossible for me to go. I wrote to thank the society for their invitation and asked why I had been invited. The reply cleared up the matter. As the convention was being held on a Monday, members of that society would miss that evening's episode of Jet Morgan and his crew, and they had hoped that, at the close of the meeting, I would be kind enough to give them an account of what had taken place.

Byron Rogers, writing in the Sunday Review of the *Sunday Telegraph* 15 June 1997, said the following:

> In a corner of my mind it will always be 7.30 on a summer's evening and I am hurrying home from play. If you know anything about summer evenings and small boys you will appreciate this is an exercise that usually requires a large posse. Certainly nothing else ever made me do it. But then nothing else in my childhood ever made me look at a clock. Over the trees, the big brass hand on the church tower is at 7.26 and I am running now for in four minutes *Journey into Space* will be on the Light Programme.

In October 1957 a letter came from the Director of Broadcasting, Falkland Islands.

> The two transcripted series of *Journey into Space* have both been fantastically popular here. We broadcast the series on Monday evenings and nobody would dare to organize an event to coincide with that half hour, for attendance would be practically nil. Even the local Defence Force had to change their drill night!

When the Transcription Service wanted to put out the first series, *Operation Luna*, it found that the BBC at that time did not automatically keep all of its recordings. So we had to re-record the whole series. One change we made was to cut out the first four episodes which were rather dull. The remake differed from the original in another respect. David Kossoff, the original 'Lemmy', received an offer to make a film at the time of the recording, so we recruited Alfie Bass in his place.

When the BBC repeated *Operation Luna* in 1958 on the Light Programme, it was the Transcription version that was used. Thenceforward Lemmy was played by Alfie Bass.

In 1954 I wrote a novel based on *Journey into Space* called *Operation Luna*, published by Herbert Jenkins; *The Red Planet* came out in January 1956 and *World in Peril* in May 1959. Many European countries also published *Journey into Space* in their own languages – Holland, Denmark, Sweden, Italy and Yugoslavia among them.

In 1955 the *Daily Express*, trying to emulate the success of Hulton Press's *Eagle* comic, decided to publish the *Express Super Colour Weekly*. They asked me if I would turn *Journey into Space* into a strip cartoon for inclusion in their new publication. I agreed, but asked who they would employ as the artist to illustrate my work. To my surprise they said that they had in mind an Italian artist who had done much work in the strip cartoon line.

'Why Italian?' I asked. 'And how are we to work together if he lives in Italy?'

'The Italians are the best for this kind of work. There are very few artists here in England who could do it', was their reply.

The *Express* arranged for Nando Tacconi to come over to England to meet me and discuss the project. And that was the beginning of a lifelong friendship with Nando and his family. He came over in the autumn of 1955 and immediately set to work on the *Journey into Space* project. We fixed him up with a studio in our attic. The first strip went out in the *Express Weekly* in April 1956.

'This is it!' screamed the *Express*, 'The day you've been waiting for! JET MORGAN appears for the first time in a strip serial! His amazing new adventures begin in today's *EXPRESS SUPER COLOUR WEEKLY*, 20 pages 4d.'

Nando and his family remained part of our lives long after the *Journey into Space* strip had finished. Our summer holidays were often spent together, sometimes in Italy, other times in England. They stayed with us when our youngest son Anthony was born in 1956.

In all his work Nando was most painstaking and determined to be accurate. If the story he was illustrating were set in England, he would ask for my help. One strip, I remember, was called *Gli Aristocrati*, a story about English aristocrats and their nefarious doings. He asked me if I would photograph some typical upper class London dwellings and also a shot showing the entrance of Scotland Yard. He was very pleased with the photos I sent him. I remember being a bit anxious when photographing Scotland Yard in case I should be arrested as a terrorist.

Nando's life was very sad towards the end. His son Rolando committed suicide, and his wife Lydia died of cancer. Nando himself became partially blind, but continued to write stories and rough out the illustrations almost to the end of his life. He was always cheerful and uncomplaining, but eventually could take no more. He died in his home in Milan in April 2006, aged 84.

Various companies featured *Journey into Space* in advertising campaigns. I remember Lyons had a coffee and chicory product called 'Bev'. An advertisement appeared in the *Daily Mail* and *Daily Express* in 1955 showing a space ship with a hatch door open and a ladder leading down to the ground. The caption read, 'Where's Jet? Gone to have a Bev.'

On 23 May 1955 the Zing Pen Company had a huge ad in the *News Chronicle*. It showed a spacecraft flying towards the moon. 'Zing – the Ballpoint of the future – retractable, reliable, and only 1/-. Jet Morgan says: Zing! What a ballpoint. Best value in the universe.'

I have been amazed by how many people involved in real space travel have told me that they listened to my programme. One was Dr J. G. Porter of the Greenwich Royal Observatory. In 1956 a new Astronomer Royal, Professor Richard van der Riet Woolley, was appointed. On his arrival at London Airport from Australia, the professor described himself as a 'straightforward scientist' and talked about space travel being 'utter bilge'. During a lecture by Dr Porter to 400 secondary school children at County Hall, he was asked why he thought the new Astronomer Royal had said this. He replied:

> I can only suggest that the Astronomer Royal is a lot more cautious than I am. I am not going to throw cold water on

space travel. I would not miss a single instalment of Jet Morgan because I follow his adventures as closely as you do.

Professor Colin Pillinger of the Open University, who instigated the Beagle 2 project aimed at landing a British spacecraft on Mars, told me that as a boy he had been fascinated by my programme, which had inspired him to begin his work as a space scientist. Pen and I were invited to the launch party of Beagle 2 on 2 June 2003 held at the BT Centre in London. In the big conference hall we all applauded as news came that Beagle 2 had successfully gone into orbit around the red planet. Pillinger told the audience how he had first become interested in space travel through listening to my programme, and I was dragged up onto the platform where I had to answer a few questions, amidst much applause. Unfortunately Beagle 2 never reached the next stage, which was the actual landing on the planet. No more was heard from it, much to the great disappointment of Pillinger and the rest of us.

Journey into Space has had a long life and is not quite dead yet. It was repeated in 1958 and again in 1981. The BBC issued cassettes and CDs of the series, and with the advent of digital Radio, *Journey into Space* still draws listeners on BBC Radio Seven.

CHAPTER SEVENTEEN:
LIFE AT KESTON

The house we moved into directly after our marriage in 1947 was 44 Bromley Common in Kent. It was detached, with a pleasant garden and open land beyond occupied by gypsies. There was a pub almost opposite the house.

We might have stayed at Bromley Common longer but for the attitude of our landlord. In 1950, when I was about to go to Tombstone, Pen was pregnant. Television was just becoming popular and I thought it would be nice for her to have a television set while I was away. So I asked our landlord, Mr Maloney, if he had any objection to this. To my dismay he wouldn't allow us to erect an aerial on the roof of his house. I was so annoyed by this that when I got back from Tombstone we began to look for a home of our own.

Our desire to move had been heightened by a rather frightening experience. One night as we were about to go to bed, we heard a noise outside the front door as if someone was trying to get in. I opened the door to find a man standing there looking quite vicious. I slammed the door shut whereupon he began hammering upon it with a milk bottle and shouting:

'Let me in, blast you. I'll count three. One, two, three!'

'We must dial 999,' I shouted to Pen who was half way upstairs on her way to bed. We dialled and waited anxiously for the police. Meanwhile the crashing and banging and shouting went on. I was afraid the intruder would break a panel of the door. At last, as we sat cowering in the hallway, we heard heavy footsteps coming up the pathway and the reassuring voices of two policemen. Feeling much braver we opened the door. The intruder stood held by the policemen. He looked at us in bewilderment.

'Come along now, sir,' said one of the policemen to the intruder. 'I think you're at the wrong house.'

It turned out that the man had come out of the pub opposite, very drunk. He'd tried unsuccessfully to open the door with his key, and when he saw me thought I was someone with his wife. Once the police had arrived and he saw us both standing together, he was gobsmacked!

We were both very ignorant about mortgages and suchlike, but were greatly helped by a man from the Prudential. He had persuaded us to take out an insurance policy and used to call every month to collect the payments. He also became our friendly financial advisor and was interested in my work at the BBC. Once I played him a record I'd found in the BBC Gramophone Library. Its refrain was: 'There's no one with endurance like the man who sells insurance. He's everybody's best friend'. He was much amused. With his help we bought a small house in Coniston Road on the other side of Bromley and moved there when our daughter Mary was three months old.

Mary's safe arrival on 13 December 1950 was a very great joy for us, particularly because in 1948 our first baby had been stillborn. In those days mothers were kept in hospital for about ten days after the birth. I, as usual, was working long hours at the office and had programmes to do on Christmas Eve and Christmas Day when Pen was due home. Eventually the hospital agreed to keep Pen and Mary in hospital on Christmas Day. They had a great time, with presents from Father Christmas (one of the specialists), turkey dinner and drinks. On Boxing Day they came home.

Neither of us knew much about bringing up babies, and we had no family nearby to help us. That first night I remember getting up at every little sound or cry from Mary's bedroom.

Was she all right? Should we change her nappy? We didn't get much sleep.

Relations between me and Pen's parents became much easier once the children started arriving. We often went up to their home in Aldeburgh, where they lived in the Red House, right on the Aldeburgh golf course, which later became the home of Benjamin Britten and Peter Pears. We had no car, but for weekend visits to Aldeburgh Pen would leave early in the day carrying Mary in a sling over her shoulder and the dog on a lead. They would catch the 47 bus that stopped right outside our front gate and took them to Liverpool Street Station where they caught a train to Saxmundham, the nearest station to Aldeburgh. I would follow in the evening when I had finished work. Once I was late and rushed out of the house carrying our suitcase, just catching a bus going to Bromley. As I got off the bus at the station I stepped into the arms of two policemen; I had been seen rushing from our house with a suitcase and was a suspected thief. Fortunately I managed to convince them I wasn't.

On one of my first visits to the Red House we went over to see Pen's grandmother who lived at Wissett, near Halesworth. At that time (1950) she was in her nineties, and lived to be 101. She asked me what programme I was working on. I told her I was writing about the American Civil War.

'Oh yes,' she said, 'I remember that well.'

To me that was amazing – I was actually talking to someone who had been alive all that time ago. She was born in 1853, so would have been about ten when the war took place.

Our first son, David, was born in 1952 when we were at Coniston Road. It was here that I learnt to drive and we bought our first car.

I kept in touch with my grandmother and her family in Sandwich Street. There were now seven in the same house: Granny, Uncle Jim and his wife Aggie, and their four children, two girls and two boys. The girls, Jill and Patsy, often came down to stay with us and loved walking the dog and playing in the garden. Aunt Aggie was now supposed to do the cooking and shopping, but most of it still seemed to fall to my grandmother. Just like Granny, Aunt Aggie used the pawnbroker to solve her monetary problems, and was always in debt. Granny was very proud to have a grandson in the BBC. When someone said to her, 'Your Charlie's done well for himself hasn't he?' she replied, 'That's because of the way I brought him up.' Pat (my uncle who I thought of as my brother), however, thought differently. When I first worked at the BBC he would say: 'Why don't you get yourself a proper job?' After the war he emigrated to Australia. My Auntie Queenie (my mother's sister) who lived in Sutton was a frequent visitor and took a great interest in both my work and my family.

Mary celebrated her first birthday at Coniston Road. I remember my present to her: a train set! It was something I had always longed for. But with two children, a dog and a cat, and my ever-increasing collection of books that by then amounted to many hundreds, Coniston Road became too crowded. We started looking for something bigger.

An estate agent took us to view several houses. He insisted on taking us to see suburban semi-detached properties in built-up areas, which were not at all what we had in mind. Then he took us to a rambling old house with a tower that housed an observatory. I was all for it but Pen dismissed it as completely out of the question as it was very dilapidated and inconvenient. Just before the tour finished he took us to the village of Keston, outside Bromley. At No. 27 Commonside stood a large, red-brick house called Millfield, so named because of the windmill that had once stood in its extensive grounds. We fell for it straight away, but the agent had little hope of us acquiring it. The most we could afford to pay was £5,000.

'The owners have just turned down an offer of £7,000,' said the agent. 'But I'll put your offer to them and see what they say.'

To our astonishment and delight our offer was accepted. To this day we have never understood why. We moved to Keston in 1954.

Being a Londoner born and bred I had never envisaged living in the country, but the house we bought faced directly on to Keston Common and Keston itself still retained a countrified village aspect, although within easy reach of London. We had nearly an acre of land, a grass tennis court and a garden where we grew vegetables. (At least Pen and a succession of one-day-a-week gardeners grew vegetables. My contributions were mainly digging up potatoes or helping to put up the nets around the tennis court.)

One thing I really appreciated about the new house and garden was the space it gave me to build a much bigger and better observatory. Here, with a new and more powerful telescope, I spent many nights photographing the moon and the stars, while Pen took notes of details that might help me with the scripts of *Journey into Space*. This was cold work, but often inspirational.

Photography, indeed, became my great hobby. I became interested in the birds and wildlife that were plentiful on the common and in our garden, and took photos of the tits, nuthatches, woodpeckers and other birds that visited our bird tables. I also bought a cine-camera so that I could record the antics of our children, both at home and on holiday. One reel caught my Granny in the garden near the paddling pool. She is laughing and skipping around as the boys chase her with the hosepipe.

Keston was a good place in which to bring up our three children. (Anthony was born there in 1956.) Mary went to a girls' school a few minutes' walk away and the boys went first as dayboys and later as weekly boarders to Carn Brea, a rather snobbish prep school near Bromley. The headmaster was very keen on the boys learning Latin and Greek and insisted that they learnt to box – which was all rather different from my school days. Boys at Carn Brea were expected to move on to public schools. Pen's great uncle had been the founder of Bradfield College so we put the boys' names down for that school. David went but never enjoyed it. He created quite a stir by criticising and refusing to comply with the fagging and caning system whereby prefects could cane younger boys. He stayed to do O levels and then announced that he was leaving do his A levels at our local grammar school. His housemaster, who had been a boy at Bradfield and then become a master there, was thoroughly shocked. Anthony went straight to Bromley Grammar after he left Carn Brea.

I never really fitted in with all this posh schooling. The parents always seemed to be bankers or stockbrokers with whom I had nothing in common and I was never at ease at the various functions we had to attend. One time at Carn Brea I attended a sports day and entered the fathers' race. I thought I might have a good chance of winning and started off at a terrific pace leading the field all the way until, a few yards before reaching the winning post, I slipped and fell flat on my face. My sons thought it very funny.

From an early age, Mary wanted to be a dancer. After leaving school she went to the Arts Educational Trust to study dancing and acting. One day she came home thrilled to bits about a new teacher called Mrs Colgan, saying how friendly she was and what a good teacher. We heard about the merits of Mrs Colgan for several weeks and then one day Mary came home even more thrilled.

'Daddy,' she said, 'Mrs Colgan says she knew you in Colombo, in Ceylon.'

Mrs Colgan turned out to be Yvonne Bradley who had helped run the Fawn Night Club where our band often performed. It was only when she heard Mary's surname that she put two and two together. It was good to see Yvonne again and to meet her husband. Mary stayed with the couple for several weeks when she had one of her first jobs in a pantomime at Windsor.

At the time of our arrival in Keston, *Journey into Space* was in full swing and there were many write-ups and interviews about it in the press. Thanks to the local papers the village became aware that I was living amongst them. Soon I was bombarded with requests to open bazaars, fetes and other festivities. Our big garden at Keston was often used for local functions. The Scouts held their annual fete there and Alfie Bass and others appeared in space suits to raise money for various good causes.

Most of our friends and neighbours followed my programmes with interest and appreciation. An exception was a man who lived next door to us. When I first met him he said, 'So you're the man who writes all that rubbish about space travel.'

Music in general had always been part of my life and I had had a great desire to be part of the amateur musical world. When we were at Keston I was able to achieve this. The recorder was revived as an instrument in the 1950s, thanks mainly to the work of Walter Bergman, and Pen and I went to a concert of recorder music at the Holborn Town Hall given by the Aeolian Recorder Quintet. We enjoyed it so much that we bought recorders and joined one of Walter's classes. When Alfie Ralston came to visit us at Keston we played him some pieces we had learned. He played piano to accompany us and was soon criticising our technique, intonation and general musicality. Then he bought a descant recorder and joined Walter's class. He never learnt the different fingering for the treble recorder, but was quite able to transpose the notes at sight without difficulty. He didn't stay in Walter's class for long but later wrote several works for different combinations of recorders and always enjoyed coming to play with us, even though his technique was much better than ours.

As well as recorder, I took up the flute and piccolo. I went to classes at the City Lit and started playing with wind groups there (one of which included the actor Warren Mitchell on clarinet). Pen took up the oboe and also went to City Lit to classes given by John Barnet who was, at that time, principal oboist at Covent Garden. We both joined an amateur orchestra run by the Pearl Assurance Company conducted by Ron Gilham. Later we joined Sid Fixman's Ben Uri Orchestra and Roy Budden's Philharmonia. We had musical evenings at home at which we played wind decets, octets and quintets or mixed combinations of flute, recorder and piano. We also went to many weekends and summer schools of wind or recorder ensembles and built up a large library of wind and recorder music.

I tried to get the children interested in music. I remember sitting on the sofa playing the guitar with Mary and David on either side of me when they were about five and three years old. Mary recalls how I sang the 'Old Sow' song to them. They all learnt the piano at school, but David was the only one who kept it up. After taking his A levels he applied to the BBC for a job as studio manager. He was told that for that or a similar job he had to have a degree. So he went to Goldsmiths College and got one, supporting himself by playing the piano in a pop group. Then he applied to the BBC again – only to be told that they had no vacancies. So he went back to the pop group, which he ran and organised, and which did quite well in various London venues.

After about a year the BBC invited David to go for an interview as there were now some vacancies. He got a job as studio manager. Later he moved to the Radiophonic Workshop that specialised in musical and other sound effects for programmes. Eventually he formed his own company called 'Essential Music', which became a recording studio for many BBC and other companies' programmes. David also composed and played a lot of background music for various programmes.

Anthony had a different career. Never brilliant at school, he left aged sixteen and got a job in 'Registry' at the BBC. I was pleased about this, but after working there for six months my son came to me and said:

'Dad, I don't know how you could have stood working there all that time – it's so boring!'

In Registry all he had to do was to file documents and papers, and so of course it *was* boring. So he left to work at the English Tourist Board, where he became involved in audio-visual productions. Eventually he, too, was able to set up his own company, which promotes and organises company functions and publicity.

Pen continued to research and type my programmes. There was a good second-hand bookshop in Bromley which, while I was working on *Riders of the Range*, she scoured for first-hand accounts of life in the American West. We both had readers' tickets for the British Museum, and when I was writing musical documentaries Pen spent many days there digging out songs and contemporary accounts of subjects I was writing about. She would then present them to me in a rough format from which I would write my scripts. I always wrote in longhand (no computers in those days), and as ideas began to flow my handwriting became more and more difficult to decipher – in fact Pen, through long years of practice, was the only one who could read it. Her final task was to type my finished script.

Because Pen spent so much time on research and typing we needed help with both the housework and the children when they were small. Maria was one of the first who worked for us. She was from the province of Udine in northern Italy. When she came she had an Italian boyfriend in Bedford, where a great many Italians worked in the brick-making trade.

One day she came to Pen in tears, who said, 'Whatever's the matter, Maria?'

'It's Giovanni – he went back to Italy and now he's had to get married!'

It seems that before he came to England Giovanni had been courting a young Italian girl in a small southern Italian village, and when he went back to Italy her family had insisted on his marrying her. Maria was very upset, but a few weeks later she came to Pen, all smiles.

'I get married, Signora.'

'Married?' said Pen. 'Who to?'

'Luciano.'

'Who's he?'

'A boy I knew in Rome three years ago. He wants to come to England and asks me to marry him. If he comes we can get work as a married couple.'

Pen was worried, because Maria had not seen Luciano for three years. She persuaded Maria to go back to Italy and see Luciano and her parents before deciding anything. Some time later Maria and Luciano came back to England and got married from our house. We all went to the wedding at the local Roman Catholic Church, where Pen had to translate parts of the service into Italian as neither of them spoke much English. Afterwards we had a party in our conservatory to which the priest came as well as a collection of Italian young men who arrived in their smart, light-blue suits on motor bikes. That night we bought fish and chips for supper. Maria and Luciano had retired to their bedroom soon after the party and we didn't want to disturb them, so we left their fish and chips outside the bedroom door.

The couple stayed with us for a while, but we couldn't really afford to pay them both. Eventually they found work in Chippenham, a small Wiltshire town to which many Italians had emigrated. After four years Luciano was allowed to work at his trade: shoe-making. They had three daughters all of whom lived and married in Chippenham.

After that we had no live-in domestic help but a succession of au pairs and weekly cleaners. The most enduring of these and one who became part of the family was Elizabeth. She came from Morpeth in Northumberland and was married to Matthews (I never knew his first name), who was about forty years older than she was. They had both worked at Holwood House in Keston, a large mansion built by Decimus Burton in

1825 on the site of an earlier building used by William Pitt who was born in the nearby village of Hayes in 1749. When Elizabeth and her husband worked there, Lord Stanley had owned it. Elizabeth worked as housemaid and Matthews as coach driver and later chauffeur.

Elizabeth had many tales to tell of the house parties held at the house and of the goings-on that occurred. A bell would be rung early in the morning to enable the guests to get back to their own bedrooms. Churchill often stayed at Holwood, but neither Elizabeth nor Matthews liked him. They said he was very mean with his tips. In 1953 Holwood was sold to the Seismograph Company and Elizabeth and Matthews were out of work. They were able to get a council flat in Hayes and Elizabeth worked for many different families in the area, eventually coming to us. Matthews, too, worked for us occasionally, even though by then he was nearly ninety. The job he liked doing best was cleaning the silver (not that we had much of that). They came to us soon after Anthony was born and both became devoted to him. He was Elizabeth's pride and joy, and she baby-sat with him from his very early years. She would do anything for us: clean, cook (she was a very good cook), baby-sit, and house-sit when we went on holiday. She had her drawbacks because she loved to talk, and would drive Pen mad by standing over her while she was typing or trying to do research, and relate all the gossip of the village. If we had visitors that she didn't like she wouldn't let them through the door.

Many holidays were spent in Italy. Just before the war Pen had lived with a family in Florence to learn Italian, and during the war had worked in the Italian section of the BBC. I was very keen to visit the country that she loved and attempt to learn a little of the language. The first time I went was in 1953, when we left Mary and David with Pen's parents. We set off by boat and train to a small resort called Zoagli on the coast near Rapallo that had been recommended to us by a travel agent. The Pensione Blue was a friendly place and we soon got to know the other people, all Italians, staying there. We spent the days visiting nearby tourist attractions or swimming and sunbathing on the small beach, which was somewhat hazardous as the little bay was still cluttered with wartime relics – bits of metal sticking up in the water or lying around on the shore.

Before I went to Italy I had always imagined Italian cafes full of musicians, singing or playing guitars, but here at Zoagli there was no music.

'Does no one play the guitar?' I asked.

One man said he had one but couldn't play it. The next night he brought it in to show me. I struck a few chords which received much applause. So I tried a song.

'There was an old woman who had an old sow,' I sang, followed by grunts, snorts and whistles after each verse. All the diners gathered round. '*Bis, bis*' [encore] they shouted when I stopped. I tried to think of other songs they might like and could join in such as 'Old Macdonald had a farm, ee-i-ee-i-o', which they loved. Thereafter each evening I, an Englishman, was entertaining Italian holiday-makers with English folk songs. I didn't know many, but that didn't matter. 'The Old Sow' and 'Old Macdonald' were their favourites and they would all join in, over and over again.

As the children grew older I always tried to keep August free so that we could go on holiday together. One year when we were feeling rather broke we decided to go on holiday in England. We booked up with a farm in Shropshire that claimed that children were welcome to help on the farm and that there was horse riding, farm produce, etc. We went by car, and on arrival found there was no one there. As we were standing wondering what to do, another family with two children arrived on foot as they had come by train.

Suddenly a car roared up the driveway. When it stopped, out stepped a tall young woman, who came rushing up to us apologising for being late and pushed us into the house.

'You must be hungry,' she said, 'I'll get the stove going and we'll have supper in no time.' She looked at Pen and Rachel, the other woman guest, saying, 'Perhaps you would wash the salad for me?'

As Rachel and Pen washed and prepared the salad, Rachel said, 'Bloody hell, I thought I was going to get away from all this for a week.'

That was the start of an extraordinary holiday. We discovered that Frances, our hostess, was a young widow who ran the place with the help of a daily woman, Gertrude, who herself was something of a character. Nothing in the house ever worked properly. There was a kitchen range that was unusable. Frances cooked for all her guests on a single gas ring. Most food was out of tins; there was no sign of farm produce. Indeed, there didn't seem to be much of a farm at all. There were a few chickens wandering around and the children asked whether they could collect the eggs.

'Sure', said Frances. She gave them a dish to put the eggs in and told them where to look.

They came back empty-handed.

'No eggs?' I asked.

'We saw some,' they said, 'but they were amongst the nettles and brambles. We couldn't get to them without stinging our hands.'

At the back of the house was a field that led down to a stream where the boys hoped to catch fish. We started off across this field and had reached the middle when a wild fury of a horse came rushing towards us. Clutching the boys I tugged them back to the safety of the farmyard. I would never cross that field again.

'Are you frightened of that horse?' asked David.

'Yes.'

'Why?' said David. 'You shouldn't be; you fought in the war, didn't you?'

The girls, Mary and Nicola, kept pestering us to ride the horse, so eventually I asked Frances whether she could arrange this.

'Okay', she said, 'I'll catch it tomorrow.'

Next morning she went into the field to catch the wild fury that had rushed at us the day before. Eventually she got it into the farmyard and saddled and bridled it. But by that time the girls were as scared as I was and never went riding.

Even so, all the children loved that holiday. They could do and go whatever and wherever they liked, and were never told off or shouted at by Frances or Gertrude. For some reason, however, Gertrude didn't like the Hills, the other family staying at the farm. She would make coffee for our family after the evening meal but would never make any for them. She delighted in telling them that it was in their bedroom that Frances' husband had committed suicide.

After that, holidays in Italy became the norm. For several summers when all our children were at school we spent our summer holiday in a small southern seaside resort called Acciaroli, some way south of Salerno. To get there we put the car on the train to Milan where we arrived early in the morning. We would be met by Nando Tacconi, whom we'd known since the days of *Journey into Space*, and who invited us to breakfast in his flat before making our way down south. On the return journey we would get back to Milan at about 8pm and find that Nando had organised a dinner for us at a favourite restaurant and had invited many of our other Italian friends who lived in Milan to share it with us. We would then leave them at about 10pm to put our car on the train to England, thinking what a good way it was to end our holiday.

Right from our first visit we liked Acciaroli immediately. From an Italian holiday guide book we had chosen a hotel called La Pineta. The beach was open to everybody and not privately owned like so many in Italy. We could hire an *ombrellone* [big sunshade] and plant it anywhere we liked. We could walk along the coast until we came to a *pineta* [little pine wood] from where you could also bathe. There were no English people, many Italians and one or two Germans. After lunch at the hotel we would try to persuade our children to take a nap, but they usually played up and made a lot of noise.

On the second day we were there someone knocked on the door of our bedroom. A woman said in Italian, 'I'm sorry, but we are in the room next to yours and I'm trying to get my two-year-old son to sleep. Could you keep your children a bit quieter?'

We apologised and let our children go back to the beach. Next morning we met the Italian family at breakfast. They, like us, had two boys and a girl. We became great friends. The Vitiellos lived in Padova but came to Acciaroli every summer as they had many relatives living in the district. From then on for several years our holidays were spent in Acciaroli. The Vitiellos found us a flat that we rented each year (much cheaper than staying in the hotel) and it became our holiday home.

The children loved it; they made friends with many Italian kids and took part in the *Sbarco dei Saraceni* [Invasion of the Saracens], which took place each year in the little harbour. Once the Saraceni arrived in a homemade boat surrounded by their dancing girls, among them Mary. As it neared the shore it gradually began to sink until the performers were knee-deep in water. The watching crowd enjoyed it immensely. Marino, a young Italian who was rather keen on Mary, played one of the Saracens. He took his performance very seriously and asked Pen if she would make up his face for the part. Pen did her best, but he was never really satisfied with the result.

Marino was also involved in another incident when, one windy day, our *ombrellone* blew over and hit Mary in the face. Pen came back from her swim to find an anxious crowd around the entrance to one of the hotels lining the beach. They all looked at her and murmured *non spaventare la mamma* [don't frighten the mother]. Pen found Mary in Marino's arms, blood streaming from a gash just above her eye.

Marino took charge. 'We must go to the doctor,' he said.

He carried her to our car and escorted us to the doctor whose house was situated a short way up the hill above the town. The doctor was out so we sat in the waiting room for a while. I was dying for a cup of tea so I went back to the flat and brought back a thermos of tea and some mugs.

Just as we started drinking, the doctor arrived.

'Well,' he said in Italian. 'It's true. English people are always drinking tea.'

He put some stitches in Mary's wound and then said she must have a tetanus injection.

'Where do we go for that?' I asked.

'It's all right,' said Marino, 'I'll get the captain. He can do it at your flat – don't worry.'

'Do you know where he lives?'

'No, but I'll go and look in the bars. He's sure to be in one of them.'

We drove back to the flat and sure enough Marino soon arrived with the captain, who asked if we had any alcohol. As it happened we hadn't.

'Perfume will do,' he said.

The captain daubed the wound with some of Mary's perfume and gave her the injection.

'How much should we give him?' I whispered to Marino. He shrugged.

'Something to buy a few drinks with,' he replied.

Next morning he came round to see how Mary was. She was fine. 'The Captain's a bit embarrassed,' said Marino.

'Why?' we asked.

'When he went back to the bar last night, all his friends accused him of having made love to the English girl.'

'Why?' we asked again.

'Because he smelt so much of perfume.'

We first met the Vitiellos at Acciaroli in 1963 and have been friends ever since. We've had holidays together, sometimes here, sometimes at their home in Padova. In 2005 we went to Padova to celebrate Salvatore's ninetieth birthday and in the summer of 2007 he and Annamaria and two of their grandchildren came to London for my ninetieth birthday.

Keston, when we lived there, had two churches: the Parish church situated some way out of the village on the road towards Westerham, and a small church called St Audrey's that was right next to our house. Apparently, Lord Sackville Cecil, who had lived in nearby Hayes, wanted his mistress, who was an organist, to play in Hayes Parish church, but the vicar would not agree to this. So he built St Audrey's, installed his mistress in what was to become our house, and arranged for her to play the organ in the new church.

When we lived there both churches were functioning. Although we were not churchgoers we nevertheless became involved in various activities organised by the church, and were on very friendly terms with the succession of rectors and their wives who lived next door. During the thirty years we lived in Keston there were six different rectors, differing widely in character and disposition. Some we liked much better than others. On one occasion the church had been asked to find families who would put up members of an American choir that was touring various churches in Britain and who were going to sing in Keston Church. We were asked if we could put up two songsters. We agreed, and two very attractive young girls, one white and one black, were assigned to us.

Before they arrived at our house the rector came and knocked on the door. 'I just want to apologise,' he said.

'What for, Rector?'

'Well I understand that one of the girls who are coming to you is coloured.'

Pen and I couldn't believe our ears and felt insulted that he could imagine we might not want a black girl in our house.

'Of course we shall be very pleased to have her, Rector,' I said.

That particular rector's wife was a small, fluttery little lady, rather prim and proper. She called on us a few days after the girls came to Keston. She rang the bell and the door opened.

'Stick 'em up,' said David, dressed in cowboy costume and brandishing his six-shooter.

'Yeah, stick 'em up,' yelled Anthony. The poor lady didn't know what had hit her. Pen had to apologise profusely.

The next rector was very different. He was involved with the Ecumenical Society that works to establish good relations between many different churches. He was asked to host two Italian Roman Catholic priests who were in England for some conferences and wanted to improve their knowledge of English. The rector knew that Pen spoke Italian and asked if she would give them English lessons. Pen agreed and the next day the two priests arrived. I had previously imagined they would be like those rather elderly, sombre black-coated men found in the towns and villages of Italy, but was very surprised when two cheerful-looking youngsters arrived named Ferruccio and Vittorio, dressed in sports jackets and flannel trousers. Every morning for about a week they came to our house to work with Pen and we grew quite friendly.

One day the rector rang up. 'I'm awfully sorry,' he said, 'but we're going on holiday next week and I wondered whether you could put up Ferruccio and Vittorio for a few days while we're away.'

So they came to stay with us. They were very different characters. Vittorio was a calm, thoughtful person, dedicated to the priesthood, but Ferruccio longed to get married and would have willingly abandoned the priesthood if he had been able to get another job. His parents, as was the case with many poor families who lived in remote country areas, had sent him to a *seminario* at an early age. This was a school and university run by the Church where young boys could receive free board and education and eventually enter the priesthood. Ferruccio still lived with his mother in a small parish near Florence. At Torquay both boys went to see the Black and White Minstrel

Show in which Mary was dancing, which they much enjoyed, but Mary was pleased that we only stayed for the weekend. She was very embarrassed when Ferruccio made a pass at her after the show.

Back home in Keston the priests stayed with us for a few more days. One day they decided to go up to London to see the sights and take in a film. When they got back in the evening, Vittorio seemed rather subdued.

'Are all British films like that?' he asked.

'Like what?'

'Naked girls,' said Ferruccio. It turned out they had gone to a blue movie somewhere in Soho.

'No, of course not,' I said when I realised what had happened. 'You went to the wrong kind of cinema.'

We had been watching television when they came in, and as we heard about their experiences the programme changed. The new one was all about a nudist camp with plenty of shots of naked girls.

'I think I'll go to bed,' said Vittorio.

'I'll be up in a minute,' said Ferruccio as he settled down in front of the telly.

We told Ferruccio we were planning to visit our friends in Padova that summer.

'Then you must come and stay with me first. My mother would be so pleased to see you.'

So we did. Ferruccio met us at Florence in his battered old car and drove us up to the little village in the Tuscan hills where he and his mother lived, which was very beautiful. We left the main road just outside the village and drove up a long, sandy drive lined with cherry trees. Ferruccio told us later that he himself had made that drive. At the top was a very small church attached to a very small house. Ferruccio's mother came out to greet us. She had been a cook at a famous restaurant in Florence, so for the three days we were there we ate like lords. In the mornings when we had breakfast we could hear Ferruccio in the church next door intoning the mass. We began to realise how frustrated he had become in this beautiful but isolated place. His parish consisted of the church attached to his house and one other small church in a neighbouring village. His parishioners were mostly elderly residents or holidaymakers who rented houses in the area in the summer. Poor Ferruccio would have been much happier working in a parish like Vittorio's, which was in a small town and much involved with many local families and their children. As well as his pastoral duties, Vittorio organised football matches and other activities for the young people in his parish – activities that Ferruccio would have been very good at and would have enjoyed.

Eventually we heard that Ferruccio had left the priesthood and had opened an antique shop on the Ponte Vecchio in Florence. We never heard whether he had married.

All our children attended Sunday School at Keston run by a friend of Pen's who lived in our road. Her husband, who was a clergyman, had been killed in France during the D-Day invasion. Kathleen lived to be 101 and was mourned by the whole parish. Our children were very fond of her and took part in the various nativity plays put on in St Audrey's at Christmas time. I remember Anthony, when very young, playing an angel. In the colour photographs that I took of the performance Anthony's eyes shone bright red, making him look more like a devil.

In 1975 Mary and David (an American) were married in the Parish church by one of our favourite rectors, Geoffrey Hyder. David's grandmother, who had brought him up, flew over for the event. She lived in a remote farming town in Wisconsin and had travelled hardly at all. She had never seen the ocean. At aged eighty, however, she took it all in her stride and thoroughly enjoyed herself. We met her at Heathrow in the car, and I remember how surprised she was on the journey home.

'All the houses are joined together!' she exclaimed in amazement.

Many of our Italian friends came over for the wedding, and our neighbours rallied round to provide accommodation for them. We had a marquee in the garden for the wedding feast; David and his pop group played; people danced; altogether it was a very happy occasion.

CHAPTER EIGHTEEN: RETURN TO AMERICA

I n spite of my new journeys into space, my interest in
America and its songs didn't lessen. One of my most
successful programmes was called *The Blue and the Gray*
which told the story of the American Civil War (1861–1865)
and was first broadcast on the Home Service on 9 November
1955. It was primarily a documentary about the songs
produced by the war. The programme showed how the Civil
War developed and some of the battles were described, using
quotations from generals and soldiers.

'The South would have won if her songs had equalled those
of the North,' said a Confederate general. His view on how the
war was lost is, perhaps, a little exaggerated; but there can be
no doubt that the songs of both sides played an important role
in what was one of the bloodiest conflicts in American history.
Every war in which the US has been engaged since the fight for
independence has produced a good crop of national songs, but
none can compare in quantity or quality with those associated
with the 'War Between the States' (as Americans call their Civil
War). They were sung and played on the march, on the
battlefield, in camp and at home behind the lines. They
covered very many subjects, from red-blooded patriotism in
rousing marching numbers such as 'The Bonnie Blue Flag' and
the 'Battle Cry of Freedom', to pathos, humour, defiance,
resentment and even downright insult in songs such as 'The
Vacant Chair', 'Goober Peas', 'A Life on the Vicksburg Bluff'
and 'O, I'm a Good Old Rebel'. It is not possible to pin down
each song as belonging exclusively to one side or the other.

Neither side hesitated to steal a song from the other and adapt it to its own needs. A small change in the words would render it as useful to the enemy as to its originators.

Song publishers didn't hesitate to print songs (with modified words) that belonged to the enemy, even going so far as to reproduce the same pictures on the music covers. 'The Drummer Boy of Shiloh', written by W. S. Hayes, tells how a drummer boy, although wounded, continues to beat his tattoo and inspire his Southern comrades to stand up against almost overwhelming odds. The original copies of this music, first printed in the South in 1862, show the boy being carried on the shoulder of an infantryman with the Confederate battle flag high-flying and defiant as a backcloth. Within a few weeks the North had pirated the same song, with exactly the same picture on the cover except for the flag which had been changed to the Stars and Stripes of the Union.

'Tenting Tonight', 'All Quiet along the Potomac Tonight', 'The Vacant Chair,' 'Grafted into the Army' were songs sung by both sides. 'Dixie', the song of the South, was written by a Northerner and was popular in New York before anybody in the South had even heard of it.

In these days, of course, the blood-stirring melodies of the Civil War are looked upon as national tunes that belong to the whole nation – all except one: 'Marching through Georgia'. Never make the mistake of singing that song to a Southerner, particularly a Georgian. It rubbed salt into the Confederacy's greatest wound: Sherman's march from Atlanta, Georgia, to the sea. This was the march that tore the Confederacy in two and virtually finished the war.

A letter from an American living in London who heard the programme appeared in the *Radio Times* on 2 December 1955:

> May I, as an American in England and a former high school teacher in the US, suggest that your programme *The Blue and the Gray* be put on tape for distribution to educational institutions in America? I cannot imagine any teacher of history not welcoming such an imaginative and inspiring

device for teaching one of the most important phases of American history. Both the dramatic narrative and the moving music combine to present a comprehensive overall picture of the period and they leave a lasting impression. This was a great production.

As a result of my programme *The Blue and the Gray*, I was approached by a representative of the British Division of the Confederate High Command, who had heard the programme. He said they would like to confer the rank of Brigadier General of the British Confederate High Command upon me and hoped I would accept. Of course I did.

Soon after that I attended an auction sale in Brighton with Frank Humphris, who was always on the lookout for old rifles or handguns. I didn't want guns but I did see something that intrigued me. It was a ship's compass. On looking at it closely I saw the name 'Alabama' and realised it must have come from the English-built ship CSS *Alabama* which was used by Confederate sailors during the Civil War. I bought it. When I heard that the High Command were trying to raise money for the battlefield I sent it to Gettysburg, hoping it would make some money for them. It did. It raised £750 at auction and the money was used as the next payment on a 118-acre farm in the middle of the battlefield area.

I also wrote a series of programmes entitled *Frontier America*, in which I presented various periods of the American drive westward in song and speech. The programme dealt with early pioneers crossing the plains, the Gold Rush of 1849, the Mormon exodus to Salt Lake City, the coming of the railways, cattle ranching, law and order and the Indian Wars.

I felt I needed more direct contact with the issues I was writing about, and in 1961 I was thrilled when the BBC agreed to send me on a three-month trip to the States to refresh my knowledge of Western history, folklore, folk music etc. I was to collect printed and recorded material with the object of using it in future BBC programmes, as well as gain an impression of

American radio methods, particularly in western and southern areas.

I decided to take Pen with me so that as well as enjoying a fantastic new experience she could help me with the organisation of the trip and the recordings I hoped to make. To plan our journey we got hold of a Greyhound Bus schedule and found that we could travel anywhere along the way the buses travelled for ninety dollars each for ninety days. The company had specific routes and we had to travel according to its schedule. We could also stop off anywhere en route and catch other buses whenever we liked.

Before we left I wrote to various US travel organisations and chambers of commerce in the States that I hoped to visit, and as a result received many letters of welcome and offers of help. At that time America was just beginning to welcome tourists. Many states, especially those in the West, were keen to help us, and in doing so help to publicise the attractions and facilities of their particular state.

Leaving our children to be looked after by Pen's mother, we set sail on Friday 16 June 1961, on the SS *United States*, and docked at New York on Wednesday 21 June. I quickly made myself known to the BBC New York office and there I collected a recording machine and a number of tapes that had been forwarded from London for my use.

Four days later we left for Washington D.C. where we met with someone who was extremely helpful in putting me in touch with radio stations of all kinds. We also met with someone else who let the states of South Dakota, Wyoming, Montana, Utah and Georgia know I was coming, with the result that when we arrived at these places we were treated as special guests, offered free accommodation, and a guide and car to take us around.

We boarded a Greyhound bus from Washington on Sunday 25 June, bound for Pierre in South Dakota. The journey took about three days. We spent one night on the bus and one in a hotel in Sioux Falls, South Dakota. As we drove further west the bus drivers became much more communicative and gave us a running commentary on the country we passed through. We imagined Sioux Falls to be a small western town, particularly as we had to change from the Greyhound Line to the Jack Rabbit Line, and we were a bit worried as to where we would find accommodation when we arrived at midnight. We needn't have worried. Sioux Falls is a typical modern American town and the Sheridan Hotel at which we stayed was right opposite the bus station. It was good to have a bath and a comfortable bed.

Back in England we had been in touch with the State officials in South Dakota and had told them that we hoped to reach Pierre at about 5pm on 27 June. We were amazed that, in spite of a delay in St Louis and the various changes of buses we had to make, as we stepped off the bus in the centre of Pierre the town clock struck five o'clock. We were welcomed by the state official who looked after us while we were there and took us to our accommodation in a small motel.

It was in South Dakota that I hoped to visit some Indian reservations, but our guide had other ideas. What he most wanted us to see were all the improvements made in Pierre since his party had won the state election. He took us first to the Oahe dam on the Missouri River, which had been built to control the river in this very dry land, and was preparing other tours of this kind when I asked how I could get to see an Indian reservation. He looked puzzled. Why would I want to do that and how would I get there?

'By train or bus?' I suggested.

'No trains around here,' he replied. 'There's only one bus a week to the Rosebud Indian reservation and that went yesterday.'

Fortunately, at a dinner given that evening in our honour, I met up with John Artichoke, the director of Indian education. I explained my problem.

'I'll see what I can do,' he said. 'Be ready to leave in the morning.'

Next morning we were up early, not knowing quite what to expect. Soon after breakfast there was knock on the door, and there stood a tall Highway Patrol police officer who told us that he had come to take us to the Rosebud Indian reservation. This and the Pine Ridge reservation were where the Dakota Sioux Indians had been confined after the last Indian wars of the nineteenth century. I asked our driver how he came to be allowed to take us to the Rosebud in an official patrol car.

'Well,' he replied, 'I just happened to be going this way on a skunk hunt.'

'Are there many skunks around here?'

'Plenty of human ones,' he replied with a grin.

The journey from Pierre to the reservation was some two hundred miles across barren-looking grasslands. I had seen many Indians in the town while we were at Pierre and asked the driver how they got there with little or no public transport.

'Oh,' he said, 'they walk.'

When we arrived at White River on 29 June 1961, we were taken to meet several Sioux families living on the reservation. Their living standards varied considerably. This was because when the reservation was set up and the land divided amongst the many Indians on the site, some who were more astute bought up the portions allocated to others and so became virtual land owners. One such owned a ranch and was about to go on holiday in Hawaii when we met him. The majority, however, lived in much poorer conditions in log cabins, and had little or no land of their own, like Jesse Whitefeather. Outside his little cabin was a large, old-fashioned automobile. I asked him whether he drove it.

'No,' he said, 'I keep my clothes in it.'

He also had a traditional sweat bath, in which stones were heated up in a kind of wickiup (wigwam).

Mr Knox (Chief Ironshell) posed so that could photograph him outside his small log cabin home in full Indian costume, complete with flowing head-dress. We were also taken to see the Indian tribal council and to meet Mrs

Leader Charge, the reservation Junior Judge. I asked her how she got her name.

'My husband led a famous charge against the white men,' she told me, 'and was called Leader Charge thenceforward.'

'And what was your name before you were married?' I asked.

'Smith,' she replied. Maybe Joseph Smith and his Mormons had passed through her village.

Mrs Leader Charge was a well-educated, delightful person. Years later when we went to see the film *Dances with Wolves* we saw her name on the credit list as Indian language adviser.

After our day at the Rosebud we were taken to Pine Ridge. It was dark by the time we got there and we were left at our sleeping place, the Pine Ridge Boys' School. The boys were on holiday so just the two of us slept in a long dormitory of about forty beds. We woke in the morning dying for a cup of tea or coffee. There was no one in the school but us, so no catering facilities were available.

Then I remembered seeing the illuminated sign 'Coca Cola' on a small building when we'd driven through the dark street the night before. Where there was Coca Cola maybe there would be coffee. We set off along the road. On either side were log cabins with Indians sitting outside. They must have wondered who we were and how we had got there as we had no car or transport of any kind. With their long braided hair hanging beneath Stetson hats they sat there silent and unmoving, only their eyes following our progress.

We reached the café. There was a bar and several tables at which Indians were sitting. We found a free table and the Indian bar tender came to see what we wanted.

'Could we have breakfast?'

'Sure. What would you like?'

'Have you a menu?'

'I think so.'

He went to the bar and came back with a dog-eared Greyhound bus menu that he handed to us. It had the typical choices of such menus: No. 1 Egg and bacon; No. 2 Sausage, beans, bacon; and so on up to the fullest category which was No. 12. I said I would have No. 2 while Pen chose No. 1. The bar tender looked at us.

'Well,' he said, 'now's the time to tell you we've only got sausage! Mind you,' he added, 'it's the best sausage on Pine Ridge – that's because it's the *only* sausage on Pine Ridge.' As we looked around the room we saw the Indians sitting at their tables covering their mouths with their hands as they laughed.

Having eaten our breakfast, we went up to the bar to pay.

'Where do you folks come from?' the bar tender asked us.

'London,' we said.

'Oh, that's in Canada, ain't it?'

'No, no, London, England.'

'England? Way across the ocean?'

'Yes.'

He thought for a moment. 'What happened? You got lost or sump'n?'

We went back to the school where the superintendent of the Pine Ridge reservation arrived to take us on a tour. Pine Ridge is the largest Indian Reservation in South Dakota, and at the time we were there contained 8,200 Sioux Indians. As on the Rosebud, we visited many places, took many photographs and interviewed a number of people.

One of the first places we visited was a factory that attached fishhooks onto cards for anglers. At that time it was the only factory on an Indian reservation. We were taken to see the Indians at work and found to our surprise that the majority were women. Mr Towle explained that they had built the factory to supply work for male Indians who had almost nothing to do. But most of the men found it impossible to adapt themselves to factory life: arriving at the same place at the same time of day and doing the same thing day after day was foreign to their former way of providing for their families by hunting, fishing or fighting. In the end they would give up, and it was their wives who found it much easier to adapt to factory life and thereby become the breadwinners of the family.

I found all the Sioux Indians I met friendly, hospitable and extremely co-operative. They had a good sense of humour and were glad of the chance to take part in recorded interviews. The superintendents were selfless and devoted people whose concern for their charges seemed greatly to outweigh their concern for themselves.

Our next port of call was Rapid City, also in South Dakota, where Paul Besselievre, manager of the Black Hills and Badlands and Lakes Association, met us at the Sheridan Hotel. I had been in touch with him from London and he was overwhelmingly helpful and enthusiastic about all my projects, providing free accommodation and free transport to wherever I wanted to go. He took us first to the Black Hills, where we saw most of the sights including the 'Shrine of Democracy' at Mount Rushmore, where the faces of Presidents Washington, Jefferson, Lincoln and Theodore Roosevelt are carved from the face of the mountain. We also saw the site of the original gold mines, whose discovery by General Custer sparked off the great Sioux wars of the 1870s. The Black Hills were sacred to the Sioux. When gold seekers began to flock into them after Custer's announcement that the region contained precious metal, war was inevitable.

To me it was incredible that I was actually in and seeing these places that I had read and written about so often. There was even a herd of buffalo grazing on the hills. We photographed them, as well as some pronghorn antelopes and wild donkeys.

On the viewing platform from which visitors gaze up at Mount Rushmore there stood the 'official' Black Hills Indian, Ben Black Elk. He looked very romantic with his long, black hair and traditional Sioux costume. He was there to answer visitors' questions, to pose for their cameras or to sign the postcards of himself that they had bought.

That evening, Ben Black Elk, his wife and family came to our motel and we spent a fascinating evening with them. At first I didn't recognise Black Elk when he arrived because his long black hair had gone. He only put it on when he was on duty. He had agreed to be interviewed and gave me some of the most valuable and interesting material of the whole trip. We talked about Indian history, language, religion, the Black Hills, music, art and folklore. Then he called his grandchildren, Little Igloo, Chase Along and Defends the Flag, together. Would we like them to dance a rain dance? We would indeed. So while Black Elk sang and beat a drum, the children danced.

It happened that there had been a long drought in South Dakota at the time, and ranchers were having to kill off some of their cattle because of the shortage of food. But that night the rain came down in torrents. Next morning, when we were getting ready to leave the motel, a group of local farmers appeared. They begged us to ask the Indians to dance another rain dance for them.

We set off for Wyoming on Sunday 2 July. Our driver and guide took us in his car to see all the interesting sights. The Devil's Tower, a huge rock formation that has many connections with Indian history and legend, stands in a National Park that is also a game preserve. Here we had our first glimpses of prairie dogs. We photographed them and I tried to record the peculiar barking noise they make, but none of them ventured to utter a sound.

Our next stop was Sheridan. To get there we had to drive some 200 miles or more across the flattest, roughest, most deserted-looking prairie country you could imagine. In the far distance we could see the outline of the Big Horn Mountains. After driving for two hours the country on either side of the flat, straight road looked exactly the same as before except that the mountains looked a little nearer. In all that time we saw only one very small bar on the side of the road where we stopped to have a drink. Ron explained that it was very important in that type of country to make sure you had drinking water in the car. If you broke down you might not see another vehicle for hours, and without water you would be in a bad way.

We spent the night at Sheridan and next day set off to cross the Big Horn Mountains. The scenery was fantastic, everything so lush and green compared with the country we had just driven through, and there were beautiful displays of wild lupins growing everywhere.

On the other side of the mountains we arrived at Cody where we visited the Buffalo Bill Cody Museum and the Whitney Gallery of Western Art (devoted entirely to western subjects). In the museum we saw the famous Deadwood Stagecoach, the oldest stagecoach in western history. That same day we drove on to Yellowstone Park, arriving there late at night. Our accommodation was at Canyon Village in a simple but comfortable log hut. Our tour of Yellowstone Canyon, with its falls, geysers and so on, lasted all the next day. In spite of the bad weather we were bowled over by it all. The famous 'Old Faithful' geyser did not erupt, but we did see many bubbling sulphur cauldrons and much wildlife including bears, deer and moose. Brown and black bears lined our route, most looking rather miserable in the pouring rain.

The Yellowstone ranger who accompanied us told us many stories about bears and stupid tourists who got out of their cars to photograph them – one couple even tried to take a picture of a child sitting on the bear's back. He also had a story about one of his own rangers who got out of his car to tell off some tourists who were behaving stupidly and dangerously. Unfortunately, in his hurry, the ranger had forgotten to shut the door of his own car and found a bear sitting in it when he got back.

Our last memory of Yellowstone was of a fantastic sunset over Yellowstone Lake. The next morning a new guide arrived to drive us over the Bear Tooth Mountains way above the tree line and among the snow banks into Custer National Park, just over the state line in Montana.

On Wednesday 5 July we set out for Billings, the Custer Battlefield and the Northern Cheyenne Reservation. Here I was able to interview Alonzo Spang, the only Cheyenne Indian at that time who had the ability or desire to win himself a university education. The Cheyenne were quite the poorest and most backward Indians I met during my travels. Alonzo told me of his plans to help better the lot of the Cheyenne, to stamp out the bad old customs and to try to convince his people that sanitation is just as important for good living as the survival of old tribal dances. A problem was the aversion the Cheyenne had towards white men's medicine. Tuberculosis was rife on the reservation, but they preferred their own tribal remedies to the reservation hospital. To show how bad the white man's medicine was they would treat patients with their tribal remedies and when they showed no signs of getting better and were about to die they allowed them to enter the hospital. When they died there, to them it showed that white men's medicine didn't work.

When we arrived, the Cheyenne were making preparations for the Sun Dance. As we looked, a special lodge was being built because the Sun Dance was to begin that night. Alonzo explained that the Sun Dance is a religious ceremony, although it has now lost some of its religious meaning. It's an annual affair where the young braves dance. Each brave has a reason for dancing and starving himself for two days and two nights – to ask a favour or to express thanks for someone's help. The last day when the Sun Dance is nearly over is the most spectacular. After fasting for two days and two nights, the Sun Dancers will run in four directions – the four points of the compass – out of the lodge and then back again. At first all that the dancers will be wearing is a black blanket wrapped around their bodies and they have a little whistle that they blow through and keep time with the music. But at the end of the second day when they run out of the lodge the dancers are painted up in brilliant colour combinations and it is a really spectacular sight. We were very sad not to have the time to see this.

The tour of Montana ended at Helena, the state capital. It had been arranged that we would meet the state Governor, Donald Nutter. He was a charming man and seemed pleased to meet us. I apologised for interrupting his busy schedule.

'Don't worry about that,' he said with a grin. 'It's such a pleasure to meet someone who doesn't want to tell me how to run the state!'

From Helena we set off once again on a Greyhound bus, heading for Utah and Salt Lake City. We found the bus journeys very interesting. At the frequent 'rest stops' for refreshment and toilets we got talking to several of our fellow passengers. I remember one woman in particular. She was a schoolteacher and sat behind us in the coach. As we drank our coffee she said:

'Are you folks from England?'

'Yes,' we said.

'Oh, do please go on talking,' she said, 'I love to hear the way you talk.'

She was thrilled to meet us. At her school she had organised classes in which the children pretended to meet and befriend people from other lands who were visiting their country, and here she was doing just that. She couldn't get over it.

We became very aware of the colour bar problem. Negroes and Indians always had to stand at the back of buses, and at places such as St Louis they were not allowed to eat at the white folks' restaurants or bars. We felt acutely angry and embarrassed by this.

At one point the bus stopped beside a stretch of sagebrush covered desert with no signs of habitation in sight. A tall Indian who had been standing at the back of the bus got out and walked into the desert.

'Where's he going?' I asked the driver.

'Home,' he replied.

We arrived in Salt Lake City at 7.15am on Friday 7 July. We were made very welcome and were guests of the Mormon Church during our stay at the Church-owned Temple Square Hotel. When we arrived we turned on the radio in our hotel bedroom, only to hear one of my own programmes! It was part of the *Frontier America* series I had done for transcription overseas and dealt with the Mormon trek westward and the building of Salt Lake City.

One of the purposes of my trip was to gain an impression of American radio methods, particularly in the West and South. What listening I managed to undertake usually took place in the hotel of the town in which I was staying. At first I listened avidly, staying up until the small hours of the morning so as to miss as little as possible. But even though I tuned from one station to another, I soon found that most local stations in the West transmitted almost identical programme fare. All music was supplied from gramophone records, which were themselves supplied by the record companies free of charge in exchange for the 'plug'. Nearly all the discs were chosen from the top twenty, thirty, fifty or hundred best sellers. All over the US the same few records were being played over and over again from thousands of local stations, interspersed with news flashes, announcements of the temperature and humidity, and the inevitable commercial.

Fortunately there was a group of broadcasters in America who aimed to raise the standards of American radio programmes. One of these was KSL at Salt Lake City, which proved to be the best radio station we heard during our whole trip. KSL is a 'clear channel station', located on a frequency which it has for its exclusive use. Its power was 50,000 watts and although there were nine radio stations in Salt Lake City, KSL was way ahead of the rest in general popularity. Compared with other American radio stations the area covered by it was vast and its output considerably more varied and interesting. The fact that I heard one of my programmes on it was proof that the station was in touch with the BBC's transcription service (the other stations I had visited had not even heard of it).

The Mormon Church owns the station. It has a symphony orchestra, the Tabernacle Choir, the resident organists at the Tabernacle, the State University and only a few miles away the Brigham Young Mormon Church University at Provo. Consequently the station had first call on most of the available talent in the area. I interviewed several of the station's organisers and they assured me that they made no attempt to force the doctrines of the Church on their listeners and that in fact many of its staff were non-Mormons. One of those I interviewed said:

> The policy of KSL is established by the L.D.S. Church. The Church does not dictate programme content but may object to certain items being included, e.g. rock-and-roll.
>
> Sometime during the day there is a programme to cater for almost every taste. But rock-and-roll is taboo on KSL unless we want to make fun of it or to make comparative analysis.

We spent the first morning being shown the historic Temple Square, the meeting house, the Tabernacle and the Temple (the outside only because 'gentiles' are not allowed inside). We attended an organ recital in the Tabernacle and on the following day a broadcast of the Mormon Tabernacle Choir.

To our surprise, our guide throughout our stay in the city was not a Mormon. He was, however, married to a Mormon. I interviewed him and his wife at their home.

'Do you think Salt Lake City is a better city than most?'

'Absolutely. The crime rate is down; there are no big slums; the city is clean; it's the place to raise your children if you're out of town. I know many people come here and take a salary cut just to have an opportunity to live here and raise their children.'

'But you are not a member of the church?'

'No sir. I am Greek Orthodox. There is a Greek Orthodox Church here; nearly every other church is represented; there's a big Catholic cathedral; there are Methodists, Jehovah's Witnesses and so on. They get along real fine with the L.D.S people.'

I asked Tom's wife whether it was difficult being married to a non-Mormon and how much time being a Mormon took up. Being married to a non-Mormon was no problem, she said. Her duties as a Mormon took up about ten hours a week. Sundays were for Sunday school and singing in the choir. During the week there was the Relief Society.

'What does the Relief Society do?'

'It takes care of any relief work the church might have. We give to the poor and needy; when someone goes to hospital to have a baby we look in on the husband and the children that are left at home. When there is a passing away we are right at the door to offer any assistance we can. There are MIA [Mutual Improvement Association] meetings for younger people of the Church: athletic programmes, dances, socials, etc. On Sunday evenings there is a meeting called the Sacrament meeting. This is the only meeting that Mormons are duty bound to attend.'

Salt Lake City was certainly the most impressive town we visited. Its wide streets, interspersed with water fountains, its historic buildings and monuments, its culture and musical heritage, all paid tribute to its original founders. As we stood by the 'This is the Place' monument, marking the spot where Brigham Young announced that the city should be built, we marvelled at the immense difficulties those early pioneers had overcome. All building materials had to be obtained from the hard rock of the encircling mountains; water had to be diverted from the mountains; crops were grown on most unfavourable land, only to be threatened by hordes of devouring locusts. The famous 'Seagull Monument' records the answer to the pioneers' prayers – a flock of seagulls flew in and devoured the locusts.

Almost twenty-four hours' travel on the Continental Line Bus from Salt Lake City brought us to Santa Fe, the ancient capital of New Mexico and the oldest town in the United States. We admired its old churches, palaces, cathedral and other places of interest to be found in the old Spanish town. From Santa Fe we were taken to Taos, also in New Mexico. We stopped off at various Indian villages and Spanish Mission churches. We also stopped at the San Juan Reservation of Pueblo Indians. These tribes are very different from the warlike Sioux of the north. They used to live in villages – pueblos – built into the side of the hills. But nowadays their homes are sun-baked adobe houses on the reservation.

A Spanish-speaking Indian named Trujillo showed us round. He took us into his house, which was clean and comfortably cool. It contained the largest television set I'd ever seen. Although the family cooking was done outside the pueblos in primitive 'bee-hive' ovens, nearly all the houses had TV aerials towering above them. We visited the house of another less well-off Pueblo Indian and admired the smooth white walls of his room.

'How did you manage to get the walls so smooth?' I asked.

'Wife with hand,' was the reply!

The next bus we caught was to Flagstaff in Arizona and the Grand Canyon. Here we planned to have two days' rest from interviewing, recording and collecting material for future programmes. To see the Grand Canyon was pure enjoyment. We took the little bus that circles round the Canyon, allowing passengers to get off at various points and see the wonders below. At each stopping place the canyon presented a different aspect, mind-boggling in its depth and coloration. I took many photographs of the canyon itself and of the half-wild chipmunks, blue jays and other creatures that were there.

Behind us in the bus sat two elderly ladies, clearly American tourists from the East. They got off with the rest of us at the first stopping point on the canyon's edge, but after that their conversation went something like this:

'Do you want to get off the bus again, Dora?'

'No. I don't think so, do you?'

'Naw – what's there to see – only a lot of old cliffs and stones!'

On the way back to Flagstaff they were looking out of the windows at some wild turkeys grazing on the hillside.

'Oh look, Dora – look at those birds!'

'What are they?'

'Ostriches I guess.'

We returned to Flagstaff for the night in a motel and caught the bus for Tombstone via Tucson early the next morning. It was a great pleasure to see all my old friends in Tombstone once again and to introduce Pen to them. The school teacher Ben Ridge and his wife Betty, with whom I had become friendly on my first trip, invited us to stay at their home and we were welcomed enthusiastically by many others.

The town itself had not changed – or rather it had changed for the better. Since the advent of television the city had experienced an all-year-round boom in tourists. Tombstone still retains nearly all its original buildings and everyone was working hard to restore the interiors of places such as the Wells Fargo Office, the Last Chance Saloon, the Bird Cage Theatre, the Nellie Cashman Sporting House and the Town Marshall's office. The entire population seemed to have gone into the museum business, scouring the country for old photographs, mining tools, old wagons, stagecoaches, and so forth, which were put on display. Even the state had stepped in and taken over the cost of restoring the courthouse to what it was in its rip-roaring days. The latest acquisition was the gallows, which had been re-erected in the courthouse yard.

I interviewed Mrs Macia, a very old lady who had arrived in the town in the early 1880s in a covered wagon.

'Could you tell me how Tombstone looked in your very young days?' I asked her. 'Was it very different from now?

'Not at all,' she replied. 'Just the same. I walk along the same streets; the same buildings were there when I was a child.

Now a window or a doorway has been changed, but the same walls, and the same outsides – in fact some of the streets are just the same as they were when I first went to school.'

'How did you, as a respectable family in Tombstone, live with the kind of life that went on there?'

'Well, I don't know how I can explain it to you, but my life was a perfectly normal and everyday life. But in the town there was a kind of life that was very different. There was a certain area my father very firmly forbade us to go into.'

Mrs Macia told me that her father thought a lot of Wyatt Earp and had been his friend. She reckoned that Earp has been painted as a grafter and not as a credit to the town. She thought the town wouldn't have sponsored such a person.

While I was interviewing Mrs Macia, we were sitting outside her house in the shade of the most magnificent rose bush I have ever seen. I asked her how it came to be there.

'This rose was sent to a young woman who came from England in the early days. Her husband was a young mining engineer. The young woman found Tombstone and its surroundings the most barren, forsaken country that she had ever seen and she was quite unhappy. So her folks in England sent her this rose – a white Banksia rose – and it was planted here at the end of the porch. It grew and grew and today Ripley says it is the world's largest rose bush. [Ripley was an American journalist who wrote a column about amazing facts, *Believe It or Not.*] It is more than seventy-five feet across in every direction. The trunk is over seven feet in circumference and there are something like sixty-nine supports under it of various kinds.'

Another great character I interviewed in Tombstone was Sid Wilson. He was eighty-two years old and had first come to the town in 1898. All his life had been spent with horses, mules and cattle. He had had freight teams which would haul silver from the mines and deliver it all over Arizona. He had driven stagecoaches for many years and had a contract with John Slaughter (who became Sheriff of Tombstone) to break horses for him at his ranch in San Bernadine near the Mexican border during the Spanish-American war. In 1900 he sailed to England as part of Buffalo Bill Cody's Wild West show and spent three weeks in London.

'Did you meet Queen Victoria?' I asked.

'Oh yes. We dined in Buckingham Palace along with all the rest of them after the performance. You would have thought we belonged to the Royal family the way we were treated. She was one of the most loveable women I ever met. Everybody with the show fell in love with Queen Victoria.'

'Can you remember what London was like then?'

'Well, not much, no. The only place I ever remembered was what they called Piccadilly Square.'

'Now your life is not so active, Sid, but would you tell our listeners what you do now?'

'Oh, I fool around this trail. I hunt a little bit sometimes, and we handle the horses in moving picture jobs; occasionally I drive stagecoaches in the pictures, or teams of any kind for freight-teams and so on. I'm not very wild any more.'

'I hear you reconstructed the O.K. Corral in Tombstone and rebuilt it to look exactly as it did.'

'Well, I just uncovered the old foundations and it was put back as far as it goes now. Originally it ran clear through the block, but they built the city hall and the jail there, which would make it impossible to put it all back like it was. But this end here is back like it was.'

'Do you remember any of the Wyatt Earp family?'

'I knew Wyatt Earp himself pretty well, but that was over in California in 1918–19. I had my teams in the oil fields at Beaconsfield, California. But I never spoke to him about Tombstone. We talked in a business way about oil leases – the pipes to be hauled – working the teams and hauling.'

The people of Tombstone were genuinely impressed that I should have bothered to visit them a second time. Before I left the town I was asked to become honorary mayor of

Tombstone, with my wife as mayoress, an honour I gladly accepted.

From Tombstone we went to San Antonio in Texas, where we attended a fiesta or Mexican folk singing and dancing and a grand barbecue at Palmetto State Park, some seventy miles from the city. On the way back a thunderstorm broke. We arrived back in the city to find many of the streets flooded to a depth of more than three feet. Some crossroads appeared to be raging torrents. A man attempting to cross the road at one badly flooded point was swept away and drowned. But in spite of the bad weather we visited many places of interest in the city, including the old Spanish Governor's Palace, La Vallita (the Mexican quarter) and, of course, the Alamo.

Our next port of call was New Orleans on Monday 24 July. We went there at the invitation of the radio station WNPS. Two members of WNPS staff took us on a tour of this beautiful city, so different in style and character from other US cities. We admired the lovely old buildings in the French district and the Rigolets Bridge, which we crossed on leaving the city. We were very distressed to read about the devastation and flooding caused by Hurricane Katrina in August 2005.

We were taken out to 'Beverley Hills' – the country was as flat as a pancake – to appear on a pre-filmed television programme, which took place alongside a swimming pool. WNPS makes use of many BBC programmes produced by the London transcription service, and we were amazed to find that all the people we met at that recording session were enthusiastic listeners of *The Goon Show*. They were delighted to know that I had produced many of the episodes and besieged us with questions about the show and other programmes.

We left next morning at 8am by train, en route for Atlanta in Georgia, a journey that took seventeen hours. I had read a great deal about Atlanta and the important part it had played during the American Civil War, so we were somewhat surprised to read the banner flying over the town. It said nothing about the war or Atlanta's part in it, even though 1961 marked the start of a four-year official centenary celebration. The banner read: 'Atlanta, The Home of Coca Cola!'

During our first morning in the city I called at the Georgia Department of Commerce at the State Capital and introduced myself to my host, Bill Hardman, who gave us a real Southern welcome. We spent the morning touring the State Capital and the Georgia Museum and were taken to the top of Atlanta's tallest skyscraper where the landmarks that featured in the Civil War battle for the city were pointed out to us. Then we toured the city, visited a number of ante-bellum style houses and the largest supermarket in the world, itself the size of a small town.

The afternoon was spent viewing the famous Cyclorama of the Battle of Atlanta, and visiting station WSB (television and radio). WSB was another high-powered 'clear channel' station, similar to the one we had visited in Salt Lake City. It was the most beautiful radio and television station I saw in all my travels, built in southern ante-bellum style and very luxuriously furnished.

The part Atlanta played in the Civil War was well documented in the town. Confederacy flags adorned many buildings and Civil War trinkets for tourists abounded in the shops. We were presented with a cigarette lighter that played 'Dixie' when operated. At a restaurant where we were taken for lunch the menu, too, reflected the Civil War atmosphere. We chose Kentucky fried chicken, but after a delay were told unfortunately there was none left; so instead we chose 'Confederate Steak with Southern Fries'.

The waiter said: 'Sorry, sir, the Confederate Steak is off. All we can offer you is Shiloh Meat Balls.'

I turned to my host, saying, 'The Civil War atmosphere is most realistic – the blockade must still be on!'

From Atlanta we travelled by train to Gettysburg. During our visit we were taken on a tour of the Battlefield. It was a great experience to stand on the site of that famous battle about which I had read and written so much.

We spent a few days with friends in Brookfield, Connecticut before returning to New York and embarking once again on the *SS United States* for England. Before leaving I arranged for the many books and pamphlets I had bought to be sent to me in England. I had to buy a large trunk in which to put them all. We arrived back in England on 9 August.

Once back at work in Aeolian Hall I immediately started putting in ideas for programmes, such as *How the West was Won*, a series of thirteen one-hour programmes on the history of the West from the Spanish conquest to modern times; *Blood on the Prairie*, an 'authentic Western drama based on the Indian wars'; *The Trampling Herd*; *The Buffalo People*; *The Longhorn*; *I Hear America Singing*; and *This is the Place*, the story of Joseph Smith, Brigham Young and the building of Salt Lake City. These and many others went out in the years following our trip.

My American experience also expanded into country and western music, following a meeting with George Hamilton IV, a country and western singer and guitarist who became very popular in England. He often came over to do tours around Britain and Ireland and recorded many shows for me. One was a series called *A-Pickin' and a-Grinnin'*, a long series for which I often had to go over to South Carolina where George lived to record the show with him and his musical group leader Arthur Smith. George became a friend and I often stayed at his house in South Carolina. He had three children, Mary the eldest and two sons, George V and George VI! He once took me to a great family reunion where I met many of his older relations. When I was introduced to his grandfather, the old man shook my hand and said, 'English are you? Well, we licked you didn't we?'

I was now a Deputy Marshal of Tombstone, Arizona; a Deputy Mayor of Tombstone; 'Chief Long Knife, of the Osage

Indians' and Brigadier General of the Confederate High Command – not bad for a cockney lad from King's Cross!

CHAPTER NINETEEN
MUSICAL DOCUMENTARIES

While writing my programmes on American subjects I often went to the American Embassy to do my research. Ironically enough it was one of the many people who helped me there, Bill Gausman, who asked why I always wrote about US songs and not about those from Britain. I didn't really know the answer to this. Possibly it was because I had been so influenced by Alistair Cooke that I hadn't considered investigating British songs that reflected British history.

I soon found out that the possibilities for writing about British songs were endless. Pen and I scoured the British Museum library and many other sources for songs reflecting various periods of history, and came up with programmes such as *A Ballad History of Samuel Pepys, Dickens' London* and *Marching to Glory* (the story of the Salvation Army).

I'd loved going to music halls as a child and wrote many programmes about them, such as *Songs that Made the Halls, A Little of What You Fancy* (about Marie Lloyd), and a long series with Roy Hudd, the presenter of the programme, called *Vintage Music Hall.*

Musical documentaries, illustrating history through song, became my forte. Someone who did a great deal to make my programmes with music so successful was Alfie Ralston. Van Phillips, who had created the music for *Journey into Space,* introduced me to him. Alfie was a born musician. He taught himself saxophone and clarinet and was often employed by

Van, both as instrumentalist and arranger. He also played the piano and had perfect pitch. He began working for me as an arranger on shows such as *Century of Song* and historical documentaries such as *The Victorian Age*. At that time, as well as the BBC Symphony Orchestra, the BBC employed a number of light music orchestras such as the Variety Orchestra, the Revue Orchestra, the Midland Light Orchestra (based in Birmingham) and the BBC Concert Orchestra. I used all these orchestras in my programmes at various times.

Alfie, like Van, became expert at arranging songs in the style and period in which they were originally written. He was one of the best musicians I've known, and became a great friend.

There were many singers who nearly always took part in a Chilton production, such as Rita Williams and Pat Whitmore. The latter could sing anything from a lively cockney song to a straight ballad and – something that didn't always happen with other performers – you could always hear what she was singing about. Charlie Young was another regular. He had a vocal group, a quartet of singers who took part on many occasions. Then there were Charles West and John Gower, baritone and bass, and Benny Lee who sang the jazz numbers. Edric Connor sang Negro songs and spirituals, and George Mitchell's minstrels were always there when needed. Instrumentalists, too, became regulars in my shows: people such as Danny Levin, violin, who tragically died very young; Billy Bell on banjo; Jack Fallon, double bass and fiddle, and many others.

Music publishers were always a bit of a problem. They were always anxious to get their songs broadcast and kept producers up to date with news of their latest offerings. Since the row, soon after the war, when a producer called Tawney Nielson was found guilty of taking objects such as fur coats from publishers in return for putting their songs on the air, one had to be very careful. I made it perfectly clear that I didn't accept bribes.

Some music publishers, such as Eddie Standring of Campbell Connelly and Company, became good friends. He told me a story about a music publisher who was trying to promote one of his songs in Blackpool. He tried to popularise the song by selling copies on the beach. It didn't go down very well at first. After a few days, however, hundreds of people suddenly started queuing up for copies. At first he was delighted, but subsequently not so pleased when he learnt the reason: the local fish-and-chip shop had run out of newspaper with which to wrap their wares!

My researches into popular song led to my accumulating a large library of songs of all kinds and of all periods. I was not looking for published songs by well-known composers: rather, songs that reflected the lives and feelings of ordinary people – popular song.

In medieval times wandering minstrels popularised songs by singing them in court and in the countryside, at fairs and taverns. After the invention of printing, ballad sellers hawked their broadsides all over England, thus becoming distributors not only of popular song but also of the news of the day. In the eighteenth century the common people learnt their songs – street ballads – through the medium of theatres and fairgrounds, taverns and pleasure gardens.

In the research for my programmes I delved into all aspects of popular song. People such as Pepys and Roxburghe started collecting the flimsy ballad sheets, which can be studied at many museums and libraries. No music was printed on these broadside ballads, but often the tune was indicated at the top of the sheet – sometimes a folk song and sometimes a popular song of the time. When there was no tune indicated it was often possible to tell by the words what tune would fit it.

At the beginning of the nineteenth century, songs were also being published in little volumes such as *The Universal Songster*. In the edition of 1828 I found this parody on the popular pleasure gardens song 'The Lass of Richmond Hill', entitled 'The Brixton Tread Mill'.

On Brixton Hill there stands a shop
Oft known to Cyprians fair
Where prigs and knowing swells oft stop
To taste the Surrey air
There you will meet
Black Sal so neat
Though much against your will
'Hard fate, my eyes'
The black nymph cries
'To tread the Brixton Mill'

These parodies and many like them, which are true reflections of social history, would have been sung at the smaller and less respectable pleasure gardens and in taverns which, by the beginning of the nineteenth century, had become a feature of drinking places all over England.

In 1815 a man arrived in London who was to be responsible for the first great boom in popular song writing and distribution. His name was James (known as Jemmy) Catnach. At the age of twenty-two he set up as a printer and publisher of 'ballads, battledores, primers, etc.' at No. 2 Monmouth Court in the Seven Dials district. Here, using an old wooden press brought with him from Alnwick where he'd previously lived, he printed and published small books for children, penny histories and halfpenny songs on flimsy sheets illustrated with crude woodcuts.

Jemmy didn't care what song he published; it might be old, new, topical, sentimental, horrific or sensational, so long as it appealed to his public, the great mass of British people. Catnach was lucky. His arrival in London was followed by a number of sensational events that provided ideal material for a ballad printer. Politics and party strife ran high. The working classes, suffering appalling conditions under a grossly unfair distribution of the country's wealth, were beginning to object. After the victory of Waterloo and final defeat of the French in 1815, conditions for the poor became even worse. Returning soldiers and sailors swelled the ranks of the unemployed;

angry mobs and riots were the order of the day. Catnach unashamedly played on the feelings of the dissatisfied poor to sell his publications.

In 1820 the death of George III sparked off a royal row that was the making of Catnach. The trial of Caroline of Brunswick, wife of the Prince Regent, now George IV, for adultery sparked off numerous caricatures, political squibs and satirical songs emanating from all sections of the press, some for the King and some for the Queen. Catnach well knew that the common people were all for the Queen. Ballads poured out of his presses in her praise.

On 24 October 1823 John Thurtell murdered William Weare in Gill's Hill Lane, near Elstree. Catnach made £500 out of this event, for as well as the ballads providing news and gory details of the murder there were news sheets about Thurtell's trial to be sold and the 'Last Dying Speech and Confession of the Murder'. Social injustice, royalty, shocking rape and murder thus became the cornerstone of the Catnach Press.

'Songs if they're over-religious,' said one ballad seller, 'don't sell at all; though a tidy moral does werry well. But a god-awful murder's the thing. I've knowed a man sell a ream a day of them – that's forty dozen you know. There's nothing beats a stunning good murder!'

Catnach died in 1841, but the trade of which he became master did not die with him. In 1871 there were still at least four ballad presses in London.

Pepys, Roxburghe, Bagford and others have preserved the earliest ballads for posterity. Sabine Baring-Gould, Thomas Crampton, Charles Hindley and many anonymous collectors have done the same for the street ballads of the nineteenth century. In the Baring-Gould collection alone there are nearly twelve thousand ballads. In the eight volumes of Crampton's collection there must be five or six thousand.

The ballad collections which I found in the British and London Libraries were a great source of material for my social history programmes. Catnach and his successors featured in my programme *Royalty, Rape and Murder*. Queen Victoria's marriage provided the Seven Dials presses with a great deal of ballad material. Albert was not popular with the Queen's subjects. He was looked upon as a poverty-stricken, obscure German prince who, in his marriage to the British sovereign, saw the means of acquiring a vast fortune and control of the British throne. A verse from one ballad reads:

> Here I am in rags
> From the land of all dirt
> To marry England's Queen
> And my name is Prince Albert

Another is entitled 'A Fine Young German Gentleman':

> I'll sing you a fine new song
> made by a modern pate
> Of a fine young prince of Saxe Gotha
> Who had a small estate
> And who lived in an old castle
> At a parsimonious rate
> With a famished porter frightening
> The poor folks from his gate
> Like a fine young German gentleman
> One of the modern kind
>
> Now wanting gold, to England old
> He posted in despair
> But when at Windsor he arrived
> He found a refuge there
> For then the homeless wanderer
> His passion did declare
> And Britain's Queen was smitten
> With the eyes and auburn hair
> Of this fine young German gentleman
> One of the modern kind

Queen Victoria was the subject of many ballads. One ballad-monger said:

'I worked on twenty-three different songs on the marriage of the Queen. They all sold – especially the one about Albert the begging prince, and the one where the Queen says she had to marry the prince because she was in a comical way. We couldn't print enough copies of that one.'

> 'The Queen of the Nice Little Islands'
> My Albert he is handsome made
> A sausage maker by his trade
> No one shall ever him degrade
> When he marries the Queen of England
> If I don't get married I'll kick up a row
> I'm in a comical way I vow
> Oh dear I feel I can't tell how
> The marriage fit comes on me now
> Don't ax'em, tax'em merrily be
> Sausages and skilly-go-lee
> Won't Prince Albert have a spree
> When he marries the Queen of England

By the mid nineteenth century, however, street ballads were on the wane. Cheap newspapers were beginning to appear which lessened their news value. The development of the music hall provided the working classes with a cheap form of entertainment and the songs to go with it.

From then on popular songs were, of course, easier to find. Songs and music were printed together, often, as was the case with popular artists of the 1850s and 1860s, with delightful coloured illustrations to each song. Later, music publishers such as Francis Day and Hunter and Feldman's issued albums of their popular songs. Some were devoted to the songs of a particular artist; others were collections of songs published during a particular year. I collected as many of these as I could find. (In the early 1960s you could find them in bookshops in Charing Cross Road.) I also consulted the BBC Music Library, which contained a great deal of published light music of the eighteenth and nineteenth centuries.

The American wars had produced many good songs, so I sought out songs relating to British military and naval exploits. There were many. I wrote and produced programmes such as *Heart of Oak*, about ships and sailors in the Napoleonic Wars; *When Boney was a Warrior*, a series on the Napoleonic Wars; *The Victory*, a biography of Nelson's ship; *Follow the Drum*, about life in the army, starting in Elizabethan times; *Cheer Boys Cheer*, about the Crimean War; and *Goodbye Dolly*, about the Boer War. In all these programmes as well as details of the battles I tried to present the life of the soldiers and sailors who took part in them, much of which was reflected in the songs they sang. I found that all major British wars, from the time of Marlborough onwards, produced soldier or sailor songs grumbling about their lives and conditions of service. An example is a song called 'Thirteen Pence a Day', written at the time of the Crimean War.

> Come and be a soldier, lads
> March, march away
> Don't you hear the fife and drum
> March, march away
> Come to the battlefield
> Make the enemy to yield
> Come and lose your eyes and limbs
> For thirteen pence a day
>
> Come and learn your exercise
> Run lads run
> Soon you'll know the use of
> Both bayonet and gun
> Then you'll go abroad, my lads
> And there you'll ne'er be warm
> By shooting men you never knew
> Who never did you harm

In the navy during the Napoleonic wars there are many songs about the hated press gang:

Thirteen of the press gang
Did my love surround
And one of the cursed gang
Lay bleeding on the ground
My love was overpowered
But he fought most manfully
Till he was obliged to yield and go
Aboard the Victory

During the Boer War British Tommies sang songs that were replicated during the First World War. In Africa one of the most hated jobs was 'rifting', that is, having to clean your kit ready for inspection.

Rifting, rifting, rifting
Always bloomin' well rifting
Rifting all the morning
And rifting till I'm sore
Grousing, grousing, grousing
Always bloomin' well grousin'
Roll on when my time is up
And I will rift no more

Another reflected the difference between civilians at home and soldiers in Africa.

O ever the blooming war was done
Or I had ceased to roam
I was a slave in Africa
And you were a toff at home

The tommies in Africa and those in France both sang with slightly different words:

'I want to go home'
I want to go home
Of hausers and pom poms
I've had quite enough
And the grub that they give us

Is so bloody tough
Take me over the sea
Where the Boers can't get at me
Oh my, I don't want to die
I want to go home

In the trenches of the Great War of 1914–1918, British tommies sang to relieve their incredible sufferings. It was their songs that inspired me to write my radio programme entitled *The Long Long Trail*.

CHAPTER TWENTY
OH WHAT A LOVELY WAR

In the summer of 1958 we planned to go for our annual holiday to Italy. In those days we went by car, stopping one or two nights on the way. Before we left, my grandmother said to me, 'When you go to Italy, do you go anywhere near Arras?'

'We don't normally,' I replied, 'but we could do. Why?'

'Could you get me a photo of your father's grave?'

'I'll try.'

So we stopped off at Arras and started looking for my father's grave. I had had no idea there were so many soldiers' cemeteries around Arras.

They were all over the place, commemorating the dead of almost all the nations who had taken part in the First World War. Eventually we found the British cemetery. It consisted of a large field of white crosses surrounded by three enormous stone arches, all looking like Marble Arch. We looked up and down the field of crosses for one with my father's name on it, but couldn't find it. Eventually I asked a British ex-service man employed to take care of the graveyard who was tending the graves if he could help us.

'Have you looked on the wall?' he asked. 'You'll find many names in alphabetical order there.'

My father's name was inscribed upon the wall, along with those of '35,942 officers and men of the Forces of the British Empire who fell in the Battle of Arras and who have no known graves'.

What could possibly have happened to a man that rendered his burial impossible? What horror could have taken place that rendered the burial of 35,942 men impossible, and all in one relatively small area?

The search for the answer to this question led to my research into the lives, feelings and songs of the men in the trenches. Songs that reflected the horror of their lives, but which also reflected the bravery and humour with which they met that horror.

There were, of course, the well-known popular songs such as 'Goodbye Tipperary' and 'Pack up your Troubles' that the troops sang as they embarked for France. But it was the songs the soldiers sang in their dugouts and trenches that enabled them to make fun of the conditions under which they lived and helped them to bear the awfulness. These were songs where soldiers created words to fit hymn tunes or popular tunes of the day; songs such as those collected by Second Lieutenant F. T. Nettleingham, RFC, dated October 1917. His collection was called *Tommy's Tunes* and was prefaced with the following verses:

To ye that have sung
Ye that have laughed
Ye that were happy
Amateurs at warcraft

Ye that have cursed
Ye that have prayed
Ye that have joked
And joking – were laid
Side by side
Britons all

Your songs were ribald
Your rhymes were rude
Your ditties doubtful
Your quips quite crude
Heroes all

I read all the material I could find about life in the trenches. I read the poems of Siegfried Sassoon, Wilfred Owen and many other war-serving poets, whose thoughts and feelings echoed those of the men in the trenches, albeit in rather more eloquent language. I read the *Wipers Times*, and the *BEF Times*, those rough and ready newspapers produced, God knows how, by writers such as Gilbert Frankau serving in the trenches. These also had songs and verses parodying popular songs or hymn tunes, with verbal digs at 'the staff', that is, those who were serving behind the lines or the people back home who eulogised 'our gallant boys' and had no idea what trench life was really like. Hence the verse 'Realising Men Must Laugh'.

> Realising men must laugh
> Some wise man devised the Staff
> Dressed them up in little dabs
> Of rich variegated tabs
> Taught them how to win the war
> On AFZ 354
> Let them lead the simple life
> Far from all our vulgar strife
> Nightly gave them downy beds
> For their weary aching heads;
> Lest their relatives might grieve
> Often, often gave them leave
> Decorations, too, galore,
> What on earth could man wish more?
> Yet, alas, or so says rumour
> He forgot a sense of humour
> (From the *Wipers Times*)

Some songs or verses I collected from men such as my uncle Jim who drank in pubs in or around Sandwich Street. Though few of them had served in the war, the soldiers' songs and feelings had lingered on.

Gradually as I read letters, accounts, diaries, newspapers, speeches, and personal experiences of the men, both German and Allies, the futility of the war became more and more obvious. The soldiers on both sides marched gaily off to the front, cheered by their womenfolk and others who stayed behind, while newspaper correspondents wrote of 'the great adventure that faces our brave lads'. There was much flag-waving and patriotic fervour.

Then came the grim reality of trench warfare. From Switzerland to the sea, the German and Allied soldiers faced each other in two long lines of mud, misery, unbelievable hardship and squalor. When the soldiers went home on leave, they found the patriotic flag-waving unchanged. In Germany they were taught an official 'Hymn of Hate'. In Britain a prelate said that to kill a German was a Christian act. Official 'hate' was organised on both sides.

In the trenches the tommies knew that the Germans were suffering as much as they were. On the first Christmas Eve of the war, Germans called to the French and British troops to meet them in no man's land and the fighting men laid down their arms and exchanged greetings and cigarettes. But the war leaders of both sides frowned on such 'fraternisation'.

I read of the courage with which the men faced this hell on earth, of the songs they sang, songs with bitter words that expressed their disgust with their conditions yet which helped them to bear them. The soldiers ended up hating those who stayed at home rather than the German soldiers with whom they had so much in common. There were people of all nations who made money out of the war, as well as the propagandists and the whole system of power politics that had led to this slaughter of the youth of Europe.

Out of all this material came my radio programme *The Long Long Trail*, first broadcast on 21 January 1961 and narrated by Andrew Faulds. On 11 November 1962 it was repeated with Bud Flanagan as narrator. This was at the request of programme planners who liked the idea of a star performer narrating the programme, particularly as Bud himself had fought in the First World War. I myself, however, always preferred the first edition, particularly because Bud, although a brilliant stage performer, found it very difficult to read a script. I had to spend a long time working with him on each bit of his narration.

In the programme I told the story of the war through the songs it produced, nearly all of which were incorporated into the subsequent stage show. Our signature tune, 'The Long Long Trail', and the song 'The Last Long Mile' covered the new recruit's entry into the army and his training at Salisbury. Then came the great recruiting campaign with songs such as 'Your King and Country Want You' and 'I'll Make a Man of You', followed by 'Belgium Put the Kibosh on the Kaiser' when Belgium was invaded.

The soldiers' going-away medley consisted of 'Hold Your Hand Out Naughty Boy' and 'Are We Downhearted? No'. When they reached France 'Madamoiselle from Armentieres' was a favourite, but was soon to be superseded by songs sung on the march such as 'Oh My What a Rotten Song', 'We're Here Because We're Here' and 'Fred Karno's Army'.

> (Tune: 'The Church's One Foundation')
> We are Fred Karno's Army
> The ragtime infantry
> Fred Karno is our Captain
> Charlie Chaplin our O.C.
> And when we get to Berlin
> The Kaiser he will say
> Hoch! Hoch! mein Gott
> What a bloody fine lot
> Are the Ragtime Infantry
> (From *Tommy's Tunes*)

Once in the trenches, the songs reflected the soldiers' plight. The shelling, whizzing and whining overhead gave rise to 'Hush Here Comes a Whizzbang' and 'Bombed Last Night'. They were issued with a ration of rum when about to go over the top, which gave rise to the song 'If the Sergeant Steals Your Rum, Never Mind'.

'Never Mind'
(Parody of a popular song of the same title)

Though your heart may ache awhile, never mind,
Though your heart may ache awhile, never mind
You'll forget about it soon
When you've had a good old spoon
And your heart, it aches no more, never mind

If the Sergeant's pinched your rum, never mind
If the Sergeant's on the bum [on the borrow] never mind
If he collars all your fags and you've nothing on but rags
It's his affair – not yours – so never mind
(From *Tommy's Tunes*)

Bad weather, torrential rain, sticky, cloying mud produced songs such as 'Grousing, grousing, grousing, Always blooming well grousing', very similar to the song quoted in the previous chapter that was sung in the Boer War.

In the Ypres Salient (the area around Ypres in Belgium), where casualties averaged 7,000 a week, death was so common that men who received wounds were considered lucky. They sang 'The Bells of Hell Go Ting-a Ling-a Ling for You but Not for Me', 'Far Far from Wipers I Long to Be, Where German Snipers Can't Get at Me' and 'Oh What a Lovely War'. During so called 'quiet' periods, few soldiers stayed in the firing line for more than a few weeks at a time. Behind the lines they were given the chance to get clean and deloused and sang 'Whiter Than the Whitewash on the Wall'. During those off-duty moments they could attend church services, go to the official canteen of NAAFI and, what they liked best, be entertained by concert parties where songs like 'Roses of Picardy' and 'Take Me Back to Dear Old Blighty' were the order of the day.

They longed for home leave, but often found themselves uncomfortable with the folks back home who did not seem able to understand what life in the trenches was like. Songs such as 'Goodby-ee' and 'I wore a tunic, a dirty khaki tunic, and you wore your civvy clothes; we fought and bled at Loos, while you were on the booze, the booze that no one here knows' reflect this. After the battle of the Somme, the cry became louder. 'I want to go home, I want to go home; I don't want to go to the trenches no more, where whiz-bangs and shrapnel, they whistle and roar', again very similar to a song sung in the Boer War.

After the battle of Arras, described as the greatest and most futile slaughter in modern times, there was 'When This Cruel War is Over, No More Soldiering for Me', and 'I Don't Want to Be a Soldier'.

> (Tune: 'Come my Lad and be a Soldier')
> I don't want to be a soldier
> I don't want to go to war
> I'd rather roam
> Here at home
> And keep myself on the earnings of a lady typist
> I don't want a bayonet in my belly
> Nor my eyelids shot away
> For I am quite happy
> With my mammy and my pappy
> So I wouldn't be a soldier any day.
> (From *Tommy's Tunes*)

Although some of the French soldiers mutinied, the British never did (even though some did go AWOL). It must have been the songs that kept them going.

Soon after the programme went on the air I received a telephone call from Gerry Raffles, the director of Theatre Workshop at Stratford East. He had heard the programme and liked it. Would I be interested in writing a stage version for Theatre Workshop? I was amazed.

'But I've never written a stage play,' I said.

'You could try. Why don't you come and see me at Stratford and we'll talk about it?'

So I did. Gerry was particularly enthusiastic about the songs. We talked a lot about the war and the soldiers, but I still insisted that it would be very difficult for me to write a stage show – especially as I had several programmes lined up to write and produce for the BBC. In the end he agreed to see if we could find another writer.

In a letter to Gerry, dated 27 March 1962, I wrote:

> I asked Spike Milligan about his collaborating with me on a stage version of 'The Long Long Trail'. Unfortunately, although Spike says he is very interested, he feels he cannot do anything about it as he is going to Australia in June and he is spending the time between now and then writing script for his Radio and TV shows. He suggested that I might contact John Antrobus who would be very keen to work on a show of this kind. Unfortunately he wasn't interested unless he had a fairly substantial advance which I am sure you wouldn't even entertain – which once more leaves just me.

Throughout this period Joan Littlewood was in Africa teaching her methods of production and stagecraft to a group of Africans. At the end of the summer of 1962, however, she returned to Britain to resume living with Gerry, her partner. Meanwhile Gerry had been trying to find other scriptwriters and two people had in fact produced possible scripts. But Joan and Gerry liked neither of them.

'I hope,' wrote Gerry to me in October, 'that you will have remembered your promise to help us and be involved.'

So involved I became. Joan Littlewood, who at first seemed not particularly interested in the show, asked me to write some ideas for scenes and send them to her. I did. I sent her the script of *The Long Long Trail*. I also wrote out my idea for the Christmas scene where Tommies and Gerries exchanged gifts on the front line, and the church scene with soldiers' songs sung to hymn tunes. As well as written scenes she asked me to talk to the cast about life in the trenches: about soldiers' attitudes to the war; the difference between their attitudes and home front propaganda; and the 'art' of bayonet fighting. I wrote down all the ideas I had had when writing and researching *The Long Long Trail* and tried to convey them to Joan and the cast. Most were incorporated into the final version of *Oh What a Lovely War*.

The BBC agreed to my taking part in the production, and for many weeks I regularly attended Joan's rehearsals and learnt much about her production methods. I would take in a scene and she would get the cast to enact it.

'Okay,' she'd say when they had done this, 'now throw away your scripts and redo the scene in your own words.'

Ideas would come and go from me, from the cast, from Joan. Gradually the show began to take shape.

Alfie Ralston was engaged to arrange the music and conduct the small pit orchestra. John Gower who had sung in *The Long Long Trail* was also taken on. But the great majority of the cast were stalwarts of Joan's Theatre Workshop. They knew her and her methods of working.

On the opening night, 19 March 1963, there was still no formal script. The billing on that first night's programme read:

Theatre Workshop Presents
Oh What a Lovely War
A musical entertainment written by
CHARLES CHILTON
And the Members of the Cast

There was no mention of Joan Littlewood. She was not convinced of its success. But the reception the show received from the Stratford audience was tremendous, and next day there were rave notices in most of the press. On the second night the programme included the words:

A THEATRE WORKSHOP GROUP PRODUCTION
Under the direction of
JOAN LITTLEWOOD

The *Evening Standard* was one of the few newspapers that gave the show a bad review in its first edition. A *Standard* reviewer rang me up, asking whether it was true that Joan Littlewood had produced the show. I said it was. In the later edition of the paper there was a very complimentary review.

Thus *Oh What a Lovely War* began its tremendously successful life. It later transferred to Wyndham's Theatre in the West End, and played in Paris, New York, Milan, Brussels, Holland, and even in East Germany before the Berlin Wall was pulled down.

It became 'Joan Littlewood's Lovely War'. I had to fight to keep my name even mentioned in the programmes. Luckily for me Max Kester, my agent, was more than a match for Gerry Raffles who controlled all the financial dealings of Theatre Workshop. Max ensured that I got a fair royalty on all productions, including those of amateur dramatic companies. Joan was always reluctant to put *Oh What a Lovely War* on in the West End because of her aversion to the established theatre. When it moved from Stratford to Wyndham's she only allowed it to continue there for a few months.

Oh What a Lovely War became a great favourite with amateur dramatic companies and still is. My earnings from the play have mainly come from this source.

The play really belongs to the men who fought and died in the trenches. It was their songs in this not-so-lovely war that inspired both me and Joan Littlewood to commemorate their gallantry.

CHAPTER TWENTY ONE
TELEVISION

M any people have asked me why I never went into television. The answer is that I tried it out but never liked it.

In 1958 the BBC had a policy of sending radio producers, myself included, on a TV course. In July that year I wrote and produced two shows that appeared on television. The first was called *Alfie's Penny Gaff* and the second *Battle Cry of Freedom*.

A 'penny gaff' was an early Victorian entertainment of London's cockney underworld. The homemade theatre would consist of two shops next door to each other. The dividing wall would be broken down and the ceilings removed so that you looked right up to the roof rafters. One shop formed the stage and the other was the auditorium. The show, or 'gaff', lasted exactly an hour and the 'gaffer' who ran it charged a penny admission. Our penny gaff lasted only fifteen minutes. It was a very short time, but it was my first television programme and perhaps I was being tested to see how well I did.

Alfie Bass, who at that time was making his name as 'Bootsie' in *The Army Game*, was our gaffer. Until I used him in my programme *Century of Song*, Alfie had never sung on the air. But he was a genuine cockney and could put over such songs as 'Villikens and his Dinah' with great panache. In this programme he also sang a cleaned-up version of 'Sam Hall' to great effect. We introduced a suitably shabby audience who sat in the gallery to heckle and applaud. They were, in fact, members of Pen's Over 60s Club, dressed in period costume.

Battle Cry of Freedom featured songs sung by the Northern troops in the American Civil War. In it I used the first war photographs taken by Matthew Brady and excerpts from the film *Birth of a Nation*.

One TV critic wrote:

> It was in rather dubious mood that I tuned into *Battle Cry of Freedom*. If there was ever a production that seemed doomed to failure it would be, I thought, this attempt to present on television thirty minutes of war songs nearly one hundred years old. The problems of satisfying the eye, as well as the ear, seemed considerable. Fine material for sound radio, yes, but not television. Despite my fears the programme more or less made the grade as television entertainment. Those early still photographs were stark and compelling and whatever ancient movie it was Chilton had dug up from the storeroom dust, it served its purpose quite well. The production numbers, I felt, were unconvincing. There was that unreal air of musical comedy about them. On several occasions I expected the stage soldiers to break out into a natty little dance routine or something lusty from *Oklahoma*. One extremely effective nicety of production was that terrible march through Georgia summarised into a few seconds by the slow tracing of a pointer across the map, with the famous song in the background and the commanding general's marching orders grating on the ear.

I agreed with everything this critic said. The production numbers were unconvincing. I was to experience this difficulty with other television productions I was involved with some years later.

My next venture into television was in 1963, when I had a phone call from the TV producer Anthony (Tony) Jay. He was in the process of trying to organise a new type of TV programme to replace the extremely popular *That Was The Week That Was*. Tony's programme was to consist of an anthology of verse, diary extracts, speeches, literature and songs, spoken or sung by actors and musicians on stage that referred to various different subjects. He had got together a team of contributors that included Dr Geoffrey Best, Professor Philip Collins, Marghanita Laski, Wynford Vaughan Thomas and many other experts on particular subjects. Each week, three or four subjects would be chosen and the experts asked to send in their contributions. They ransacked diaries, volumes of letters (both published and unpublished), ancient newspapers, encyclopaedias, street ballads, popular songs, as well as more conventional sources such as novels, essays, plays and volumes of poems. An example of the sort of subjects these experts were asked to produce material for was 'The Brush Off'. Tony would phone a university don, asking whether he or she had ever heard of a more splendid brush-off than Napoleon's to his empress. The don might reply that Molière did better. A second don, asked if he had ever heard of a more perfect brush-off than Molière's, might say: 'Yes. Ben Jonson's.' And it would continue thus. Everyone started 'digging' and producing 'rhubarb, rhubarb, rhubarb'.

I didn't see how I fitted in with this intellectual bunch, but Tony explained this in his book entitled *Pick of the Rhubarb*:

> Having seen Charles Chilton's brilliant documentary *Oh What a Lovely War* I spent a long time trying to find out about him before I discovered he was a fellow BBC producer, with an encyclopaedic knowledge of songs, and an extraordinary talent for using them in a documentary way.

Eventually I became the associate producer and Pen was asked to join the research team. We had a meeting to try to think of a name for the programme. Script editors Nicholas Garland and Bamber Gascoigne were there, as well as directors Bill Hays and Terry Yarwood and members of the research team. 'Dig the rhubarb,' said Pen, putting rhubarb and digging up the past together, not really thinking of it as a title. But Bamber Gascoigne hung on to the phrase, saying, '*Dig This Rhubarb*. What do you think?' Everyone present agreed it was possible and *Dig This Rhubarb* the show became.

The first programme went out on 7 October 1963. Reviews were pretty good, though many thought the title silly. The *Leicester Chronicle* came up with the following on 11 October:

> It used to be the fashion to keep a commonplace book into which notable sayings and passages could be written and in which cuttings could be pasted. *Dig This Rhubarb* – unhappiest of titles – is TV's commonplace book and I found the first volume uncommonly entertaining.
>
> The actors include clever young men from *Beyond the Fringe* and *Oh What a Lovely War* and I note with satisfaction and without surprise that Charles Chilton is the associate producer.
>
> Chilton suggested the mixture of fact and song which was turned into the *Lovely War* show. The pattern, if not the contents, of the *Rhubarb* programme is similar. Sunday's script provided by novelists, poets, playwrights, diarists and statesmen was highly satisfying, particularly the irreverent sequence concerning Royalty and lampooning the Three Georges. [This was one of my contributions.] The delivery of the script by a hand-picked cast was impeccable.

I wrote short pieces involving letters, quotations and songs on subjects such as 'Trafalgar', 'John Brown's Body', 'Jim Crow', 'The Buffalo,' 'Street ballads on Royalty', 'Grimaldi the clown', 'Botany Bay', 'The Press Gang' and many others during the course of the year-long show.

Pen and I also searched our library for quotations on other subjects to be presented in each programme. In particular I remember one contribution we made to a piece that dealt with older people's views on young people through the ages. Someone had found details of an ancient Egyptian manuscript denouncing the young in just the same terms as today: too many drugs, too much drink, sex, violence, etc.

Apparently the original pictograph was in a museum in Turin, Italy. As Pen spoke Italian, Tony asked her to ring the museum and ask if they could send us a copy of the picture so that we could use it in the programme.

Pen found the museum quite willing to help, except that the curator in a somewhat dubious voice asked, 'Do you want all of it?'

'Yes, please,' said Pen very confidently.

'Are you sure?' said the curator even more doubtfully.

'Yes. Why not?'

The curator didn't answer, but said that he would send the copy as soon as possible.

Some days later it arrived. When we looked at it we realised why the curator had grave doubts about the pictograph. It was one of the most pornographic scenes I have ever seen. We were able to use parts of it to illustrate our item, but by no means all. After the show I went into the studio to retrieve the picture. Too late. Someone in the technical department had already made off with it.

Dig This Rhubarb was a most enjoyable programme to work on. It ran for about a year, going out every other Sunday night. When it finished I put in some other ideas for television programmes that I wanted to write and produce. The result was that I was allowed to stay on at the television centre in White City for another six months or so, with the proviso that I worked in conjunction with a regular TV producer. His name was John Furness.

The show was called *Songs for the Times*. The first three programmes in the series were entitled *The British at the Seaside*, *In the Trenches* and *Stop Press Seven Dials*. The last programme dealt with the street ballads published by James Catnach and others between 1817 and 1850. I wanted to call it *Royalty, Rape and Murder*, but John and other TV pundits thought this title too strong.

I soon found that you lost the ability to be in sole control of a production. Too many people were involved. There were directors, cameramen and technicians of all kinds: they all had to be consulted before anything could be done. Also, I was always at odds with other members of the team, in particular as regards illustrating the programmes. I wanted certain programmes to be illustrated not by members of the cast dressed in costume but by using still pictures. *The British at the Seaside* worked well with actors in costume but *In the Trenches* I thought needed only background photographs to illustrate the horrors of war. I had my way with this latter programme, and the resulting reviews backed my ideas. From the *Evening News* 5 August 1964:

> *Songs from the Trenches* made superb television... The still photographs were skilfully made to come alive and for thirty-five minutes the boys of 'Fred Karno's Army' were on the march again. Matched against the mud, the pain, the weariness and the optimism were the strong voices of the George Mitchell Singers.
>
> Charles Chilton's script was brilliant. The pictures and words, plus those earthy songs, told younger generations more about the Great War than anything which has gone before.
>
> The programme must be repeated – and considered for annual honours.

In May 1966 we were booked to do another six programmes in the series: *The Victory* (the story of Nelson's flagship); *London's Pleasure Gardens*; *London Pilgrimage* (illustrated by the pictures in Gustave Doré's *London: A Pilgrimage*); *Botany Bay* (the story of the convicts sent to Australia); *The Longhorn* (about the famous longhorned cattle who made the first long trails from Texas to the railway in Kansas); and *The Spirit of '76*. This went out on 4 July and showed how most of the songs inspired by the American War of Independence were adaptations of British songs. In all the programmes the songs inspired by the subjects were the most important part of the production.

That series was the last of my excursions into television. I had only been on loan to TV and back at Aeolian Hall the powers that be were demanding that I came back to radio. I did, and was glad to do so.

CHAPTER TWENTY TWO
FINALE

Back at Aeolian Hall I continued to write and produce a great many musical documentaries. I redid all the television *Songs for the Times* for radio, and for the first time managed to get the Third Programme to accept a programme about popular song. Called *The Music Goes Round*, it examined the musical content and effect that the talking film and the gramophone had on shaping the popular song of the 1930s. I'm glad to say that it went down well with the critics and viewers.

Other programmes I produced during this period (1967 to 1977) were: *Work Boys Work*, celebrating the anniversary of the TUC; *Don't Go down the Mine, Daddy*; *The Birth of Broadcasting* (starting with Marconi and going up to the birth of the BBC); *Cry with the Wind* (the story of the suffragette movement); *Victorian Top of the Pops* (a series with the pianist Joseph Cooper); and many programmes and series for the World Service.

In 1968 I was very pleased to once again meet Alistair Cooke. The BBC gave him a dinner to celebrate the thousandth broadcast of *Letter from America*, to which Pen and I were invited. Then in 1972 Alistair asked me to help him with the music for his television programme *America*, which I was glad to do. It turned out that helping Alistair Cooke was one of the first and last things I did during my time at the BBC.

Radio was my life. On looking through the lists of my programmes, I've found that the total number of titles of shows I wrote, produced and often presented amounted to more than 150. These do not take into account the many long series involved. Neither do they include programmes that I merely produced as part of my work in the Light Entertainment Department.

The greatest surprise of my life came in a letter dated 1 January 1972. It was from Buckingham Palace to say that I had been awarded an MBE for 'Services to Radio'. I couldn't believe it. Me? Getting honours? But it was true; and on 15 February 1972, accompanied by my wife and daughter Mary, I went to Buckingham Palace to receive the honour from the Queen Mother (the Queen was on a trip abroad). One of the things that have stuck in my mind about this occasion was that Mary, who at that time was studying ballet, danced her way up and down the long red-carpeted gallery leading to the room where the presentations took place.

On the same day, Pen and I had something else to look forward to: our Silver Wedding anniversary. After the presentation at the palace we went to lunch with Pen's mother who had a flat in Gloucester Square to celebrate with the rest of the family. Our youngest son Anthony was supposed to bring with him any cards or presents that had arrived at our house. Unfortunately he left the bag they were in on the bus. As we knew some of the letters contained cheques we were rather worried and poor Anthony was completely distraught. We rang the bus depot near our home and they told us to come to the depot that evening about 9pm when most of the buses would have returned. We went, but nothing had been found. As we were about to give up, however, one more bus arrived, the last one due in. We saw the conductor walking up to the office with a bag in his hand – containing the missing Silver Wedding presents.

On 15 June 1977 I was 60 years old. At that time if you worked for the BBC you had to retire at the age of 60. It was devastating to think this had to happen. Nevertheless retire I had to, although the BBC did let me finish some programmes I was currently working on.

I received many letters wishing me well, from the Director General downwards, and the Department gave me a big dinner party. They also gave me an autograph book that had been signed not only by all the heads of department and producers I had known but also by people who worked in the Music Library, Effects Department, post-room, canteen, boys, messengers, those working in Broadcasting House and Aeolian reception, School Radio as well as many other BBC venues and departments. One entry reads:

> I'll miss you and your lovely cup o' tea
> Lots of love from ME!

Unfortunately I can't remember who 'ME' was!

For a while things didn't seem very different as I still continued to go to the office to finish programmes I had started, but towards the end of 1977 the fact that I had been retired became a reality. I had put up the idea for a long series called *Songs of Protest* that had been accepted for the World Service. I was allowed to write this, but as I was no longer a producer was not allowed to produce it. John Dyas did this.

Worse was to come. In 1981 the BBC repeated the whole of the recorded version of *Journey into Space*. Once this finished I was asked to write another single episode. This I did, which I called *The Return from Mars*. I was not allowed to produce it. I didn't mind so much about *Songs of Protest* because it was produced by someone from my department whom I knew well. But someone I didn't know at all who had very different ideas from me produced *The Return from Mars*. He needed the script many weeks before the recording – no more writing at the last minute – and he could cut and edit as he liked. Worst of all, he could choose the actors to play the parts of Jet, Lemmy and co. The actor who played Lemmy was a Welshman. How could he possibly be the cheeky cockney

Londoner that was Lemmy? I had to put up with this, however, and also with another producer when I wrote the series *Space Force* in 1984.

Nevertheless, *Journey into Space* has served me well. The BBC has issued the series on cassettes and CDs, and Radio 7 still puts out the series from time to time.

During my retirement I still had many contacts with radio and the BBC in various forms. I did audio-visual lectures for the Museum of London entitled 'Radio Comes to London' and 'BBC and the Blitz'. I also gave three lectures, with sound, film and still photographs, for the Museum of the Moving Image (MOMI), covering 'Broadcasting in Britain' from its earliest days.

For three years starting in 1986 I taught a class in Kensington, near the Victoria and Albert Museum, called 'Communications' to American students who were over here to study radio and television. As part of my course they had to write and produce a documentary programme on an aspect of London life. They all enjoyed it, though some of their efforts were not brilliant. One girl student, however, wrote to me after she returned to America to thank me for all she had learned in the class and to let me know that she had just landed a job in an American television station.

In 1984 we moved from Keston back to London. The children had all left home and the house and garden seemed to have grown too large for us. Thanks to our daughter Mary, who was by then working as an actress, we found a new home. Mary was playing in *Noises Off*, and the actress Phyllida Law was in the cast. Her husband, Eric Thompson, had recently died. Phyllida had asked Mary if she knew anyone who wanted to buy a house in London. Mary told her we had been thinking about moving to London and eventually we bought Phyllida's delightful house in West Hampstead. Many of our friends in Keston thought we were mad to move to London away from the countryside, but we found it suited us well as most of the things we did were in London. Also we were nearer to our children.

David's recording studio provided me with yet another contact with the BBC. He was often asked to provide 'onsite locations' for the plays he recorded – locations that could provide more atmosphere than a studio. One of the programmes he was scheduled to do for the BBC was *The Picture of Dorian Gray*, to be produced by Gordon House who wanted a location with attic rooms and creaking staircases, all of which we were able to provide. That was the first of many radio programmes to be recorded in our house and/or garden. In many cases it meant that we were reunited with people I had previously worked with in the Corporation.

I was quite often interviewed for programmes about *Journey into Space*, *Oh What a Lovely War*, or to talk about people I had worked with such as George Mitchell. The Archive Hour on Radio 4 put out a whole programme simply entitled *Charles Chilton*.

So the BBC remained part of my life, sometimes directly, but often more indirectly in the hobbies and interests I had. Since my childhood I had been a fan of the music hall, and had written many programmes about it. Now that I was retired I presented audio-visual programmes on music hall in many venues, ranging from the Museum of London to classes for the over 60s at the Mary Ward Centre.

Another activity during my retirement was being a guide for 'Original London Walks'. Our daughter Mary had married an American journalist, David Tucker, who took over this institution from its founders and turned it into a flourishing company with over 140 walks on offer, both in London and other well-known tourist places such as Oxford, Cambridge, Bath and Stonehenge. David asked me if I would do a Hampstead walk, which I did every Sunday morning for many years until walking the hills of Hampstead became too much for someone aged nearly ninety.

In February 2007 Pen and I celebrated our Diamond Wedding anniversary, surrounded by our three children and ten grandchildren. My ninetieth birthday fell on 15 June of that same year.

As I look back at the forty-six years I worked at the BBC, I often wonder what my life would have been like if I had not walked through those heavy entrance doors to Broadcasting House when I was fifteen years old. Would I have become a builder and decorator like most of the male members of my family? Or maybe a sheet metal worker. Or, worst of all, if I had not been so keen on the cinema might I have been caught stealing from lorries and ended up in Borstal?

In 1924 Reith's vision was of a BBC which would inform, entertain and educate all those who wished to listen, wherever they were and whatever their financial circumstances, so that at the end of the day they could feel enriched. In my case these aims were certainly fulfilled. The BBC became my university, my music college, my introduction to literature and drama and the place where I was able to develop the skills necessary to become a writer and producer of programmes.

I could not have asked for a better job.

Also available from

fantom
publishing

Charles Chilton
JOURNEY INTO SPACE

Between 1953 and 1958, millions of people tuned in to the radio adventures of Jet Morgan and his crew as they left earth to investigate the universe. Chilton went on to write three best-selling novels based on the groundbreaking radio series.

Reprinted for the first time in forty years, Fantom Publishing presents Charles Chilton's tales of space expedition – released over three special hardback editions – each title limited to only 200 copies.

OPERATION LUNA

Destination: the Moon! No adventurers had ever faced greater hazards than the crew of rocket-ship Luna when she hurtled into space. Jet Morgan, ace pilot, was her captain. With him were her Australian designer, Mitch; Lemmy, the Cockney radio-operator; and Doc, whose diary astonished everyone. ISBN: 978-1-906263-73-7

THE RED PLANET (available November 2011)

Jet Morgan leads the first fleet of rocket ships to reach the 'Red Planet', Mars. But right from the beginning the expedition is ill-omened. Uncanny happenings test their courage to breaking point, both on the long space flight and on the hostile planet itself. ISBN: 978-1-906263-74-4

THE WORLD IN PERIL (available February 2012)

Jet Morgan and the crew of the Discovery return to Mars on the most dangerous and vital mission ever undertaken by man – to obtain the Martian plan for the conquest of Earth. Too late, they find themselves part of the invasion fleet. ISBN: 978-1-906263-75-1

Available in hardback from
www.fantomfilms.co.uk

Also available from

fantom
publishing

FRED HAMILTON
ZOOM IN WHEN YOU SEE THE TEARS
30 ADVENTUROUS YEARS AT THE BBC

After emigrating to Britain in the 1950s, Fred Hamilton joined the BBC's Film Department where he was soon promoted to Film Cameraman. Coverage of sports events soon became his bread and butter job, followed by assignments to armed conflict areas in many parts of the world. Obtaining footage to be broadcast on *Panorama* and other current-affairs programmes, often under perilous circumstances, he survived the jungles of Borneo, the battlefields of Vietnam and the Middle East.

As a member of the Film Department, he contributed to iconic shows such as *Doctor Who*, *Z Cars*, *Out of the Unknown*, *Doomwatch*, *Colditz* and *Hitchhikers Guide to the Galaxy*. With colour television still in its infancy, Fred became a man for 'action scenes' before the phrase even entered the BBC vocabulary, always on the lookout for that unusual, extra dynamic shot.

Committing his memories of an impressively colourful professional life to paper, Fred Hamilton tells the story of a man totally dedicated to his job, whose accounts are enriched by hilarious anecdotes involving many BBC legends. This autobiography is a fascinating insider's view of the BBC, lavishly illustrated with never-before-seen exclusive photographs from Fred's personal archives.

ISBN 978-1-906263-67-6

Available in paperback from

www.fantomfilms.co.uk

Also available from

fantom
publishing

Victor Pemberton's
THE SLIDE
And Other Radio Dramas

FOREWORD BY DAVID SPENSER
AFTERWORD BY JOHN TYDEMAN

Victor Pemberton is a well established author and playwright who over the past 45 years has contributed to iconic cult series such as *Ace of Wands*, *Timeslip*, *Tightrope* and of course *Doctor Who*. He has also written prolifically for radio, and this volume brings together five of his most celebrated radio scripts; complete with original notes, deleted scenes and alternative lines.

THE GOLD WATCH – From 1961, Victor's first script for radio is based on the extraordinary circumstances of his father's retirement.

THE SLIDE – One of Victor's most famous radio plays is this seven-part science-fiction thriller from 1966.

KILL THE PHARAOH! – An eight-episode adventure from 1967, in which a London doctor finds herself plunged into a nightmare of international crime and intrigue on a holiday to Egypt…

THE FALL OF MR HUMPTY – A 'Nightmare for Radio' from 1975 in which a man has a strange meeting on the last train of the night…

DARK – A supernatural thriller from 1978. An American woman living in London is haunted by the spirit of her dead husband.

This collection of scripts is printed here for the very first time alongside newly written introductions by Victor Pemberton himself.

ISBN 978-1-906263-46-1

Available in paperback from
www.fantomfilms.co.uk